SECOND EDITION

The Homemaker/
Home Health Aide
Pocket Guide

SECOND EDITION

The Homemaker/ Home Health Aide Pocket Guide

Elana Zucker R.N., M.S.N

Consultant/Former Chief Nursing Officer
Overlook Hospital
Summit, New Jersey

Prentice
Hall

Upper Saddle River, New Jersey 07458

Library of Congress Cataloging-in-Publication Data
Zucker, Elana D., 1941-
    The homemaker/home health aide pocket guide/Elana Zucker.—2nd ed.
        p. cm.
    Companion volume to: Being a homemaker/home health aide, 5th ed.,
    c2000.
    Includes index.
    ISBN 0-13-032184-2
    1. Home health aides—Handbooks, manuals, etc. 2. Home care
services—Handbooks, manuals, etc. 3. Home nursing—Handbooks,
manuals, etc. I. Being a homemaker/home health aide. II. Title.
RA645.3 .Z826 2001
649.8—dc21

                                                            2001021688

*To Brian without whom nothing would be possible and the world and our
family would be poorer.*

Publisher: Julie Alexander
Executive Editor: Maura Connor
Acquisitions Editor: Barbara Krawiec
Director of Manufacturing and Production: Bruce Johnson
Managing Editor: Patrick Walsh
Production Editor: Clarinda Publication Services
Production Liaison: Mary Treacy
Editorial Assistant: Michael Sirinides
Manufacturing Manager: Ilene Sanford
Creative Director: Cheryl Asherman
Cover Design: Gary J. Sella
Interior Design: Clarinda Publication Services
Composition: The Clarinda Company
Printing and Binding: RR Donnelley and Sons
All photos are copyright Prentice Hall unless noted next to photo.

Pearson Education LTD.
Pearson Education Australia PTY, Limited
Pearson Education Singapore, Pte. Ltd.
Pearson Education North Asia Ltd.
Pearson Education Canada, Ltd.
Pearson Education de Mexico, S.A. de C.V.
Pearson Education—Japan
Pearson Education Malaysia, Pte. Ltd.
Pearson Education, Upper Saddle River, New Jersey

10 9 8 7 6 5 4 3 2 1
ISBN 0-13-032184-2

Preface

The Homemaker/Home Health Aide Pocket Guide, Second Edition has been created as a reference for you to use as you care for your client. Many times, while performing your duties, you have a question or want to check your information; this book is designed for those quick reviews. It can also be used when you are planning care and want to be sure that all important points have been covered in your plan, or as a handy quick reference when you want to review a specific idea you had learned in class.

Though this is currently an occupation held mainly by women, more and more men are entering the home health field. However, for convenience and ease of presentation, the text will normally refer to the supervisor as *she* or *her* and to the clients as *he* or *him.*

Keeping in mind that your most important task is caring for your client, the content is arranged for easy quick reference. Tables, lists, and illustrations are used throughout. Procedures have been shortened to reflect the fact that those people using the book will all be experienced health-care workers. Should more complete explanation be needed, you are referred to the textbook, *Being a Homemaker/Home Health Aide,* Fifth Edition.

You are encouraged to familiarize yourself with the layout of the book so that you will be able to find the information quickly. Write in the book and make notes. Use the book as a teaching tool for your clients. Use it as a quick review as you provide care.

Contributors to the Fifth Edition of *Being a Homemaker/ Home Health Aide*, to whom we are very grateful, include:

Joan B. Kane BS, RPT
  Registered Physical Therapist, Private Practice, New Jersey

Theodosia T. Kelsey OTR
  Occupational Therapist, Private Practice, New Jersey

Janne Litzelman MS CCC
  Speech Pathologist, Private Practice, New Jersey

Elaine Muller MA
  Private Practice, New Jersey

Patricia Taboloski RN, MSN
  Research Assistant, University of Rochester School of Nursing, New York (Family Health, Nurse Clinician Practitioner)

Eleanor Bannon RN
  Enterostomal Therapist, Overlook Hospital, Summit, New Jersey

Gloria J. Bizjak
  The Maryland Fire and Rescue Institute at the University of Maryland

Special thanks to these careful reviewers:

Clara McElroy, RN, MA, LMT
  President, First Call Medical, Florida Health Academy & CEUonline, Bonita Springs, Florida

Paula Eining, RN, SDC
New York, NY

Elana Zucker

Introduction

*Y*OUR RESPONSIBILITY AS AN EMPLOYEE OF A HOME CARE AGENCY

It is your responsibility to perform the tasks you are assigned to the best of your ability. Perform *only* those tasks that are part of your assignment. If you do not know a procedure or have a question be sure to *ask*! You are expected to care for the clients in a thoughtful, respectful, and considerate manner. It is also expected that you will share your ideas, thoughts, and observations with your supervisor and fellow employees.

You will be expected to use many different pieces of equipment. Be sure you are familiar with each one. If you do not know how to use a piece of equipment safely and easily be sure to *ask*! Sometimes you may need to ask the client, sometimes you will ask a family member, and sometimes you will ask your supervisor. It is important to ask for instructions before you use the equipment so that you do not harm the client or yourself.

When you receive your assignment ask your supervisor the following:

- What equipment is needed for the client's care?
- Who will obtain the needed equipment? Will the family buy it? Will the nurse bring it? Will it be delivered?

- Are the necessary tools and equipment to keep the house clean available? Will the family purchase any needed equipment or supplies?

Try to use equipment and supplies that are already in the house. The client and his family are used to these. If you have tried to use the equipment and supplies that have been provided and you still find that you need something, discuss this with your supervisor. She may have suggestions for ways in which you can improvise or ways in which the equipment or supplies you require can be obtained. Keep in mind that one of your responsibilities is to set up the client's care so that he can continue it on his own when you leave. Your use of equipment and supplies that are familiar to him is part of this process.

YOUR RESPONSIBILITIES AS A HOMEMAKER/HOME HEALTH AIDE

You are expected to be familiar with your job description. This includes understanding what your role is within the agency and as part of the home care team. It is your responsibility to perform the assigned tasks to the best of your ability. You are to perform *only* those tasks that are part of your assignment.

When you first meet the client and the other members of his household, remember that you are a stranger to them. There will be a period of time when you will all have to get to know one another. Helpful hints to make this period easier are:

- *Wear your uniform.* This identifies you as a member of the health team.

- *Wear your name pin.* This tells the family that you are who you say you are.
- *Introduce yourself.* Write down your name and the name of your agency if the client cannot remember them. Write down the telephone number that the client can call to ask questions or to reach you or your supervisor.
- *Discuss with the client and his family what you can do and what you cannot do.* Tell them how long you will be there. Involve the client and his family in the plan of care. Assure them that you will structure your care so that the client is comfortable.
- *Answer the client's questions.* Be honest. If he asks for information you do not have or are not supposed to discuss, you might say, "I do not have the answer now, but I will get you the information." Then call your supervisor and work out a response for the client. Be sure to give the client an answer the next time you see him, and be sure it is an honest one. Do not lie because the client may never trust you again.

*Y*OUR NEEDS AS A HOMEMAKER/HOME HEALTH AIDE

It is important that you meet your needs as a person and as a homemaker/home health aide, but not at the expense of your client. There are many times when you will have to put aside your needs until you leave your client. When you feel you can no longer do this, speak, to your supervisor. As you care for your client, ask yourself:

- Are you meeting your needs or your client's needs?

- Do you perform a procedure with the client because he enjoys having you help or do you feel you *must* do it?
- Does helping a client become independent make you feel good or useless?

NOTICE

It is the intent of the author and publishers that this textbook be used as part of a formal Homemaker/Home Health Aide course taught by a qualified instructor. The Procedures presented here represent accepted practices in the United States. They are not offered as a standard of care. Home health care is to be performed under the authority and guidance of qualified supervisory personnel. It is the reader's responsibility to know and follow local care protocols as provided by the medical advisors directing the system to which he or she belongs. Also, it is the reader's responsibility to stay informed of home health care procedure changes.

The material in this textbook contains the most current information available at the time of publication. However, federal, state and local guidelines concerning clinical practices, including without limitation, those governing infection control and standard precautions, change rapidly. The reader should note, therefore, that new regulations may require changes in some procedures.

It is the responsibility of the reader to familiarize himself or herself with the policies and procedures set by federal, state and local agencies, as well as the institution or agency where the reader is employed. The authors and the publishers of this textbook, and the supplements written to accompany it, disclaim any liability, loss or risk resulting directly or indirectly from the suggested procedures and theory, from any undetected errors, or from the reader's misunderstanding of the text. It is the reader's responsibility to stay informed of any new changes or recommendations made by any federal, state and local agency as well as by his or her employing health care institution or agency.

Contents

CHAPTER 1

Communication Skills

COMMUNICATION

Communication means exchanging information with others. We exchange information about feelings, opinions, or facts. People let others know how they feel or what they want all day and even during the night. They can tell the same about you. Communication takes place through verbal exchange, written words, and body language or nonverbal methods. Communication is necessary so that people can function together—in other words, so they can "get along." Developing the ability to get along with people—clients, visitors, fellow workers—is a very important part of your job. Being a good communicator is essential.

Different cultures communicate differently. Some cultures speak softly, others more loudly; some use hand gestures, others do not; some touch people to whom they are speaking, others consider this rude behavior. Different cultures traditionally communicate different pieces of information to different family members. In some cultures, finances are always discussed with the eldest male and intimate health-related information is always discussed with the eldest female. Determining whom to talk to about specific information will save time and misunderstandings.

Clients who do not speak English have the right to safe, effective communication. If you speak more than one language, let your agency know so they can assign you accordingly. Clients feel safer when their caregivers speak their language. You can also use an interpreter to communicate with the client. Be sure the client approves of the interpreter and wants to share information with the person and that the interpreter does not violate the client's confidentiality.

Verbal Communication

Verbal communication is the exchange of ideas or information through the spoken word. The tone of your voice, the speed at which you speak, your inflection, and your actual choice of words are part of the verbal picture you paint as you speak.

Written Communication

Any time you write or draw, you are communicating through writing. The way in which you write tells a great deal about you and how you feel about the subject and your activity. The neatness, the legibility, the choice of words, and how you give the written work to the reader sets the scene for how it is received.

Nonverbal Communication

The way in which we hold our bodies is called body language. No words are spoken, but the message is given and received by others. Body language includes:

- the way we look (or do not look) at people
- the way we stand
- where we stand

- what else we may be while speaking
- how we are dressed and groomed

Answering When the Client Calls

Every client needs a way to signal other people: a hand bell, a stick used to bang on the bed or the floor, or a voice signal. Use whatever method is most appropriate in the house where you are working. When the client signals, go to him and ask him what he would like.

Basic Rules for Communicating

Be a Nonjudgmental Observer and Listener

It is important to learn to receive and give information in an accepting manner without expressing your opinions. If you are asked your opinion, you might say, "This is your house and how you feel is more important than how I feel."

Be a Careful Listener

Listen to what the person says. Listen to what information is left out of the conversation. Listen for the tone of voice of the speaker and his breathing pattern. Do the words make sense? Is it appropriate to ask questions?

Be Sensitive

When the client does not want to talk, respect his moods. Being near the client in a moment of trouble may be the most comforting message of all.

Be Courteous and Tactful

Courtesy means being polite. Courtesy and tact are important in your relationships with your fellow workers. Show them you are willing to hear what they have to say and then reply in a thoughtful manner.

If you are not clear as to what you have heard, summarize what you think you heard. For example, "I heard you say that John was going to the store, then coming home and fixing you dinner before he went to the doctor's. Is that correct?"

Tact means doing and saying the right thing at the right time. Before you make a remark to a client or his family, think! Is this the right time? Is this the right word to use? What is the best way to express the idea to this person? Do not speak within hearing distance of the client if you do not want him to hear you, even if you think he is asleep, under the influence of medication, or unconscious.

Emotional Control

The stress level of a client and members of the family may affect their ability to communicate and listen. Speak in simple terms. Do not be upset if you have to repeat yourself.

Learn to take constructive criticism and accept suggestions from your supervisor and coworkers. If you do not agree with what is said to you, answer in a polite, courteous manner. Discuss the criticism, not the person who is giving it.

Be Truthful

The client may ask you a question about his doctor or his diagnosis. Do not lie to the client! Do not tell him you do not know when you are aware of the information. If you say you do not know, you close the conversation. Tell the client you will get him an answer. Then call and talk to your supervisor. When you promise to get an answer for a client, do it!

FAMILY AND VISITORS

Visitors are often the highlight of the day for clients who must remain at home. Visitors may be worried and upset over the illness of your client. They, too, need kindness and patience. Pleasant comments, privacy, and polite, efficient manners will make them feel at ease. If it appears that visitors are upsetting or tiring your client, you may have to tactfully suggest that the client rest. Remember, you are in the house to care for the client, not to wait on or socialize with the visitors.

- Listen to the visitors and family members. Some suggestions by visitors can be very helpful. Some complaints may be valid, others not.
- Try not to get involved in family affairs. Never take sides in a family quarrel.
- If visitors have questions about your client and you are not sure you should answer, tell them you will get the information. Discuss these questions with your client to be sure he wants the information given to his visitors.
- If a visitor or family member asks how he or she may help, give some suggestions.
- Visitors may arrive at the house and give you orders. Be open about your responsibilities. Explain

that your supervisor sets up the plan of care and that you will discuss all changes with her.

■ Report the roles family and visitors play in the life of your client. Report changes in the family functions, relationships, and roles both as you observe them and as the client relates them.

*O*BSERVING, REPORTING, AND RECORDING YOUR OBSERVATIONS

Observation of the client is a continuous process, which includes listening to the client, talking to him, and asking questions. Be extra alert to any unusual things. Changes in the client's condition or appearance are most important. Watch also for changes in the client's attitude or moods and the way in which he interacts with other people. Pay attention to complaints of pain or discomfort as well as to complaints that do not seem to have a reason. Be alert when the client relates events that took place in your absence. Observation of the client's family and friends is also important and may have great implications for the client's future care. Table 1.1 lists general client observations.

TABLE 1.1 *G*ENERAL CLIENT OBSERVATIONS

Concern	Observations
General appearance	Has it changed? If so, in what way? Is there a noticeable odor or smell in the client's room?
	Does he always complain about the heat or cold?

TABLE 1.1 (*continued*)

Concern	Observations
General mood	Describe the client's actions rather than your interpretation of them. ("The client threw a shoe at his daughter" rather than "The client was angry at his daughter.") Has his mood changed? Does he talk a lot or very little? Does he make sense? Can he report things to you accurately? Does he hallucinate (see or hear things)? Is he oriented (know where he is, who he is, and who you are)? Is he anxious, calm, excited, or worried? Does he talk about pain? Does he speak rapidly or slowly? Does he look at you when he speaks? Can he be understood when he speaks? Can he remember? Is he confused or forgetful?
Sleeping habits	Have these changed? Is the client a quiet or restless sleeper? Does he complain about lack of sleep? Does his report agree with your observations? How many pillows does he sleep with? How much does he sleep?
Pain	Where is the pain? How long does the client say he has had it? Is it new pain? How does he describe it? Is it constant or does it come and go? Is it sharp, dull, or aching? Has he had medicine for the pain? Does the medicine relieve the pain? Is there any activity that brings on the pain?

(*continues*)

TABLE 1.1 GENERAL CLIENT OBSERVATIONS (*continued*)

Concern	Observations
Daily activities	Does the client dress himself? Does he walk with or without help? What kind of help?
Personal care	Can the client bathe himself? Can the client brush his teeth, comb his hair, go to the bathroom, or wash his face? Does he ask for assistance?
Movements	Does the client limp?
Skeletal system	Does the client have pain, limited movement, swelling in joints, warm tender joints, unusual positioning of any body part, or redness in joints?
Muscular system movement	Does the client have painful swelling, limited movement? What is the color of the skin over painful areas? Does he lie still? Does he change position frequently? What is his favorite position?
Skin	Temperature, texture, moisture, bruises, healing of bruises, incision appearance, and mouth condition. Has it changed? Is the client's skin unusually pale (pallor)? Is it flushed (red)? Are his lips or fingernails turning blue (cyanosis)? Is there any swelling (edema) noticeable? Are there reddened or tender areas? Where are they? Is the skin shiny? Is there any puffiness?
Circulatory system	Does the client have chest pain? Swelling of fingers, toes, feet, ankles, or around the eyes? Good pulse rate

TABLE 1.1   (*continued*)

Concern	Observations
	and quality? Full color of lips, nails, fingers, or toes? Any headaches? Any pain in legs when walking?
Respiratory system	Does the client have pain while breathing? Good rate and quality of respirations? Any cough, sputum (color and consistency), wheezing, shortness of breath? Full color of fingers and toes?
Gastrointestinal system	Does the client have pain? Good appetite? Flatus? Any vomiting (color of vomitus)? Feces (color, amount, frequency, odor)? Any discomfort before or after eating? Can the client control his bowels? Have his eating habits changed? Does he complain he has no appetite? Does he dislike his food? What and how much does he eat? Is he always thirsty? Does he seldom ask for fluids? Is it difficult for him to eat or swallow?
Nervous system	Does the client have painful areas of body, twitching, involuntary movement, inability to move, or inability to feel stimuli?
Urinary system	Does the client have pain during urination; urinary continence; urine color, odor, amount, and frequency; blood in urine; pain in kidney area?
Eyes	Does the client have pain, discharge, redness, sensitivity to light, vision change?

(*continues*)

TABLE 1.1 *(continued)*

Concern	Observations
Ears	Does the client have pain, discharge, hearing change?
Nose	Does the client have pain, discharge, bleeding, smell?
Female genitals	Does the client have menstrual periods (frequency, amount of flow, pain), vaginal discharge (color, odor, amount), breasts (lumps), discharge, soreness, parasites, or draining sores?
Male genitals	Does the client have pain, discharge, parasites, or draining sores?

Methods of Observation

Use all of your senses when making observations. You can:

- See some signs of change in a client's condition.
- Feel some signs with your finger.
- Hear some signs.
- Smell some signs.
- Listen to the client talking for other changes in his condition.

Subjective and Objective Reporting

Subjective reporting means giving your opinion about something or stating what you think. When you report your opinion to your supervisor, be sure you say that it is your opinion. Objective reporting means reporting exactly what you observe—that is, reporting what you see, hear, feel, or smell.

*B*ASIC RULES FOR REPORTING

Knowing What to Report, When to Report, and to Whom

Important questions to ask yourself include:

- Is there a special time for me to call the office?
- Is there a special telephone number to call to reach my supervisor?
- If my supervisor is not in the office, who can help me?
- Can I call from the client's home? If not, where is the nearest telephone?
- What information does the agency give by telephone, and what is given in writing?
- Where do I document information?

*G*uidelines—*Reporting and Recording*

To accurately report and record, be sure that you:

Upon Taking an Assignment

- Know to whom to report.
- Know when to report.
- Record any specific observations that members of the health care team need.
- Know the basic observations you should always be aware of as you interact with the client.
- Know what types of information must be written and what should be reported verbally.

- Assess details about the client's condition.
- Be sure about your information.
- Obtain complete information.

General Reporting

- Report objectively. When reporting subjectively, say so.
- Report all changes in a client's condition.
- Report the events in the order in which they occurred. Include the persons present at the event. You may find it helpful to indicate exact times.
- Report the condition of both sides of the body (for example, "the left leg is cooler than the right leg").
- Report and record soon after the event occurs.

TEACHING CLIENTS

Teaching clients is an important part of your job. You will teach clients by example, by discussion, or by taking part in activities with them. You will teach them new skills, help them relearn old skills, and help them gain independence in as many activities as possible. Everybody learns differently; therefore, you must have a teaching plan that is individualized to each client.

Reasons for differences in learning include:

- Life experiences
- Disease processes
- Motivation for learning
- Family dynamics
- Language skills
- Past experiences with learning
- General abilities

- Teaching skills of teacher
- Age of client

Clients who are not fluent in English may have to learn with the help of a family member. When this occurs, be sure you confirm that involving another person is acceptable to the client and the interpreter. Also, be sensitive to the information you are discussing because you may have to review very personal information and activities.

Points to Remember when Teaching a Client

- Be sure the client is paying attention and is not distracted.
- Be sure the client wants to learn.
- Be sure you are familiar with the material you will teach the client.
- Speak slowly and clearly.
- Tell the client the reasons you are doing each step.
- Do not try to teach too much at once.
- Teach at the time of day most convenient for the client.
- Use written material so the client will have something to refer to when you are gone. If the client cannot read, pictures may help.

CHAPTER 2

Working with People

BASIC NEEDS

Every person has certain basic needs that must be met so that he can survive. A need is a requirement for survival. Sometimes an individual can satisfy his needs himself, and sometimes he requires help. When a person becomes your client, it means he is unable to satisfy all his needs himself. All physical and psychological needs do not all have to be met completely each day, but a person whose needs are fulfilled will have a better quality of life and a healthy emotional and social outlook.

The needs of children are usually met by family members. During the adult years, most people are expected to meet some or most of their own needs. Needs overlap and affect each other. Each person determines his own particular balance. When one need is out of balance due to illness, the other needs are also affected (Figure 2.1).

Several factors affect the way in which we balance a client's needs:

- Client knowledge
- Disease state
- Family support
- Mental state

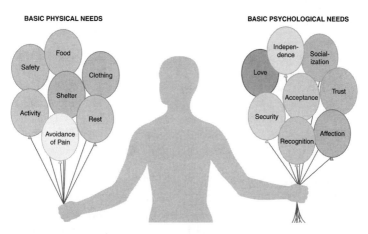

BASIC PHYSICAL NEEDS

BASIC PSYCHOLOGICAL NEEDS

FIGURE 2.1 When a client is unable to meet his own physical or psychological needs, it is your role to assist him.

- Age
- Available resources
- Culture
- Financial resources

The ways in which these elements interact will determine how the client's needs are met and how all other family members' needs are satisfied.

*F*AMILY NEEDS

If your client is part of a family unit, his change in status will affect all other members of the family. Every member of the family has a set of basic needs and these needs must continue to be met even though one of its members, your client, now has a changed status. Discuss with your supervisor a plan of care that can be established to best meet all these needs.

PAIN

Pain means different things to different people. Some people think pain is normal and must be tolerated. Some feel it is a punishment. Some do not want to complain. Some are afraid of medications, and some are afraid that if they complain, their caregivers will leave them.

Pain causes many reactions, some you can see, and some you cannot see. A client who is in pain may:

- Have a rapid pulse or shallow, rapid breathing
- Have increased fatigue
- Have increased anxiety
- Have increased stress
- Withdraw and decrease communication
- Decrease food and fluid intake
- Make faces and make gestures with his hands
- Moan and talk in baby talk and cry
- Demonstrate angry behavior

People of some cultures may hang a charm near the bed; some may say special prayers; some may burn candles; and some may dress the client in special clothes. Support these actions even if they may seem unusual to you. Some people do not want to take medication because they are afraid they will become addicted. Encourage your client to take medication as prescribed.

Help the client and his family manage the pain.

- Ask the client what usually decreases the pain. Do not change his routine!
- Talk to the client. Explain what you will do and how he may help.
- Allow the client to move at his own pace.
- Support the medication schedule. Encourage the client to take medication before the pain becomes severe.
- Encourage the family to support the client as he deals with the pain.
- Observe the client for any increase of pain, and alter your care accordingly.
- Encourage the client to share feelings about his pain.
- Encourage the family to share their feelings about the client's pain, his reaction to it, and its effect on them.

*F*AMILY UNITS

Most people live in some sort of family unit. It may be an extended family with several generations living in the same house. It may be a single-parent family. It may be a unit made up of friends who live together. Different cultures define family in different ways. In the broadest sense, a family is a unit bound together by common interests working to maintain the well-being and meet the needs of all members.

Each family has needs and rules of its own and interact in different ways. Observe the client's family. Do members care for one another? Do they punish their members with violence? Do they speak lovingly to each other? Do they stop speaking to one member when they are angry? Do they tease each other?

Culture and the Family

Many factors influence the functioning of families, including:

- Decision-making roles
- View of illness and pain
- Number of members
- Economic resources
- Each member's needs
- Culture of the members
- Culture of the country in which they live

Sometimes, a family functions within the rules of its native country but lives in the United States. This may often cause a conflict between the roles of family members and the relationship and expectations of the health care team. Understanding a culture means understanding its members' basic ideas about themselves, their relationship to their family members, and their ideas about health care.

Family Members and Their Roles

A role is the part a person has in his family or situation. Sometimes these roles are learned from older members of the family; sometimes, if there is no role model, the role must be shaped to the best of the person's ability. Family members may each have several roles; for example, a woman may be a mother, a daughter, a wife, and a grandmother. Each role demands different behavior and a different set of responsibilities.

Economics

All families have some money or use something to barter services with others. All families spend their money according to their own rules and beliefs based on family history, needs, culture, and the state of the client's disease.

It is most important not to inflict your opinions about money on the client or his family, even if asked. For example, all that you need to say is, "I'm not really in a position to comment on this situation. I suggest that you discuss your feelings with your son."

ILLNESS AND DEPENDENCY

Every person reacts to illness, being disabled, and being dependent in a different way. Individual reactions are determined by age, family, culture, emotional health, and all the other aspects that make up a particular person. It is important to remember that you bring certain feelings about illness with you when you care for a client. Identify these feelings and do not let them get in the way of your work.

Illness is the absence of good health. An illness usually has associated pain and discomfort, which may be acute or chronic. An acute illness starts suddenly and does not last very long. A chronic illness continues for a long time.

A disability is a condition that produces a physical or mental limitation that may or may not respond to adaptive aids. Usually, a body function that is normally taken for granted is impaired. A chronic illness may cause a disability. A disability may or may not be painful or cause discomfort. A disability usually is permanent.

Reactions of families to illness, disability, and crisis vary. This method of functioning has been shaped over many years. Support systems are people or actions used to help a person adjust to a new or difficult situation.

The support systems a family chooses should allow them to continue functioning—even in time of crisis. Examples of support systems include:

- Informal systems: people help one another because they want to.

- Formal systems: people help because they are paid to do so, or they have a particular knowledge necessary, or an outside agency or government says they must do so.

- Support groups: people gather, usually with a leader or facilitator, to discuss and share similar problems, help each other, and gain knowledge from each other.

Denial

Denial is used by some people when they meet a situation with which they cannot cope at the time. They simply say, "This doesn't really exist." Denial is a way people shield themselves from situations. Sometimes, a person will deny an event or situation and then come to accept it later when he is emotionally able to do so.

You may be asked to take part in this process of denial. When a person has an illness, the family may wish to keep it from him. They will deny that there is a problem and will ask your help in keeping the secret. It is most difficult, and you may become angry that the client or his family is denying the truth and involving you in this lie. The family and the client have a right to deny a situation if that is their method of coping and if the client is not negatively affected.

Abusive Words and Difficult Behavior

A client may show his impatience to one member of the family or only to you. Often, he is angry at the situation, not at you, but you are the closest person to whom he can react. He may become irritable due to pain, the general situation, or a feeling of helplessness. Remain calm and try to put the client's actions and words into perspective.

Clients may say things to you that they would not say to their relatives. They may use unpleasant or nasty, abusive words. Because you are paid to care for the client, a client may feel that you will return even if he isn't nice because it is "your job." A visiting family member does not have to care for the client, and if the client is unpleasant, the family member may not return. Some clients may say and do things to test you and the limits of the situation. Often, clients will be very nice to you but not to their families. These actions may be to make family members jealous and show them that the clients are still in control of the situation. Some clients do or say unpleasant things but are not aware that their behavior is a problem to anyone. If you tell a client that something he does makes you uncomfortable, he often will stop it.

*A*DVANCE DIRECTIVES FOR HEALTH CARE

Each client has the right to determine the kind of health care he wants if and when he cannot actively make the decision. A document, often called a living will, indicates to others what the client's wishes are concerning heroic measures, accepting or refusing treatment, or withdrawing life support. It is always a good idea to discuss the presence or absence of a living will before you accept an assignment. The contents of this living will influence the plan of care and your activities in the home. If a client tells you that he is interested in making a living will, contact your supervisor so that the appropriate person can be called to assist the client.

MENTAL HEALTH AND MENTAL DISABILITY

Mental health is the ability to function effectively and satisfactorily in society. Mental health is a condition of the whole person, and it reflects how a person deals with daily life and crises. Mental health is the basis for our behavior and relationships with others. Mental health is also a matter of degree. The difference between a mentally healthy person and one with a mental disability is that the latter adopts characteristics or behaviors that no longer enable him to function within society. Mentally healthy people can:

- Adapt to change
- Give and receive affection and love
- Tolerate stress to varying degrees
- Accept responsibility for their own feelings and actions
- Distinguish between reality and unreality
- Form and keep relationships with people

Not long ago, mental disability, whether temporary or permanent, was thought to be a punishment or a curse. Many people thought mental disabilities were contagious. People who were mentally disabled were put into institutions so that the rest of society would not catch their disease.

Mental disabilities often start slowly. Because there are many levels of mental dysfunction, you should avoid labeling a mentally disabled client. Just treat him with respect, support him and his family, see to his safety, and follow the plan of care.

Some of the causes of mental disability are:

- Isolation
- Environment
- Medication
- Chronic stress
- Drugs
- Alcohol
- High fever
- Specific traumatic event
- Family and interpersonal relationships
- Heredity
- Circulatory diseases

Besides reacting to illness and disability in physical ways, people also have mental and emotional reactions. Some people become mentally disabled as a result of a physical ailment.

Symptoms of mental disability include:

- Hallucinations
- Decreased memory
- Withdrawal
- Sleeplessness
- Disorientation
- Mood swings

- Fears
- Forgetfulness
- Change in behavior patterns

Care of the mentally disabled client is very similar to the care of any other client. One of the important aspects of your care will be to support the client's family. Encourage family members to discuss their feelings and concerns with the client's doctor. For the client to reach his maximum ability, it is necessary that his environment be an accepting one.

Defense Mechanisms

When a person is subjected to stress, he reacts with certain defenses. A defense mechanism is a thought used unconsciously to protect oneself against painful or unpleasant feelings. When defense mechanisms are used to such an extent that a person is not in touch with reality, he is said to be mentally disabled. The most common defense mechanisms are:

- Denial—"It's not happening."
- Depression—"It's no use. It's hopeless."
- Regression—acting like a child or becoming very dependent.
- Repression—forgetting about the situation, putting it out of the mind.
- Projection—"It's not my fault but the fault of the medical people."
- Rationalization—explaining how one's behavior is acceptable even though it isn't.
- Aggression—behavior that attacks everyone regardless of cause.

- Overdependence—taking no responsibility for personal decisions; relying on others for all needs.

Depression

Depression may be a mental illness, a way in which a person deals with illness, the result of an illness, or a side effect of medication. The primary sign of depression is lack of any interest in the present situation and environment. Other signs of depression include:

- Poor appetite
- Disinterest in people and things that were previously of interest
- Statements like "I'm not up to that" and "What does it matter anyway?"
- Being overappreciative of help
- Lack of activity or social interaction
- Lack of expression in face or voice
- Sleep disturbances
- Changes in appetite

Allow the client to take part in as much of his care as he wants and is able to. Encourage his decisions and opinions. Establish routines that benefit the client and have a high rate of success.

SUBSTANCE ABUSE

The definition of substance abuse is the continued use of a substance despite adverse consequences that impact major life areas and alter the ability to interact in society.

There are many types of substance abuse. A person can abuse drugs, alcohol, or a combination. The drugs may be prescription or illegal. Substance abuse is seen in all ages and in all economic levels. Abuse may be obvious or subtle. Common signs of substance abuse are shown in Figure 2.2.

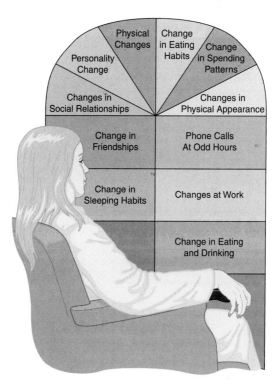

FIGURE 2.2 Be alert to subtle changes in behavior of both clients and family members.

General misconceptions held by abusers about substance abuse include:

- ▪ "Everyone does it."
- ▪ "I can control it."
- ▪ "No one will know."

Working in the Home of a Substance Abuser

You may be assigned to care for a client who lives with a drug user or an alcoholic. First, you must be sure your client is in no danger and that the substance abuser is not likely to harm your client—or you. Discuss the situation with your supervisor so that a plan can be made to offer help to the abuser. Do not try to obtain help on your own. Offering help to a long-time abuser can be complicated and must be carefully planned. It is important that the correct help be offered and that the most appropriate community resource be used. Your supervisor will know how to plan this.

Do not tell the abuser he must stop. The chances are he would if he could but is unable to do so without help. Do not make the family members feel guilty that they have permitted the situation to continue. They may not know what to do. Families of abusers need a great deal of support. Your understanding and demonstration of nonjudgmental behavior will be very important in this household.

If you are assigned to a client who is presently under treatment for having been an abuser, you should act in the manner discussed. Be observant to detect if the client has reverted back to previous habits of abuse. Report to your supervisor any actions that suggest the client is not drug- or alcohol-free. Follow the care plan carefully, and support the client appropriately.

CHAPTER 3

Caring for a Geriatric Client

THE AGED

The elderly population is growing faster than any other segment of our society.

The world has changed so much in the last 50 years that the elderly are often unfamiliar with what now exists. It is not that they cannot learn about the new machines or the new systems, but rather that no one has ever taken the time to teach them. They often find themselves in a strange world. The adjustment to all the changes is often difficult for clients and their families. Although many clients have a well-tested and strong system of coping, enabling them to adjust to changes and new roles, many elderly people are unable to cope with all the changes.

AGING

Aging is universal and starts the moment we are born. The way in which society views the aging citizen varies. In some cultures, the aged are of no value and are often neglected because they are unable to contribute to society. In some cultures and some professions, the aged are well-respected and cared for and are given a place of honor. American society often appears to value youth for its beauty and not to value the contributions of its elderly citizens. At this time, however, it seems that society is also gaining a greater understanding of the aged.

Some facts to remember as you care for older people:

- They want to remain independent.
- They enjoy sexual relationships.
- They can maintain good health.
- Senility is not the same as old age.
- They want to be contributing members of society.
- They can learn, although they often take longer to do so than younger people.

The aging process has many phases. The exact combinations of physical, mental, and social changes vary from person to person. Some changes are obvious and some are not. Some changes are easily acceptable and some are not.

MEETING THE NEEDS OF THE ELDERLY

The needs of the elderly are the same as the needs of all other people, but these needs are met differently.

- Assist with all phases of personal care. A complete bath may not be necessary every day. Remember that many clients have dry, flaky, fragile skin. Lubricate the skin with lotion or oil as the client wishes.

- Observe the client for irritation, redness, bruises, and areas on the body that do not heal.
- Teach the client how to maintain his own personal hygiene when you are not in the home.
- Provide an environment for safe and simple exercise.
- Plan your care around the client's usual household schedule and ethnic customs.
- Provide for warmth and ventilation in the home. Protect the client from extreme heat or cold. Dress and groom the client in what makes him comfortable and is appropriate for his age.
- Do not disturb personal belongings, letters, or pictures unless you discuss it with the client first.
- Do not use baby talk with the client. Speak slowly and clearly.
- Do not speak about the client to others as though he were not there.
- Always show patience and respect.

Physical Changes

TABLE 3.1 *P*HYSICAL CHANGES OF AGING

Body System or Organ	"Normal" Aging Change	Possible Problems Consequence
Skin	Decreased response to pain sensation, temperature changes, and vibration	Accidents; inability to feel hot and/or cold objects, weather changes, injury and/or pain

(continues)

Table 3.1   (*continued*)

Body System or Organ	"Normal" Aging Change	Possible Problems Consequence
Skin, continued	Loss of fat under skin (subcutaneous fat) and fatty padding over bony prominences (i.e., hips); change in number of blood vessels	Veins appear more prominent; wrinkles, (especially facial) and folds in skin appear; occurrence of pressure sores (bedsores); slower healing; loss of hair; fluid balance of skin is difficult to maintain
	Decrease in number of sweat glands	Difficulty in regulating body temperature
	Decrease in oil production	Dry skin, itching, easily injured
	Formation of pigment cell clusters	Moles and "old-age spots" (liver spots), graying of hair
Eyes	Clouding of lens	Development of cataracts
	Decrease in ability to focus	Difficulty seeing at night or in fluorescent lighting
	Decrease in production of tears	Dry eyes
	Inability to blink as quickly	Easier to get a foreign body in the eye
	Muscle degeneration in 50 percent of people over age 70	Central vision loss
	Less light reaching retina	Need for adequate lighting
	Eyelids tend to evert or invert	Irritation

Table 3.1   (continued)

Body System or Organ	"Normal" Aging Change	Possible Problems Consequence
Ear	Decrease in ability to hear high-frequency sounds (presbycusis)	Hearing loss
	Stiffness and inflexibility of ear structure	Distortion of sound and pain if volume is too high
Sense of taste	Decrease in number of taste buds	Food may become tasteless
	Salty taste decreases the most, sweet next	Overuse of salt and sugar
	Sense of smell generally declines	Difficulty smelling smoke, gas, etc., or enjoying pleasant odors
Mouth and teeth	Loss of gum and bone structure around teeth	Periodontal disease, loss of teeth
Brain	Change in reaction time and in verbal and vocabulary skills	Slowed reactions and reflexes; inability to learn quickly
	Memory loss may occur after age 50	Recall, recognition may be slightly slowed (i.e., "Where are my keys?")
	Decrease in deep sleep	Periods of wakefulness during sleep hours
	Decrease in need for sleep	Hours of sleep may change

(continues)

Table 3.1 *(continued)*

Body System or Organ	"Normal" Aging Change	Possible Problems Consequence
Lungs and chest	Stiffness of respiratory muscles	Expansion of the lungs
	Decrease in elasticity of rib cage	Mild barrel chest due to structural changes
	Decrease in area for oxygen and carbon dioxide exchange	Less oxygen available during physical exercise and activity
	Diminished activity of cilia (help to clean lungs) and diminished cough reflex	Difficulty coughing and eliminating foreign particles from lung; increased incidence of bronchitis and pneumonia
Heart and circulatory system	Decrease in cardiac muscle strength	Cardiac output is decreased
	Narrowing of arteries and veins	Blood pressure is increased
Musculoskeletal system	Decrease in absorption of calcium	Osteoporosis (thinning of bone)
	Decrease in bone replacement	Incidence of fractures is increased
	Loss of muscle mass and tone	Fatigue and weakness
Balance	Less-efficient balancing mechanisms and reactions	Incidence of falls is increased; standing position tends to be with flexed hip and knees
Gastrointestinal system	Decrease in esophageal muscle action	Indigestion is more frequent; digestion is slower

Table 3.1   *(continued)*

Body System or Organ	"Normal" Aging Change	Possible Problems Consequence
	Decrease in large-bowel mobility, nervous stimulation	Constipation, diminished frequency of bowel movements (BMs), incomplete emptying of the bowel
	Decreased sensitivity to thirst	Dehydration
Renal system	Decrease in size of urinary bladder	Increased frequency of urination
	Decrease in kidney size	Increased sensitivity to medications
	Slowing of filtration, blood flow to kidney	Decreased ability to eliminate toxic wastes
Genitals	*Men* Enlarged prostate gland	Urinary system obstruction Increased time needed to urinate Increased urinary
retention,		frequency, and infections
	Penis may be less hard	Decreased ability to delay ejaculation
	Women Decreased vaginal and cervical secretions, thinning of vaginal walls	Uncomfortable intercourse, longer time to experience orgasm
	Changes in estrogen levels after menopause	Changes in secondary sexual characteristics
Hormones	Decreased insulin response	Blood glucose (sugar) elevation

Mental Changes

All older people do not get confused, forgetful, and dependent. Those who do must be treated carefully just as you would treat any other impaired client, not as an object of pity or as a child. Some changes are temporary, and some are permanent. Obvious changes in brain function are forgetfulness, disorientation, and irritability.

A physical change may cause some mental changes. Other mental changes are brought about as a reaction to social changes.

Dementia is the gradual decrease in a person's ability to make judgments. This is not a normal part of the aging process. The presence of dementia and the type of dementia can be diagnosed only by a physician. Dementia is the condition that used to be called senility. Reversible dementia is often caused by a physical, social, or chemical stimulus. When that stimulus is removed, the person reverts to his pre-dementia status. Irreversible dementia can be caused by small portions of the brain losing function due to small strokes. This condition leads to confusion, decreased mental acuity, decreased physical abilities, and decreased ability to make judgments. The client may not have the same problems all the time; he may have "good days" and "bad days." Irreversible dementia can also be caused by Alzheimer's disease.

For aged clients who are confused and forgetful, it may be necessary to remind them where they are, who they are, and who you are. Safety is the key to the care of these clients because they are unable to make judgments on their own.

The family of a client suffering from dementia is often stressed and needs help in balancing the multiple needs of the client, the family, and their personal needs.

- Encourage them to seek support from professional groups and community resources for coping mechanisms, financial assistance, and assistance with the physical care of the client.
- Encourage members to attend support groups appropriate for their age.
- Encourage them to establish and maintain meaningful activities outside the house.
- Encourage them to "take a break" from the care of the client without feeling guilty.
- Encourage the family to take an active part in organizations that act on legislation pertaining to the client's condition.
- Encourage them to ASK FOR HELP!!!

Social Changes

There are many kinds of social changes that affect the elderly, including:

- Retirement
- Change in income
- Change in level of activity
- Fear of illness
- Isolation from friends and family
- Death of a spouse
- Change in housing
- Increased dependence on others

Changes in behavior that should be reported immediately include:

- Change in mood, such as withdrawal from activities, becoming anxious or afraid

- Change in activity, either increase or decrease
- Change in eating habits
- Change in sleeping habits
- Change in interests, such as stopping long-established hobbies

Reality Orientation

Reality orientation is a technique utilizing the remaining brain cells to reduce the confusion often seen in clients with dementia. This program must be carefully individualized by your supervisor and requires the continued backup of the client's family and caretakers. Usually, the reality orientation board (Figure 3.1), which is visible to the client, contains simple information useful to him so that he can function at home.

Remember the following as you use this program:

- The program must be individualized for each client. Be sure to consult your supervisor before it is started.
- The client's family is an important part of this program and they must take an active part. If they do not feel they can support this activity, discuss this with your supervisor before the program is started.

Report the following as the program is used:

- Does the client understand the subjects on the board?
- Does the client remember the information? For how long?
- Is the family supportive of the reality orientation program?
- Any other observations you may make.

FIGURE 3.1 Orienting a client to his surroundings assists him in feeling secure.

SPECIAL CONSIDERATIONS IN CARING FOR THE ELDERLY

Safety

It is easier to prevent an accident than to heal its consequences. If you are asked to take part in an activity which you believe is unsafe, refuse tactfully and discuss this with your supervisor.

- Encourage your client to think realistically about his abilities as they change.
- Help provide good lighting and accessible light switches for all tasks.
- Encourage the use of grab bars in bathrooms, showers, and tubs.
- Encourage the use of banisters on all stairs.
- Teach your client to test the washing and bathing water before he uses it. Run cold water through the faucet after using it for hot water. This will prevent burns if someone touches the metal.
- Have the thermostat of the water heater set at a safe level.
- Encourage and demonstrate safe practices in the kitchen, such as not wearing clothes that are long and flowing; turning pot handles inward on the stove so they will not be a danger; watching cooking pots so they do not burn, bubble over, or catch fire.
- Plan emergency exits from the house.
- Discuss the presence and use of smoke detectors with your client and/or the family.
- Encourage your client to discuss his driving capabilities with his physician.
- Do not permit any client to smoke in bed unattended.

Exercise

Health professionals now feel that planned exercise is important for everyone. The benefits are many:

- A feeling of well-being

- Increased strength of bones
- Increased cardiac and respiratory capacity
- Increased strength and tone of muscles
- Decreased weight
- Decreased blood pressure
- Decreased anxiety
- Better sleep habits

All clients should consult their physician before they start an exercise regimen.

Sleep Changes

Many elderly clients experience changes in their sleep patterns. Among the changes may be the total hours of sleep, the time of sleep, and the effect of medications. Before you suggest changes to your client's routine, try to determine what the routine was before his illness. In that way, you will be able to compare his former activity with his present activity. Consider the following suggestions as you discuss the sleep regimen best for your client.

- Limit the amount of caffeinated drinks.
- Create a relaxing, pleasant atmosphere before going to sleep.
- Develop a regular sleep schedule.
- Limit naps and time spent without activity.
- Create a regular exercise routine.
- Review medications.

Sleep is necessary to the body for optimum function. A rested client is better able to take an active part in his care and interact with others in an alert and calm manner.

If your client is not able to create a regular, healthful sleep routine, discuss this with your supervisor.

Medications

Elderly clients react to medications differently than do younger clients. Often elderly clients have several diseases and disabilities and take several medications for each one. The interaction of these medications often results in unexpected side effects. Be alert for any of the following:

- A client who forgets he has taken medications and repeats them.
- A client who saves medications that become outdated and then starts taking them again.
- A client who has several physicians, each of whom may not be aware of all the medications that have been prescribed by other physicians.
- A client who stops taking medication for financial reasons.

Assist your client with maintaining a safe medication schedule. Help your client maintain a foolproof, organized method of taking his medications. This method should be established by your supervisor with input from you and the client. Be sure all your client's medications are prescribed for him. Borrowing medications can be dangerous! Report all side effects, no matter how slight, to your supervisor.

- Be sure your client knows why he is taking his medication and the possible side effects.
- When your client visits a physician, encourage him to take all his medications with him.

- Encourage your client to throw out old, outdated medications and to return medications that are not his.

Help your client get his medications packaged in containers that are easy for him to open and close. Often, clients will not take their medication because they cannot open the bottle.

Sexuality

The need for intimacy does not disappear with age, although there is a gradual slowing of response in sexual activity and a decreasing frequency of activity. Sex and the need for closeness, companionship, and touching are not the same thing. Sexual performance may decrease, but the need for human companionship does not. Sexual desire, response, and activity are also often affected by medications. Therefore, any change in sexual activity or any concern expressed by your client should be referred to your supervisor immediately. Some medications can affect sexual desire and performance. When that is the case, some people stop the medications rather than discuss the problem with their physician. Some diseases affect sexual performance and desire. If you are uncomfortable discussing this or do not have the answers to your client's questions, refer them to your supervisor. Do not forget about them. The fact that the client has discussed this with you indicates this is of great concern to him and his family (Figure 3.2).

You may have preconceived notions and feelings about sexual activity between older people. It is important for you to prevent these ideas from interfering with your relationship with your client. If you are caring for a couple,

FIGURE 3.2 Closeness and sexuality are necessary at all ages.

respect their privacy and confidentiality. Clients may have sexual practices that are unfamiliar to you. If you have concerns or questions, talk to your supervisor.

Abuse or Neglect

Abuse is any act that causes another person harm. Abuse of the elderly is especially disturbing because the abused are helpless to fight back and are often unable to call for help.

Be alert for signs of abuse or neglect. Some of the signs are:

- Bruises on a client that are hard to explain
- Client's fear of one particular person
- A request from a client not to be left alone with a particular person
- Conflicting stories from family members
- A "feeling" that things are not right
- Lack of nourishment and care for the client
- Lack of family concern for the safety of the client
- Exchange of abusive words between family members
- Unexpected deterioration of the client's health

The accusation that a person is abusing an elderly client is a very serious one. Do not make it lightly. But do report *immediately* all activities you see that indicate the possibility of abuse. Most states require that any case of suspected elder abuse be reported. It is your responsibility to become familiar with the laws of your state and the proper reporting agency in your area. Remember, most abuse or neglect is inflicted by a family member or caregiver. *Be alert*!

CHAPTER 4

Working with Children

CARING FOR A CHILD

You will act as one or more of the following when caring for a child:

- Teacher
- Primary caregiver
- Observer
- Stabilizer
- Assistant caregiver

Try to maintain the routine familiar to the family. The fewer the changes, the better. Familiarity maintains a feeling of security.

Report all your observations of behavior changes of the child and the adults in the house. You may notice many changes or very few. When caring for children, remember that they are part of a unit and they depend on that unit. Therefore, the behavior of other family members is important.

Be alert for observations concerning behavior in the home when you are not there! What does the child say? Do your observations agree with the child's report or the adult's report? Your personal opinions as to the responsibilities children should or should not have are not important at this time. The most important point is what works in this house!

Basic NEEDS OF CHILDREN

Children often depend on adults for the fulfillment of their needs. Their needs change in importance and fulfillment. Depending on the age of the child, certain needs may take on more importance. Children are not little adults. Their reactions and needs are based on their experiences as children. Researchers feel that a child must successfully meet specific needs at a certain age before he can mature. Often, when the child is ill or a family member is ill, the family will be unable to completely meet the needs of the child. That is your most important role—to meet the needs of the child (Figure 4.1).

Congenital Anomalies (Birth Defects)

A congenital anomaly, another term to describe birth defects, is defined as "any abnormal organ or part of an organ present at birth, even though it may not be noted at that time." Conditions may result from a genetic disorder or from external factors, such as exposure to toxic substances, drug use, or alcohol abuse during pregnancy. Some congenital anomalies are visible, such as a child born with a shorter arm. Some anomalies are not visible, such as a child with a malformation of the heart.

BASIC NEEDS OF CHILDREN

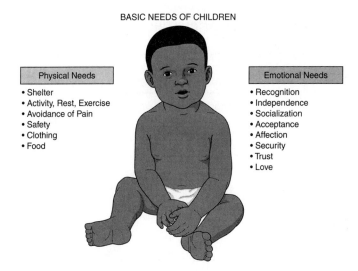

Physical Needs

• Shelter
• Activity, Rest, Exercise
• Avoidance of Pain
• Safety
• Clothing
• Food

Emotional Needs

• Recognition
• Independence
• Socialization
• Acceptance
• Affection
• Security
• Trust
• Love

FIGURE 4.1 Children are often unable to meet their own needs and may not be able to ask to have them fulfilled. Be alert to signals that your help is needed.

When you work in a home with a child who has a congenital anomaly, you will be called on to assist family members as they learn to cope with the situation. It is not unusual for the family to experience anger, guilt, denial, and emotional difficulties as they learn to care for this child.

Discuss your feelings with your supervisor so that your actions will complement the plan of care for the whole family (Table 4.1).

Developmental Disabilities

A developmental disability is any condition that interferes with the proper development of a person. Although these

TABLE 4.1 STAGES OF CHILDHOOD FROM BIRTH TO ADOLESCENCE

Stage of Development	Age	Key Characteristics or Tasks of the Age	Guidelines for Activities
Infancy	Birth to 1 yr.	Rapid growth; totally dependent on adults; experiences first relationship; starts to distinguish the world through the senses	Provide calm routine, taking into account infant's schedule; encourage family to participate in care; stimulation includes brightly colored objects held high or tied to crib, music, different shapes and textures, swings, carriages, rockers; toys infant can put into larger containers, smooth objects that do not injure
Training period	1 to 3 yrs.	Attachment to mother and regular caregivers is strong; begins independence and exploration; learns to say "no"; puts everything in mouth; shows food likes and dislikes; frightened of loud noises and absence of primary caregiver; can understand simple, honest explanation; may or may not share; usually starts to toilet train by age 3	Tell familiar stories again and again; do not lie, because the child does not know fact from fiction; help child become familiar with those objects that are part of his care; help toilet train as the family wishes, without punishment but with positive reinforcement; provide pull toys, balls, stackable objects, mirrors,

Table 4.1 *(continued)*

Stage of Development	Age	Key Characteristics or Tasks of the Age	Guidelines for Activities
			threads, large beads, windup toys
Love triangle	3 to 5 yrs.	Girls mature more quickly; discovers sharing of friends and parents; affection and jealousy apparent; imitation; attempts to please; assumes some of his own personal care; assists with simple household chores; vivid imagination leads to stories; likes to use familiar objects over and over; approval of family important; older children like to take active part in care	Activities with hands and crayons, simple puzzles; simple ball games, and tag; always give simple reasons for activities
Middle childhood	6 to 12 yrs.	Peer acceptance important; easily embarrassed; asserts independence and makes friendships; secretive and argues with adults; growth spurts at 10 to 12 yrs; sexual curiosity	Reasons for actions important; explain; give time frame for schedule; provide scientific play, jigsaw puzzles, table games, board games, electronic and video games, music, puppets, sewing and crafts, model building

(continues)

Table 4.1   *(continued)*

Stage of Development	Age	Key Characteristics or Tasks of the Age	Guidelines for Activities
Adolescence	13 to 18 yrs.	Rapid changes physically and emotionally; sexual development; mood changes; relationship very sensitive; need for privacy; peer relationships important; independence very important; enjoys reading, use of telephone, music; may reject familiar objects or foods; exerts own opinions, may reject suggestions from parents or caregivers but accept them from strangers; idol worship is common; concern for appearance and virility	Respect need for privacy, sexual concerns; explain all actions logically, honestly; encourage child to express his desires and interests.

conditions are permanent, with proper care and teaching these people can live productive and happy lives.

The exact reason some people are born with developmental disabilities is not known. However, these conditions are not contagious. Four reasons some people have developmental disabilities are:

1. Deficiency in the development of the fetus
2. Infection or injury during birth

3. Accident during developmental stages of a child

4. Heredity

Children with developmental disabilities have the same needs as other children. If your client cannot meet all his needs, you or another adult will have to continue to help him meet his needs throughout his life.

You will be instructed in the ways to specially feed, carry, and ambulate your client. In addition, it is necessary to establish a plan the family can follow when you are not in the home and they must assume the care of the client.

Stimulation of the client is important. You may be asked to "play" with the client. This activity is necessary for proper development of the senses. However, there are different activities that are appropriate for different ages and stages of development, so do not assume one activity is correct until you discuss it with your supervisor. Your activities will fall into one of these categories:

- Supporting the family in the form of demonstration, respite, or discussion
- Encouraging independence up to the ability of the client
- Providing physical and emotional care
- Providing a safe general environment, particularly with feeding and ambulation

Observe the family dynamics. How do the members of the family interact with each other? With the client? Do they consider him a part of the family or merely an imposition? Are the family members following the care plan when you are not in the home? The care of a developmentally disabled child can be a draining experience on all family members. Each one is affected in a different way. With prompt reporting, your supervisor can intervene and provide support, counseling, or other aid to the family.

Children under Stress

Everyone reacts to stress and change differently. Children are especially sensitive to threats to their security and familiar routines whether they are ill or another family member is ill. You may notice a child behave in a manner that is unusual, offensive, and difficult to explain. You may notice:

- Refusal to follow familiar household routines
- Shyness, fear, or withdrawal
- Aggressive behavior
- Jealousy
- Nightmares and fears
- Denial of the condition
- Overdependence
- Bed-wetting
- Regression

When illness is present in a home, many things affect the child indirectly. Some of these are:

- Noise restrictions
- Attention restrictions
- Financial conditions
- Family fears
- Activity restrictions

Report changes to your supervisor so that the plan of care can be modified.

Discipline and Punishment

You may be faced with the subject of discipline or punishment. There is a difference. Discipline is a set of rules that govern conduct and actions, resulting in orderly behavior. Discipline can be strict or loose. The rules can be well-known or not well-known. Discipline can be accepted or just followed for fear of punishment. Punishment is a harsh act given as a result of an offense or wrongdoing, as when a rule or discipline is broken.

The goal of directing children is to teach them behavior that will be accepted by society and will foster self-reliance and independence. Children must feel good about themselves and their actions. They should not act only because it will prevent punishment. Self-esteem is developed early in a child's life and is directly related to the way in which behavior is taught and reinforced.

Your role is to maintain the discipline in the home. If you are going to set up new rules in the house, your supervisor will plan this carefully with you. You will be leaving this house but the other people will stay. You must set up rules they can live with when you are gone. Should you be unable to follow the discipline already in the household, or if discipline seems unusually harsh or punishment seems severe, report this to your supervisor with objective data. Punishment is *not* within your role as a homemaker/home health aide; discuss this with your supervisor. As you work with children, remember:

- Treat each child as an individual.
- Discuss with the child the expectations related to his behavior or a particular task: "I expect _____. Do you understand?"
- Encourage and praise children whenever possible.

- Use positive suggestions—avoid saying "Don't." Rather, say, "Please make your bed. Thank you."

- Explain the limits set on the behavior before the child makes a mistake. "You may play outside until it is dark. Then you are to come in. Do you understand?"

- Make mealtime a pleasure. Prepare food the child enjoys.

- Encourage parents to take an active part in making decisions.

- Do not take sides in arguments.

- Suggest that people separate during an argument before harsh words are said or physical punishment takes place.

- Do not be judgmental.

- Report changes in family members or family activities to your supervisor immediately.

- Report feelings or suggestions and the objective happenings that lead you to your suspicions.

- Report child abuse or neglect to your supervisor immediately.

CHILD ABUSE

Abuse is any act that is considered to be improper and that usually causes harm or pain to another person. Even if it occurs only occasionally or even once, it must be reported to protect the child and help the family as a whole.

No matter what the reasons for the abuse of children, all of them result in children being either physically or emotionally traumatized. Sometimes the children report these events; but most often, they do not.

Some Reasons for Abuse

- The abuser was also abused and learned this type of behavior.
- The abuser cannot cope with the stress of having children.
- The abuser is not the parent, but the parent is unable to stop the event.

Reasons Children do not Report Abuse

- They are ashamed.
- They do not know whom to tell.
- They do not know any other type of behavior.
- They are afraid the abuse will increase.
- They feel they deserve it.

Types of Abuse

There are three main types of child abuse (see Figure 4.2):

1. *Physical.* This abuse is seen when a child is beaten, tied up, and/or burned. The evidence of this abuse is usually visible, except in the case of broken bones when the evidence must be verified by x-ray.
2. *Emotional.* This abuse is seen when a child is scared, neglected, screamed at, not permitted to feel safe, or is confined.
3. *Sexual.* This abuse exists when a child is forced to submit to sexual acts because of fear of either physical or emotional harm or because the child cannot prevent it.

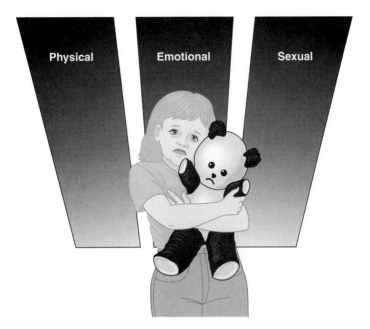

FIGURE 4.2 Abuse comes in many forms. Be alert and report any concerns you have regarding abuse or neglect.

Your Feelings About Child Abuse

Many people have strong feelings about child abuse and the punishments they feel are appropriate for abusers. It is important to be able to work in a home where there has been abuse without judging the people. Your responsibility will be to care for the child in the family without punishing the parent or family member who is the abuser. If you feel you are unable to work in a home where abuse has occurred, report your feeling to your supervisor immediately.

In some cases, the parent will be removed from the house and you will be placed there instead. In this case, you will act in a supportive way to the child and provide a safe, calm environment.

It is possible you will be assigned a client who is a member of a family where abuse is taking place. In this case, you will come by this information by accident. Report it immediately! In some states, it is a crime not to report such information.

No matter what the case, if you are in a home where child abuse has taken place, here are some general guidelines:

- Do not be judgmental. Do not compare one case with another. Be supportive to the parents.
- Be observant! Observe the family dynamics. How do the people in the family interact? Do they scream? Do they tease? Do they talk nicely to one member and in a hostile tone to another?
- Are there any signs of further abuse? Do the children have marks on them? Are they fed? Is there food in the house? Do they have a place to sleep? Are they clean? Do they laugh? Do they play? Do they seem afraid?
- Have you noticed any unusual behavior?
- Your feelings are important in these cases. If you suspect that something is wrong in the family dynamics, report your feelings and the objective observations to your supervisor immediately! Do not wait! Children cannot always protect themselves. They need adults to do it for them.
- Do the parents have activities that can be considered "adult"? Do they have friends? Do they go out?
- Is the family keeping its counseling appointments?

■ Listen to what the children say. If you do not understand what they are saying, report the entire conversation to your supervisor word for word.

Care of the Infant in the Home

The most important part of your role in this house is to teach by example.

Most infants are fed six times a day or about every 3 to 4 hours. Nursing babies, however, may be fed as often as every 2 hours. It is important to remember that some will eat more often and some less. Stick to the schedule already in place in the house. If the mother is breast-feeding her baby, it may be your responsibility to bring the baby to her when it is time for feeding. If the baby is being bottle-fed, you may need to prepare the formula. You will be given detailed instructions by your supervisor about your responsibilities. If you have a question, ask.

Children's diets vary. It is important to support the family members as they learn to follow the diet their physician has prescribed. Do not change a diet or routine without discussing it with your supervisor.

Observe the pediatric client for his acceptance of the diet. If you notice the child has a great deal of gas following a meal, cries a great deal, has diarrhea or is constipated, or refuses food on a regular basis, report this to your supervisor immediately.

Carrying an Infant

Carrying an infant is a big responsibility.

■ Always support the child's head (Figure 4.3).
■ Hold the infant close to you.

FIGURE 4.3 Always support the child's head.

- Do not carry other objects while you are carrying a baby.
- Do not hold an infant while you are talking on the phone or cooking at the stove.
- Do not carry a baby into a dark room. Turn on the light before you enter.
- Be alert to basic household hazards, such as liquid spills, shoes, clothing on the floor, and loose rugs.
- Be alert while carrying a baby up and down stairs.
- Wear good supporting shoes with nonskid soles while you are carrying a baby.

Assisting with Feeding Infants

Breast-feeding is a natural act. Most babies and mothers learn how to do this while the mother is still in the hospital.

The mother's body makes milk about 2 to 4 days after the birth. The clear yellow fluid in the breast before that time is called colostrum. This is a nourishing substance and contains antibodies the baby needs. When the breasts starts to fill with milk, they become hard and full and may be uncomfortable. As the baby nurses, the body regulates the amount of milk needed to satisfy the baby, the discomfort disappears, and the breasts become soft. As the baby grows and needs more milk, the body will adjust the supply.

During the first few days after birth, nursing may stimulate the client's uterus to contract. Sometimes this is very uncomfortable. Encourage the client to discuss any discomfort with her physician before she takes medication to relieve the pain.

Most experts recommend feeding the baby from both breasts at each feeding—usually 6 to 8 minutes to start at each breast. The nutrition of the mother greatly influences the quality of the milk the body produces. The mother should eat a balanced diet, take vitamins if the physician recommends them, and increase the calorie intake slightly. Some medication, alcohol, and caffeine will pass through the bloodstream to the milk and to the baby. It is generally advised to avoid these substances while nursing. The client should drink 6 to 8 glasses of fluid each day. If the baby sleeps well and nurses 7 to 10 times a day during the first months of life, the milk is sufficient and the baby is nursing well.

Some families feel comfortable with having a mother feed her baby while other family members are present. Some women prefer privacy. Support the mother and the family in their decision.

Help the mother ready herself to breast-feed by assisting her in getting comfortable, removing distractions, or bringing the baby, after you have changed the diaper.

Some women nurse sitting up and some nurse lying on their side.

The mother may have questions about the timing of the feeding, ways in which to interest the baby in feeding, her diet, or the care of her breasts. Assist the mother in reading the material given to her by her physician and the hospital. If this material does not answer her questions or if you have questions, call your supervisor.

*G*uidelines—*Assisting with Breast-Feeding*

- Remind the mother to wash her hands before each feeding with a mild soap. Washing the nipples before each feeding is not usually necessary. Normal bathing is usually sufficient to keep the breasts clean.

- Assist the mother with nursing aids, such as breast shields or pumps. Be familiar with the breast-feeding process (Figures 4.4, 4.5, and 4.6).

FIGURE 4.4 Stimulate the baby to turn towards the breast.

FIGURE 4.5 Keep breast tissue away from the baby's nose so he can breath more easily.

FIGURE 4.6 Break the suction before removing the nipple from the baby's mouth.

- The decision to stop nursing is a personal one. Suggest that the mother discuss this with her physician before any decision is made.
- If milk drips from the breast not being sucked, clean the breast. Dripping is normal.
- The routine of feeding and the length of nursing will vary and should be decided by the mother and baby.

Bottle-Feeding

The decision to bottle-feed an infant, or to supplement breast-feedings with formula, is made by the mother and her physician. Choosing the type of formula is also made with medical advice. Your role is to support the mother and the family with their decision. In some cases, the mother will use a special pump to remove her breast milk and put it in a bottle for use later.

Sterilizing Bottles and Nipples

Bottles and nipples are sterilized to destroy bacteria that might cause illness. There are many opinions as to the age when sterilizing bottles is no longer necessary. Do not alter the procedure without being given permission to do so.

Some people sterilize bottles and their nipples in the dishwasher. Some people have found microwave ovens to be acceptable. The most common method of sterilizing bottles and their nipples, however, is on the top of the stove.

PROCEDURE

Sterilizing Bottles

1. Assemble your equipment:

Bottles	Bottle brush
Nipples, caps, and jar	Dish detergent
Hot water from the tap	Tap water
Large pot with cover	Stove or heat source
or a special sterilizing	for cooking
pot for baby bottles	Timer, watch, or clock
Small towel	Tongs

2. Wash your hands.

3. Scrub bottles, nipples, and caps with hot soapy water. Use the bottle brush to clean inside the bottles. Always squirt hot soapy water through the holes in the nipples to clean out any dried-on formula.

4. Rinse thoroughly with hot water.

5. Fold the small towel to fit in the bottom of the pot, and lay it there. This will prevent the bottles from breaking. (This is done when you do not have a bottle rack.)

6. Stand the washed bottles on the towel in a circle around the inside of the pot.

7. Place the caps and nipples into the clean, empty jar. Place into the pot at the center of the bottles.

8. Pour water into and around the bottles and into the jar with the nipples until two-thirds of each bottle is under water.

9. Cover the pot.

10. Place the pot on the stove burner, and turn on the burner to the high or full setting.

11. When the water comes to a full boil, begin timing. Allow the water to remain at a full boil for 25 minutes.

12. Remove the jar with the nipple and caps 10 to 15 minutes after the full boil begins. With the nipples still inside the jar, stand the jar on the table to cool. Allow the bottles to boil a full 25 minutes.

13. Turn off the burner.

14. Take the cover off the pot, and allow it to cool.

15. Remove the sterile bottles from the pot with sterile tongs.

16. Empty the water out of the pot. The pot is now sterilized, so you can use it for mixing the formula.

17. Wash your hands.

*T*hree Types of Formula

*R*eady-to-Feed Formula

- Wash the top of the can before opening with a sterilized can opener.
- Shake the can before opening.
- Refrigerate the can after opening all unused bottles.
- Pour the contents into a sterilized bottle and cap with a sterilized nipple.
- Prefilled ready-to-use bottles should be capped with sterilized nipples right before they are used.
- Refrigerate the unused portions of the bottles.

*P*owdered Formula and Concentrated Liquid Formula

- Wash and dry all cans before opening with a sterilized can opener.
- Follow the directions on the can carefully.
- Be sure to use sterilized water and sterilized utensils when mixing the formula.
- Pour the mixed formula into sterilized bottles and cap with sterilized nipples.
- Refrigerate all mixed bottles until they are needed.

*G*uidelines—*Assisting with Bottle-Feeding*
Using Formula

- Make sure that the formula is fresh and the bottles have been properly stored.

FIGURE 4.7

FIGURE 4.8

- Follow the mother's wishes as to the temperature of the bottles when the baby is fed (Figure 4.7).
- Babies should be held while they are given bottles. Do not prop bottles. Do not leave babies unattended while they are drinking bottles (Figure 4.8).

FIGURE 4.9

- Hold the bottle so that the nipple is full of formula and the baby does not suck air (Figure 4.9).

Guidelines—*Storing Formula*

- Formula can be refrigerated for 2 days without spoiling. After 2 days, it must be thrown away. If you do not know how long formula has been in the refrigerator, discard it. Mark the new can with the date when you open it.
- Formula will begin to spoil within 2 hours when left at room temperature. Keep the bottle refrigerated until 10 minutes before the feeding.
- If refrigeration is not available, discuss this with your supervisor immediately, and she will arrange some way to keep the formula safe.

FIGURE 4.10 Burping method A: Support the baby against your shoulder as you gently pat his back.

Burping the Infant

Most infants swallow some air while drinking. You can prevent a buildup of air by feeding the infant slowly and stopping after every 2 ounces to burp the baby. Burping helps the baby get rid of this excess air. There are two methods for burping a baby:

Method A: Cover your shoulder with a clean cloth, such as a towel or a cloth diaper. Hold the baby in a vertical position so his head is resting on your shoulder. Gently rub and/or pat the infant's back until you hear the burp (Figure 4.10).

Method B: Sit the infant on your leg so his feet are dangling on your side. Put one of your hands on the infant's chest, and lean the baby over so your hand supports him. Gently rub and pat the baby's back with your other hand until you hear the burp (Figure 4.11).

FIGURE 4.11 Burping method B: Support the baby as you pat his back. Be sure his head is well-supported.

Observing the Infant's Stool

You will need to observe the infant's stool or bowel movement at each diaper change to detect constipation or diarrhea. A baby is constipated when the stool is hard and well-formed. A baby has diarrhea when he has frequent, watery bowel movements. When you observe a change from what has been normal for your client, report your observations to your supervisor and to the mother.

The bottle-fed infant will have stools that are yellowish or mustard-colored. They will be lumpy, but soft. One to three bowel movements each day is normal for an infant who is bottle-fed every 3 to 4 hours. It is not unusual for the stools of bottle-fed babies to look as if there are tiny seeds in them.

The breast-fed infant will have stools that are yellowish or mustard-colored, but the color may change slightly and may appear to have a greenish tint, depending on the mother's diet. The stools of infants who are breast-fed will be looser and smoother than those of bottle-fed infants.

A bowel movement after every feeding or only once or twice a day is usual for an infant who is breast-fed every 3 to 4 hours.

Diarrhea in infants can be a very serious problem and requires immediate attention. The stools may appear green and watery, running right out of the diaper. There may be a foul odor, and the frequency of the stools will increase compared with the infant's normal habit. Report to your supervisor at the first sign of diarrhea.

Diapers

Diapers are used to catch the urine and stool that babies expel. By using diapers, you help keep the babies and their environment clean and free of waste material. The methods used to diaper a baby and the types of diapers used vary from house to house. It is important for you to follow the wishes of the family as you care for the baby.

*G*uidelines—*Changing Diapers*

- Change the diapers often to decrease odor and irritation of the baby's skin.
- Clean the baby's genital area each time you change the diaper. Apply lotion or cream as you have been instructed.
- If you use cloth diapers, rinse the stool from them in the toilet before you put them into a diaper pail.
- If you use rubber pants on top of cloth diapers, be sure the elastic is loose enough to allow air to circulate in the pants.
- Do not use rubber pants over disposable diapers, because they already have a rubberized protection.

- Do not flush disposable diapers down a toilet. Dispose of them as the family wishes and as you know to be aseptically correct.
- Observe the skin of the baby each time you change the diaper for change of color, texture, and discharge. Report any changes to your supervisor.

Care of the Umbilical Cord

Before birth, the umbilical cord serves as a lifeline, connecting the fetus with the mother's placenta. All nourishment is passed from mother to fetus through the umbilical cord. At the time of delivery, the cord is clamped and cut and the healing process of the umbilicus begins. Within 5 to 10 days, the cord will be dry, turn black, and eventually fall off, forming the umbilicus. This does not hurt the baby.

*G*uidelines—*Care of the Umbilical Cord*

- Keep the diaper folded down away from the cord. A wet diaper on top of the cord could cause an infection.
- Ask how to care for the umbilical cord.
- One way to care for the cord is at every diaper change, wash the cord with plain rubbing alcohol on a cotton ball. The alcohol will help speed up the drying process and will keep the cord clean.
- Never pull on the cord. Let it fall off by itself. Laying the infant on his abdomen will not hurt the cord. Binders or belly bands are not advised.
- Never give the infant a tub bath until the cord has fallen off.

Circumcision

Circumcision is the surgical removal of the loose piece of skin, the prepuce (foreskin), from the end of the penis. It may be done to increase the cleanliness of the penis. Circumcision can be done in the operating room before the baby comes home. It is always done on a voluntary basis. That means that the mother of the baby must give her permission to have it done. In the Jewish faith, there is a ritual circumcision on the seventh day after birth. This is done either in the hospital or at home.

The physician will give the mother special instructions as to the care of the penis. Be sure and follow these instructions carefully to prevent complications.

*G*uidelines—*After Circumcision*

- Keep the penis protected from rubbing on a diaper. The pediatrician will leave instructions.
- Ask about bathing the child. If the physician does not leave instructions about bathing the baby, ask your supervisor.
- Keep the penis clean and free of fecal matter.
- Observe for bleeding or drainage. Report this to your supervisor.

Bathing the Infant

Sponge Baths

While the umbilical cord is still attached to the baby, a sponge bath with warm water or baby lotion can be given daily. More frequent bathing is usually not necessary. A tub bath is not permitted until the cord has fallen off.

Sponge bathing an infant means gently washing each part of the baby's body with mild soap and warm water, but not submerging the infant in water. Safety of the infant is very important. Whenever in doubt about anything, call your supervisor.

- A safe table or counter is a convenient place to give a sponge bath.
- Clear off the counter and wash it well.
- Spread a towel on the counter to make a soft, warm place on which to place the baby.
- Prepare warm water, mild soap, washcloth, blankets, and towels before bringing the baby to the counter.
- Only one part of the body is washed at a time. Wash, rinse, and dry each body part or area very well. Then cover the body part right away with a towel or blanket.

Tub Baths

After the cord has fallen off, the infant can be given a tub bath. You can use a large sink or a baby bathtub. If you are using a sink, be sure to clean the sink and counter. Scrub the sink with a cleanser and rinse it thoroughly. Assemble your equipment before you begin so you will not need to leave the room to get something that you may have forgotten. You cannot leave the infant in the tub or on the counter, so remove all distractions. Do not do anything else while bathing the baby.

Bath time should be a pleasant and enjoyable time for the mother and baby. Try to involve the mother as much as she is able, and take the opportunity to teach her how to care for the baby. The infant's safety is your first responsibility. Keep your hands and eyes on the baby throughout the bath.

PROCEDURE

Giving an Infant a Tub Bath

1. Assemble your equipment:
   Infant tub or sink
   Two bath towels (soft)
   Cotton balls
   Baby soap
   Baby shampoo (optional)
   Baby powder, lotion, or cream
   Washcloth
   Warm water (warm to
   the touch of the elbow)
   Clean diaper
   Clean clothes

2. Wash your hands.

3. Wash the sink or tub with a disinfectant cleanser and rinse thoroughly.

4. Line the sink or tub with a bath towel.

5. Place a towel on the counter next to the sink or tub, as you may want to lay the infant down to dry him.

6. Fill the tub or sink with 1 to 2 inches of warm water (warm to the touch of the elbow).

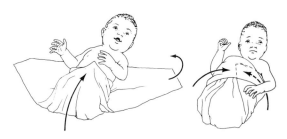

Fold lower
corner of blanket
over the legs
and feet.

Fold the two side
corners under the arms
and over the chest.

FIGURE 4.12

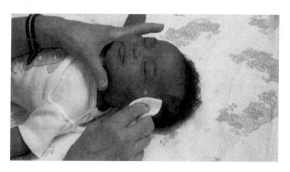

FIGURE 4.13

7. Undress the infant, wrap him in a towel or blanket, and bring him to the tub or sink (Figure 4.12).

8. Using a washcloth moistened with warm water and squeezed out, gently wipe the infant's eyes from the nose toward the ears. Use a clean part of the washcloth for each eye (Figure 4.13).

9. To wash the hair, hold the infant in the football hold, with the baby's head over the sink or tub. This will free your

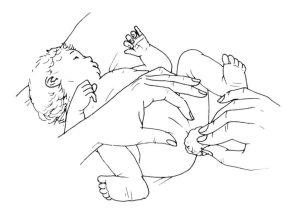

FIGURE 4.14

other arm to wet the hair, apply a small amount of shampoo, and rinse the hair.

10. Dry the infant's head with a towel.

11. Unwrap the infant and gently place him on the towel in the sink or tub. One of your hands should always be holding the baby. Never let go, not even for a second.

12. Wash the infant's body with the soap and the washcloth, being careful to wash between the folds (creases) of the skin.

13. If the infant is female, always wash the perineal area from front to back (Figure 4.14).

14. If the infant is male, clean the foreskin by gently retracting it. If the child has been circumcised, this is not necessary.

15. Rinse the infant thoroughly with warm water.

16. Lift the infant out of the water and onto the towel you laid out on the counter.

17. Dry the infant well, being careful to dry between the folds of the skin.

FIGURE 4.15

18. Now you can apply powder, lotion, or cream to the infant, whichever the mother prefers or as instructed by your supervisor.
19. Diaper and dress the infant (Figure 4.15).
20. Place the infant in his crib, or allow the mother to hold him. Show the mother how to hold the infant in either the upright or the cradle position.
21. Clean and return the equipment and supplies to their proper place.
22. Clean the area where the bath was given.
23. Wash your hands.

Infant Safety

When you are caring for an infant, you must take special precautions to protect the baby from preventable accidents. Even if an infant has not yet learned to roll over, he can wiggle and kick until he falls off a bed, chair, table, or counter. Never leave an infant unattended on any of these surfaces. If you are far from the infant's crib and you must leave him unattended for a few seconds, put him on the floor. The safest place for an infant is in his crib with the side rails up. Some people keep babies in a carriage or a drawer because they do not have a crib. Here are other things you can do to prevent accidents when caring for an infant:

- Wash your hands before handling the infant or his supplies.
- Place the infant on his side or belly after feeding to prevent aspiration.

- Keep the crib rails in the up position when the infant is sleeping or playing.
- Use only 1 to 2 inches of bath water, and never leave the infant alone in the water.
- Never place an infant in an infant seat on tables, chairs, beds, or counters.
- Keep all medications and cleaning solutions out of the reach of all children.

Assisting with Medication

Sometimes, the child you are caring for will require medication. In that case, the family will take the responsibility for giving the medication. Although you may assist, you are not the person who assumes the responsibility of giving the medication.

Your role is to observe the child after he has received the medication. If you notice any change in the behavior of the child, call your supervisor immediately.

Some of the more common changes that should be reported are:

- Rash or any change in the skin color or texture
- Irritability, confusion, or unusual "fussiness"
- Change in sleep pattern
- Pain that persists and is not relieved by the medication
- Vomiting, diarrhea, or constipation
- Change in breathing pattern
- Confusion
- Seizures

CHAPTER 5

Care of the Dying

DYING

You may feel uncomfortable around a person who is dying and not know how to act or what to say to him. Sometimes, to deal with our feelings, we try to avoid working with the person who is dying, or we rush through our tasks as quickly as possible so that we can leave the room. This often leaves the dying person feeling isolated, lonely, or deserted.

By using the same caring, consideration, and understanding you would use with clients who will recover, you will be able to work with clients who are dying.

Many clients are told they are dying. This must be done by a family member or physician. If a family decides not to let your client know he is dying, you are obligated to carry out their wishes even though, at times, keeping up this charade is most difficult.

STEPS IN THE DYING PROCESS

Dr. Elisabeth Kübler-Ross spent many years talking with dying people and studying how people die. She found there are certain stages or steps involved. It is most important to remember that:

- All clients are different.
- The family of the person who is dying will go through all of these steps at different rates and in different orders.
- Clients and families will go from step to step at any time.
- Clients do not go through these steps in any given order.

Step 1: Denial—"Not me!"
Step 2: Anger—"Why me?"
Step 3: Bargaining—"Me, but ..."
Step 4: Depression—"Ah, me."
Step 5: Acceptance—"Yes, me."

SPECIAL EMOTIONAL NEEDS OF THE DYING

Clients who are dying are still living people and have the same needs as your other clients.

- The need to be normal: to know that the thoughts and feelings they are having are like those of others in their situation.
- The need for meaningful relations: a chance to talk to friends and family members on a meaningful level.
- The need for love: to feel that they are the object of someone's love. (Couples may have sexual exchanges.)

- The need for recreation: some way to pass the time, such as knitting, playing cards, watching TV, reading books, or talking to loved ones.
- The need for safety and security: to know that they will be cared for carefully up until the moment of death.

Be a Good Listener

When a client suspects that he is going to die, he may react in various ways:

- He may ask everyone about his chances for recovery.
- He may be afraid to be alone and want a lot of attention from you.
- He may ask a lot of questions.
- He may seem to complain constantly.
- He may make requests that seem unreasonable.

Usually, when a client asks questions of his caregivers, he is sending a signal that he wants information. Assure the client that you will either get the information or provide someone who will.

1. Be honest. If you don't know, be honest and say so.
2. Do not offer false hope or reassurance. Offer realistic short-term goals or say nothing.
3. Do not say too much. A caring look, an unhurried manner, a nod, or a word at the right time tells the client that you care.
4. Let the client take the lead. Often, a question represents a fear or concern of the client. He may feel relieved if you allow him to express the concern.

5. Do not destroy hope. If the client really feels that he will recover, even if you know he won't, do not destroy this hope. The client who has hope usually lives longer than the client who does not.

Many areas of the country have hospice programs. These are organized systems of professional care that help families care for dying clients at home up to and including the time of death. The hospice concept is not appropriate for everyone because not everyone is able to die at home without any heroic methods.

Most hospice clients do not wish any treatment except to remain comfortable and pain-free. These programs provide the support and help to the dying client and his family, without the use of curative methods, and include:

- Treating the client and family as a unit of care.
- Allowing the client and family as much choice as possible in determining care in the home.
- Making use of team professionals who are experienced in home health care.
- Helping the family through the dying process.
- Helping the family after the death of their loved one.

Hospice programs use trained volunteers to help with transportation, shopping, and assisting the client with hobbies and other important things that paid employees seldom have time to do.

Do Not Resuscitate

In some states, a client who is at home may elect a DNR or "Do Not Resuscitate" status. This means that if his heart stops or he stops breathing, no medical procedures will be started to reverse the status. This wish may be indicated by a special color bracelet or a signed paper kept in a prominent place. This is a physician order and is always discussed by the patient and the physician when the client is still able to make the decision and understand the consequences. A client may always change his mind and cancel the order. Different states have different practices, so it is important that you are familiar with the practice in your state. It is also important to know if the Emergency Medical Squads honor these orders when they are called to a client's home.

*P*HYSICAL NEEDS

The client who is dying usually needs careful attention to physical needs.

- *Skin care.* Bathe daily, with partial bathing as necessary. The skin may be fragile, so wash gently with mild soap. Apply lotion to bony prominences and protect them with padding.

- *Positioning.* Do not use tight clothing, stockings, garters, or tight bed linens. Use pillows and rolled blankets for careful positioning. Change the client's position often, at least every 1½ to 2 hours. Change soiled linens and protective pads immediately. Change nonsterile dressings when soiled. Reinforce sterile dressings.

- *Mouth care.* Cleanse teeth and mouth at least twice daily. Remove dentures, or brush teeth. Cleanse mucous membranes with glycerine swabs, as needed.

- *Bowel care.* Keep a careful record of bowel movements, and notify the nurse if the client has not had a bowel movement in several days.

- *Circulation.* The circulation slows as death approaches, and the arms and legs may feel cold and look ashen. Elevate the limbs as needed to aid blood return and do not allow the limbs to be in a "dependent position."

- *Food and water.* Assist the client to a comfortable position. Wash his hands, refresh the linen. Air the room of any odors. Do not try to mask odors with perfume or spray, but remove the source of the odors. Ask the client and his family about food choices, and try to get as much variety as possible. Offer small portions of food and frequent sips of water. Arrange portions in a neat, appetizing manner.

- *Breathing.* Remove secretions from the mouth as necessary. Urge the client to cough up mucous. Elevate the head of the bed or prop the client on pillows if this makes breathing easier.

*T*HE MOMENT OF DEATH

Many clients are now choosing to die at home rather than to return to the hospital. Usually, the nurse has prepared the family for the moment of death and the other events which will occur.

Dying is a spiritual process for some people. Many clients and families will ask to see a priest, minister, rabbi, or person who shares the same concept of spirituality. As the time of death nears, services or prayer rituals may be held at the bedside, and privacy will be requested.

Breathing may become very irregular and stop for periods of up to 30 seconds or more. This breathing is called Cheyne-Stokes breathing, and although it may be upsetting to the family, it is a very usual occurrence. As death approaches, the gurgling breathing called the death rattle may begin. At this time, the client is usually unconscious, so it does not bother him, but it may be distressing to the family.

Talk openly and in a concerned way to the client, even when he is seemingly unconscious. Hearing is the last sense to be lost, and loving words from a family member, up until the moment of death, are comforting. Plan with your supervisor exactly what you will be expected to do when the death occurs. Whom should you call? What should you do?

Your reaction to the actual death depends on your experience with death, your culture, your religion, and how open you are in expressing and voicing your feelings. The agency you work for may hold special "support sessions" for those aides and nurses who have had a client die, so that they can discuss their feelings and help each other.

Postmortem Care

Care of the body after death is called postmortem care. Most of the time when death occurs at home, the family has been prepared for what to do by the doctor and nurse who care for the client. Usually, the client's doctor, the nurse from the home health agency, and the funeral director are notified. If the client's doctor or nurse is not available to make a home visit, an ambulance may have to be called to take the client to the emergency department so a physician can pronounce him dead. Check with your agency for the policies and procedures to be followed at the time of death.

The body must be prepared for removal in any case. After death occurs, the family may sit at the bedside and say their final goodbyes. Families handle grief in many ways, and they should have time and privacy as they need it. Be sure to inquire as to specific religious practices that should be observed at this time.

When appropriate, prepare the body in the following manner:

- Remove all pillows except one under the head.
- Bathe the body, removing secretions and reinforce dressings.
- Place dentures in the mouth if possible.
- Close the eyes, but do not press on the eyeballs.
- Keep the body flat on its back, straightening the arms and legs.
- Move the body gently to avoid bruising.
- Check with the family regarding any jewelry the client may be wearing.
- Fold the arms over the abdomen.
- Check your agency's policy about the removal of catheters. Usually, you will not be asked to remove a tube after death if you did not care for it when the client was alive.

After the body is removed from the home, strip the bed and air the room. Remove any equipment. Check with the family regarding the proper disposal of these items. Place personal items carefully at the bedside so family members can remove them at the appropriate time.

CHAPTER 6

Infection Control

MEDICAL ASEPSIS IN THE HOME

About 500 years ago, scientists began to suspect that some diseases were caused by very small living things called microorganisms. *Micro* means very small. *Organism* means a living thing. Microorganisms can be seen only under a microscope. Some microorganisms are helpful to people. Microorganisms in the human digestive system break down foods not used by the body and turn them into waste products (feces). Disease-producing microorganisms are called pathogens. Pathogens destroy human tissue by using it as their food and give off waste products called toxins. Toxins are poisonous to the human body. Every living organism has its own natural environment where it can exist without causing disease. When an organism moves out of its normal environment and into a foreign one, it can become a pathogen. For example, the bacterium *Escherichia coli* belongs in the colon where it helps to digest our food. When it gets into the bladder or into the bloodstream, it can cause a urinary tract infection or a blood infection. Pathogens may enter the body through any opening, such as the mouth, nose, or a cut in the skin.

Microorganisms need five conditions to grow:

- Moisture
- Correct temperature
- Oxygen
- Darkness
- Food

Medical Asepsis

Medical asepsis means creating an environment that is free of disease-causing organisms by preventing the conditions that allow pathogens to live, multiply, and spread. Medical asepsis:

- Helps the client overcome a current infection or prevent the spread of that infection.
- Protects the client against a second infection by the same microorganism. This is called reinfection.
- Protects the client against infection by a new or different type of microorganism contracted from a visitor or member of the health care team. This is called cross-infection.
- Protects the family and health care team against infection by microorganisms passed from caregiver to client, or client to caregiver. Diseases that can be passed from person to person are called communicable diseases.
- Protects the client from infection from his own organisms. This is called self-inoculation.

CLEAN AND DIRTY AREAS IN THE HOUSE

One way to control the spread of disease is to have a clean area in the house and a dirty one. The kitchen is considered clean, and the toilet is considered dirty.

Clean: This means uncontaminated. It refers to those articles and places from which disease cannot be spread. Clean areas contain food, dishes, and clean equipment. No waste material is ever brought into this area.

Dirty: This refers to those areas that have come in contact with disease-causing or disease-carrying agents. In the home, there are differing degrees of dirty. We make a distinction between items that are dirty with human waste, such as wound drainage or fecal matter, and bed sheets that are only soiled. Articles that are dirty with potentially infectious material are brought into the dirty area for initial cleaning or disposal. This could be linen, bath water, or equipment. Articles that are only soiled are cleaned in the usual way.

Microorganisms live in many places:

- In the air we breathe
- On or inside our bodies
- On our clothing
- In liquids
- In food
- On or inside animals
- In human waste
- In animal waste

Microorganisms are spread in many ways:

- Touching secretions, urine, feces
- Touching objects (dishes, bed linen, clothing, instruments, belongings)
- Sneezing, coughing, talking
- Contaminated food, drugs, water, blood
- Dust particles and moisture in the air

*T*HE IMPORTANCE OF HANDWASHING

Washing your hands frequently with a lot of soap and friction is the best way to prevent the transfer of microorganisms from your hands to a client or from a client to you.

*G*uidelines—*Handwashing*

- Handwashing must be done before and after each task, and before and after direct client contact.
- Handwashing should be done before you put on gloves for a procedure and again after you remove the gloves.
- The water faucet is always considered dirty. Use paper towels to turn the faucet on and off.
- If your hands accidentally touch the inside of the sink, start the whole procedure again.
- Take soap from a dispenser, if possible, rather than using bar soap. Bar soap leaves pools of soapy water in the soap dish.

*P*ROCEDURE

Handwashing

1. Assemble your equipment:
   Soap or detergent
   Paper towels
   Warm running water
   (if possible)

   Wastepaper basket
   Nail brush

2. Open a paper towel near the sink. This is considered your clean area. Put all your equipment on it. Leave it there until you are ready to leave the house.

3. Turn the faucet on with a paper towel held between your hands and the faucet. Adjust the water to a comfortable temperature.

4. Discard the paper towel in the wastepaper basket.

5. Completely wet your hands and wrists under the running water. Keep your fingertips pointed downward. Hold your hands lower than your elbows while washing. This is to prevent microorganisms from contaminating your arms. Holding your hands down prevents backflow over unwashed skin (Figure 6.1).

FIGURE 6.1

6. Apply soap.

7. Work up a good lather. Spread it over the entire area of your hands and wrists. Get soap under your nails and between your fingers. Add water to the soap while washing. This keeps the soap from becoming too dry.

8. Use the nail brush on your nails.

9. Use a rotating and rubbing (friction) motion for 1 full minute.

   a. Rub vigorously.

   b. Rub one hand against the other hand and wrist.

   c. Rub between your fingers by interlacing them.

   d. Rub up and down to reach all skin surfaces on your hands and between your fingers.

   e. Rub the tips of your fingers against your palms to clean with friction around the nailbeds.

10. Wash at least 2 inches above your wrists.

11. Rinse well one hand at a time. Rinse from 2 inches above your wrists to hands. Hold your hands and fingertips down under the water.

12. Dry thoroughly with paper towels.

13. Use a paper towel to turn off the faucet. Never touch the faucet with your hands after washing.

14. Throw the paper towel into the waste-paper basket. Do not touch the basket.

*D*ISINFECTION AND STERILIZATION

Two other important methods for killing microorganisms or keeping them under control are:

1. *Disinfection.* The process of destroying as many harmful organisms as possible. It also means

slowing down the growth and activity of the organisms that cannot be destroyed.

2. *Sterilization*. The process of killing all micro-organisms, including spores, in a certain area.

Spores are bacteria that have formed hard shells around themselves as a defense. Spores are very difficult to kill. The specialized equipment necessary to kill them does not exist.

Sterilization is done in one of two ways: wet heat or dry heat.

P ROCEDURE

Wet-Heat Sterilization

1. Assemble your equipment:

Items to be sterilized, cleaned, and dried	Timer or clock
Clean, covered pot large enough to hold items	Sterilized tongs
	Potholder
Cold water to cover the items in the pot	Source of heat (stove, Sterno, fire)

2. Wash your hands

3. Place the equipment in the pot so that water touches all parts of it. If there are glass parts, put a clean piece of cloth in the bottom of the pot to protect them.

4. Cover the contents of the pot with cold water. Be sure there is head room left in the pot.

5. Put the pot on a source of heat that is big enough to heat it. Turn handles away from the edge of the burner.

6. Bring water to a boil. Do not open the pot. Note the steam escaping under the cover.

7. Boil the contents undisturbed and covered for 20 minutes.

FIGURE 6.2

8. Turn off the heat.
9. Allow the contents to cool undisturbed. Leave the equipment in the pot until you are ready to use it.
10. Using the sterilized tongs, remove the contents to a sterilized holder (Figure 6.2).

*C*ARE OF CLIENTS WITH TRANSMITTABLE DISEASES

The discovery of certain diseases within the last 15 years has alerted health care workers to the need to lower the chance of transmission of these diseases from client to caregiver. These diseases are spread through exposure to blood and body fluids and are called blood-borne pathogens. Two of these diseases are Acquired Immuno-deficiency syndrome (AIDS) and hepatitis B. Another problem is our personal feelings. These diseases may awaken negative feelings because of fear or because some of the victims may have an unfamiliar lifestyle. The physicians and your agency will determine if isolation precautions should be instituted for a particular client. Remember, all clients with AIDS and hepatitis B do not have to be on isolation precautions. However, standard precautions should be observed all the time. The chance of transmitting a disease such as AIDS or hepatitis B from any client to a caregiver is very small if caregivers follow the current regulations from the U.S. Centers for Disease Control and Prevention (CDC) and the Occupational Safety and Health Administration (OSHA). However, remember that each agency may also have specific policies and procedures that should be followed when caring for clients.

Standard Precautions

Medical tests and careful medical history are often not enough to identify clients who have blood-borne pathogens. Therefore, the CDC requires health care workers to decrease the risks for being exposed to all body fluids except sweat. These basic activities are called standard precautions. An important point to remember is that standard precautions are actions taken on a routine basis for all clients. It is the law that standard precautions be incorporated into the routine tasks of all health care workers. In addition to standard precautions, if a definite diagnosis is made, then specific types of isolation, called transmission-based precautions, will be added to the patient's plan of care.

Each agency has a policy discussing standard precautions and the use of protective barriers. Protective barriers are equipment to protect you from splashes, spills, droplets, or other sources of contamination. These include gloves, gowns, aprons, masks, face shields, and goggles.

Your agency is required to provide you with this equipment. If you do not have it available, be sure to ask for it.

Using the Standard Precautions Guidelines

Standard precautions are common-sense guidelines. Clients often feel uncomfortable when being cared for by somebody wearing gloves. Explain to them that this is the new standard of care for all clients, and that it is required. If you injure yourself while caring for a client, report it immediately. If you have any cuts or injuries on your hands or body, report to your supervisor before you start to care for your client, and wear gloves while giving care.

Exposure to Body Fluids or Blood

Wear gloves if a chance exists for contamination. If splattering is possible, wear a gown or protective apron and mask. Flush waste products down the toilet. Spills should be wiped up with soap and water by a person wearing disposable gloves, then wiped with a solution of 1 part household bleach to 10 parts of water. The rag should be thrown out. Gloves should be changed frequently. When removing gloves, do not touch the outside of the gloves (Figure 6.3).

- *Personal items*. Items such as tampons or peripads are not considered medical waste and should be disposed of as you would any dressing.
- *Sharp objects, needles, blades, or razors*. Handle carefully to prevent cutting yourself. These objects should be placed in a puncture-resistant container and disposed of according to local rules. Do not bend needles or try to recap them.

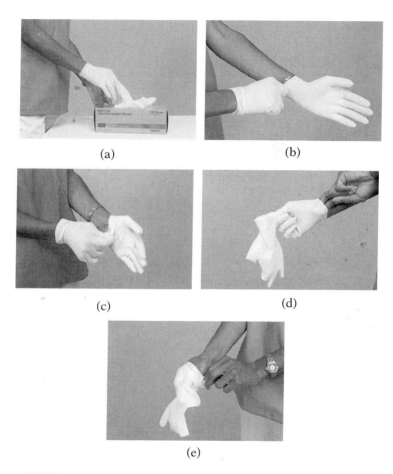

FIGURE 6.3 (a) Use a clean pair of gloves for each client contact. (b) Grasp the glove just below the cuff. (c) Pull the glove over your hand while turning the glove inside out. (d) Place the ungloved index finger and middle finger inside cuff of the glove, turning the cuff downward. (e) Pull the cuff and glove inside out as you remove your hand from the glove.

■ *Dressings*. Wrap these items in a plastic bag and dispose of them according to local law. You may have to double-bag them if you are transporting them as medical waste. Check with your supervisor.

■ *Plates, glasses, dishes*. Use separate utensils—disposable, if necessary. Clean reusable utensils in hot water and detergent. Use hot water and friction, and then dry. Do not let dishes drip dry.

■ *Laundry*. Unsoiled laundry needs no special attention. Soiled linen should be separated and handled with disposable gloves. Keep soiled linen in a double plastic bag lined with a cloth bag or pillowcase. Empty the contents of the plastic bag into the washing machine without touching the items, then throw away the plastic bag. Wash soiled linen each day.

Machine washing (colorfast)	1 cup of household bleach in hot water and laundry detergent.
Hand washing (colorfast)	2 tablespoons of household bleach in 1 gallon of warm water and laundry detergent; soak for 10 minutes and rinse.
Machine washing (noncolorfast)	1 cup of Lysol® in warm water and laundry detergent; wash again with water only to remove Lysol.
Hand washing (noncolorfast)	2 tablespoons of Lysol in 1 gallon of warm water and laundry detergent; rinse at least 3 times to remove Lysol.

*C*DC Guidelines—*Standard Precautions*

- *Disposable Gloves*. Must be worn when contact is possible with blood, all body fluids except sweat (whether or not they contain blood you can see), skin that has breaks in it, and all mucous membranes. This includes activities during direct care and care of equipment.

- *Gowns or Aprons*. Must be worn during procedures or situations when there may be an exposure to blood, body fluids (except sweat), draining wounds, or mucous membranes.

- *Masks, Face-shields, or Goggles*. Must be worn during procedures that are likely to generate droplets of blood or body fluids (except sweat), or when the client is coughing excessively. Discuss with your supervisor the agency policy for reusing masks.

- *Handwashing*. Hands must be washed before gloving and after gloves are removed. Hands and other skin surfaces must be washed immediately and thoroughly if contaminated with blood or body fluids (except sweat) and after all client care activities. Caregivers who have open cuts, sores, or dermatitis on their hands must wear gloves for all client contact or be removed from client contact until the hands are healed.

- *Transportation*. When transporting (moving) any client who may have an infection, ensure that care is taken to use standard precautions to minimize the risk for transmission of microorganisms to others and to limit the contamination of environmental surfaces or equipment.

- Use resuscitation devices as an alternative to mouth-to-mouth resuscitation.

Isolation Techniques (Transmission-based Precautions)

Beyond standard precautions, additional precautions may need to be taken when caring for a client with a highly contagious disease. This is necessary to decrease the chance of spreading the disease to others. Also, when a client is highly susceptible to diseases, caregivers may have to protect the client until his body is able to fight an infection. The physician will determine the type of isolation precaution to use. Check with your supervisor for instructions on agency policy regarding these procedures.

The use of gown, gloves, and mask should be discussed with your supervisor and individualized. A gown is put on to protect you and the client. A mask is worn to decrease the spread of airborne pathogens. It filters the air the wearer breathes. Sometimes, a mask is worn to protect the client, too. There are different types of masks, but they all filter the air and should be applied the same way and changed after every patient encounter.

Basic handwashing is necessary even though gloves are worn. Wash your hands before and after every client contact. The client may have additional restrictions placed on his activity and the washing of his linen, and may need to use disposable dishes. There will be additional laundry.

Remember, standard precautions require that you protect yourself against contact with blood and body fluids. The use of isolation status may mean some additional activities, but basic standard precautions must always be used. Double-bagging is a technique of placing contaminated articles in a plastic bag in the isolation room and then placing the closed bag into another plastic bag as it is held outside the doorway. This can be done by either one person or two.

Guidelines—*Basic Isolation—Five Areas of Concern*

- *Dressings*. Always dispose of dressings in plastic bags and according to local regulations. If the dressings are heavily soiled, double-bag them.

- *Urine/feces*. Flush down the toilet immediately. Clean urinal, bedpan, or commode thoroughly with disinfectant.

- *Dishes*. Use disposable dishes and cups, if available. Wash dishes separately in hot water and soap. Do not let dishes soak or remain in the sink.

- *Linen*. Transport to laundry area in separate plastic bags. If heavily soiled, double-bag. Wash separately in hot water. Dry immediately.

- *Cleaning equipment*. Use a disinfectant. Dispose of cleaning water down the toilet. Dispose of cleaning rags in plastic bags.

Guidelines—*Using a Gown and Mask*

- Gown should be long enough to cover your clothing. The outside is considered contaminated. A wet gown is considered contaminated and should be discarded. Do not touch the outside of the gown when you remove it. A new clean gown should be worn for each client contact (Figure 6.4).

- Apron should be worn to cover clothing during routine client care.

- Masks should fit snugly over the nose and mouth. A wet mask is considered contaminated, as is the front of the mask. Do not wear a mask around your neck. A new clean mask should be worn for each client contact.

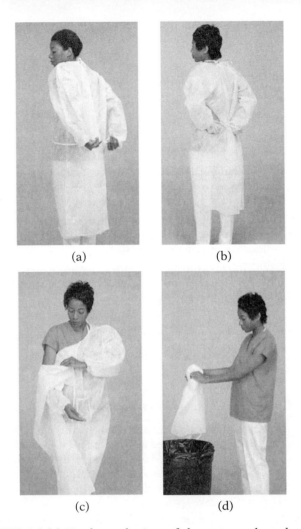

FIGURE 6.4 (a) Tie the neck piece of the gown and overlap the back flaps. (b) Tie the gown securely. put on gloves now if you need them. (c) To take off a gown, take off your gloves if you are wearing them. Untie neck and waist. Grasp shoulders. Turn gown inside out as you take it off. (d) Fold up the gown and discard. Do not reuse a gown. Wash your hands.

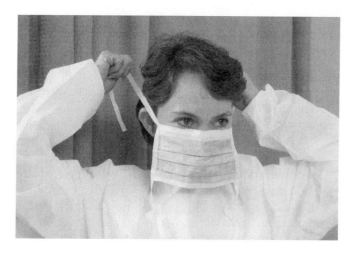

FIGURE 6.5 The face mask that covers both mouth and nose is worn to prevent exposure to blood or body fluids, or when patient is coughing excessively.

There are several different types of masks. Discuss with your supervisor which one is appropriate for your client (Figure 6.5).

REGULATED MEDICAL WASTE

Regulated medical waste is defined as blood, blood products, sharp medical instruments such as needles, and dressings contaminated with body fluids. In many communities, there are regulations that specify how the residents may dispose of regulated medical waste. It is important that you know this information so that you are able to assist the client and his family with proper disposal. In many cases, if the medical waste is not disposed of according to the local regulations, the client can be fined. Some towns make pick-ups, and some require residents to bring the waste to a central disposal site.

- *Human waste products*. These should be flushed down the toilet immediately and not discarded in the street, backyard, or street sewers.

- *Blood and bloody fluids*. These should be cleaned up immediately. If the liquid can be flushed down the toilet, that is the best disposal method. Contaminated clothes should be washed separately in hot water and dried. Dressings and cleaning rags should be double-bagged in plastic and disposed of according to local regulations.

- *Needles (sharps)*. These should be kept in a metal container, such as a coffee tin. Secure the top and dispose of the can according to local regulations. Some items may be kept; some must be disposed of immediately. Discuss with your supervisor the best method of disposal.

- *Medical equipment*. If contaminated, it should be emptied and the equipment double-bagged and disposed of according to local regulations. Discuss with your supervisor whether the used equipment can be kept or must be disposed of immediately.

CHAPTER 7

Care of the Client's Environment

HOMEMAKING

Clean environments keep harmful bacteria under control. Foods stored in specific places are easy to find and can be used more often with less time and energy being spent to look for them. Accidents are prevented in areas that are kept orderly. It is especially important to keep clutter away from stairways and areas where people walk frequently.

Clean environments also tend to make us feel better. When things are looking their best, we are more often relaxed and comfortable. It also gives us a feeling of pride when others visit.

CLEANING A CLIENT'S HOME

"Clean" usually refers to an area that is free of pathogens and clutter.

You may find that what is clean to one person may not be considered clean by another. These differences in values

107

are important to recognize. Try to meet the client's values. If your values and the client's needs are very different, consult your supervisor.

The equipment available to you in your client's house may be different than the equipment in your house. Do not use any equipment unless you are sure how it works. If the equipment is not in good condition, do not use it. Report anything that is unsafe to your supervisor. Encourage the family to check all equipment regularly and maintain it in perfect working order. This prevents accidents and assists with maintaining a clean and healthful environment. Use equipment only for the purpose for which it was intended.

Encourage all family members to make suggestions and offer help. Remember, the family is in a crisis situation and people who may not usually help with housekeeping may be willing to help at this difficult time. A spirit of cooperation and flexibility should be encouraged. Children are important members of families. Do not overlook them. If someone is willing to help but does not know how, a "teacher" (either you or a family member) could be found. In teaching, remember:

- Make the explanation of the job as simple as possible.
- Help the people, but do not do it for them.
- Let them do it their way if it gets the same results.
- It is helpful to write down all the tasks and who will do them (Table 7.1).

How to Keep a House Clean

Make a list of what you need to keep the house clean. Remember to use those products that are already in the

TABLE 7.1   SAMPLE WORK PLAN

Day	Task	Who Will Do It
Monday		
Tuesday		
Wednesday		
Thursday		
Friday		
Saturday		
Sunday		

home. Do not insist that the client purchase your preferred brand of cleaning products. Your list might look like this:

Necessary Supplies	Nice to Have
Hot water	Dustpan
Soap or detergent	Vacuum cleaner
Broom	Scouring pads
Vinegar (white)	Mop
Scrub pad, scrub brush	Wastebaskets
Baking soda, baking powder	Rubber gloves
Bucket	
Trash container	

Be sure you know how to use the appliances in the house. If you are not sure, ask! When using equipment, the following safety points should be kept in mind:

- Keep electrical equipment away from water. Never soak this equipment unless the manufacturer says that you can.
- Use equipment only for its intended use.
- Do not put sharp objects, such as hairpins, knives, or screwdrivers, into electrical equipment.
- Before repairing or cleaning an electrical object, unplug it!

Be sure all equipment is in good condition and does not have frayed cords.

When using any cleaning product:

- Read the instructions on the label. Follow the directions in the order they are given, and use the amount suggested (Table 7.2).

TABLE 7.2 *B*ASIC KINDS OF CLEANING PRODUCTS

Products	Form	Uses	Cautions
Soaps and detergents	Liquid Powder Solid	All types of cleaning; personal cleaning	Read label; protect eyes
All-purpose cleaner	Liquid Powder Solid	All types of cleaning	Read label; protect eyes
Abrasives/ bleach	Liquid Powder	Surface soil; kills certain pathogens	Read label; protect eyes and skin
Specialty cleaners	Foam Liquid Powder Spray	Specific jobs: metal, windows, etc.	Read label

- Do not mix cleaning products unless you have been instructed to do so. Mixed products may cause a chemical reaction that will hurt you and/or the surface you are cleaning (Table 7.3).

- Do not leave cleaners on a surface for a long time. Use care in how much you scrub a surface.

- Change the cleaning water when it is only moderately dirty and rinse, if needed, to avoid streaking or filming.

- Store all cleaning products safely away from children and pets, away from heat sources, and in their original containers. Store cleaning tools and supplies safely as close as possible to where you will use them.

- Line garbage pails with plastic or paper bags. Do not put wet objects directly into paper bags. Wrap them first.

Dusting

Dusting is done to prevent the spread of bacteria. In homes where people are particularly sensitive to dust, you may have to dust often.

- Dampen a lint-free rag with a light spray of water or a commercial spray to keep the dust from spreading.

- Dust with motions that will gather the dust into the rag and away from you.

- Dust from top to bottom.

- Dust pictures on walls, then objects on tables, and finally tables and cabinets.

- If the rag becomes soiled, change it.

- Wash dust rags separately from clothes.

TABLE 7.3 USING COMMON CLEANING PRODUCTS

Task	Product	Use
Bathtub stains	White vinegar or paste of hydrogen peroxide and baking powder	Rub stain with rag dipped in vinegar; leave paste on stain overnight; rinse
Tile cleaner	Baking soda	Sprinkle on, rub with damp rag or sponge; rinse, because solution makes tile slippery
Windows and painted surfaces	Mix carefully: 5 cups water 1 teaspoon detergent 1 pint rubbing alcohol 1/2 cup sudsy ammonia	Wash area carefully; rinse well; dry
Mattress stain solution	1/2 cup water 1/2 cup white vinegar	Dab solution on stain and let dry; rub area with water and detergent; leave on for 10 minutes; blot dry; rinse; let mattress dry

Washing Dishes

Dishes should be washed soon after meals. If a dishwasher is used or dishes are to be washed at a later time, scrape the food off the dish (a rubber spatula is a good tool to use for this job). Then rinse or soak the dishes in a basin of water.

If washing dishes by hand:

- Place dishes on the counter in the order in which they are to be washed—least dirty first (glasses, silverware, plates, cups, and saucers), most dirty last (pots and roasting pans).
- Wash dishes in hot, soapy water and rinse in clear water. If water is not plentiful, use a dishpan in which you wash the dishes instead of letting the water run as you wash.
- Drain dishes on drainboard.
- Dry dishes with a clean cloth. If none are available, allow dishes to air dry.
- When water is not plentiful, use water from rinsing dishes for another cleaning task, such as washing the floor. Wash dishes in water hot enough to clean the grease from them and destroy as many micro-organisms as possible.

Keeping the kitchen clean is important. Just as food keeps us alive, it is also used by bacteria. Cleaning spills and taking proper care of leftover food is very important.

- Trash should be disposed of regularly (before it falls out of the container). If the trash is wet, put it into a plastic bag first and then into the garbage can. Keep the garbage can clean. Wash it often!
- The stove should be wiped up regularly with soapy water to prevent spills from becoming "cooked on."
- The refrigerator (or the place where food is kept cold) should be wiped out on a regular basis. If the refrigerator needs defrosting, discuss this with the family and/or your supervisor. Do not use sharp

objects to poke at ice clumps when defrosting the refrigerator. If the refrigerator is self-defrosting, clean up spills promptly. Food tends to dry out faster in these models.

■ Small appliances can be wiped down with soap and water or an all-purpose cleaner after they have been disconnected.

■ Countertops should be free of food spills and grease. Areas around drawer handles and door pulls should be kept clean by wiping with a cloth (or sponge) and warm soapy water.

Cleaning Bathrooms

Because of the constant moisture in the air, bathrooms need regular cleaning to keep them free of bacteria and odors. If bathroom floors are ceramic tile, any water spilled on them can make them slippery and dangerous. Keep the floors dry.

Safety in bathrooms should always be on your mind. Before a client uses a bathroom, check it:

■ Are there nonskid mats in the tub?

■ Are there nonskid rugs on the tile floor?

■ Are there grab bars in the shower or tub?

■ Is there good lighting?

■ Is there ventilation?

■ Cleaning shower walls and bathtubs can be kept to a minimum if everyone will wipe the area out after each use. Keep a rag or old towel handy for them to use.

■ Sinks and other bathroom fixtures should be cleaned regularly with cleanser and a rag. Do not destroy the surface of enamel fixtures by using cleaners that will scratch them.

■ To clean the toilet bowl, you will need: soap or detergent, a toilet bowl brush, and a rag or sponge. Note: Do not wipe anything else with this rag or sponge. Wash it after this task.

1. Lift up the seat and put soap or detergent into the bowl.
2. Scrub the inside of the bowl with a toilet bowl brush. Get under the rim of the bowl.
3. Let the suds stay in the bowl while you wash the outside.
4. To avoid a possible chemical reaction, do not mix toilet bowl cleaner with any other cleanser.
5. Use clean hot water to rinse off all parts of the toilet with the sponge or rag.
6. If there are water stains such as rust in the bowl, shake in 1/4 cup of toilet bowl cleaner. Let stand about 30 minutes, then scrub and flush.

Laundry

Before washing any clothes, repair all tears, loose buttons, and jammed zippers. If you cannot do this, put the clothes aside and either repair them later or tell your client about the need for the repairs. Before washing, sort clothes by:

■ Color. Dark colors should be washed separately from light colors.
■ Fabric. Delicate fabrics cannot take as much scrubbing as can heavy-duty fabrics.

■ Degree of dirt. Heavily soiled items should not be washed with lightly soiled ones.

Ask the client how to operate the washer correctly or read the instructions in the "use and care" booklet from the appliance manufacturer.

After sorting clothes, load the machine, being careful not to overload it. Put in the recommended amount of detergent and select the water temperature and amount of agitation. Add bleach and fabric softener (if needed) after the water has soaked all the clothes.

Clothes dried out of doors conserve energy and have a fresh, clean smell. Take dry clothes immediately from a dryer; they will then need less ironing.

Some homes do not have a washing machine. After you have found out how the laundry is usually done in the home, discuss with your supervisor what your responsibilities will be. Bending and lifting wet, heavy pieces of linen could cause you to injure your back. If you must do this, use good body mechanics! Protect your back!

Care of Rugs and Carpeting

Ask your client how to care for the carpets and rugs. Frequent vacuuming or sweeping will preserve the rugs and decrease the lint and dust.

If the client has a vacuum cleaner, remember:

■ Ask how to change the dirt collection bag inside.
■ Use the vacuum cleaner at a convenient time for the family when it will not disturb them.

When you find stains on a carpet or rug, you may treat them as follows:

■ If it is an old stain, you will probably not be able to get it out. If it is a new stain, you may try to remove it.

- You may use commercial stain removers.
- You may mix water and baking soda into a solution and rub it into the stain. After it dries, vacuum.
- If the spot is sticky, sprinkle baking soda on it, then vacuum.

Care of Floors

Clean floors also decrease the spread of bacteria and provide a safe path in which people can walk.

- Sweep floors frequently, especially before washing them.
- Ask the family members how they usually clean the floors. Wood floors often require special cleaners and are not cleaned with water.
- Use the detergent or cleanser according to directions. Do not let water remain on the floor.
- Most households will have a mop for this job. If you do not find one, discuss this with your supervisor.
- Let the floor dry before walking on it or putting furniture back in place.

Pests and Bugs

Pests and bugs may carry diseases and be annoying to you and your client. They may bite, cause skin irritations, or even frighten people. The best way to keep an area free of bugs, rodents, and other pests is to keep it clean and free of clutter.

- Put food away in closed containers; metal, glass, and plastic are best.

- Clean up spills and crumbs.
- Take out garbage and trash.
- Keep garbage and trash in covered containers.
- Roaches and mice can pass through small cracks in walls and near pipes. Talk to your supervisor about having someone caulk up such holes.
- Do not let water stand inside or outside the house.

If you or any family member wish to use a commercial product to get rid of bugs or rodents, check with your supervisor to be sure that it is safe.

*B*ED MAKING

You may care for a client in his own bed. Your client may decide to sleep on a couch or a hospital bed in his home. Your client may have side rails on his bed. Side rails are used both to protect the client and to assist him as he moves in the bed by providing him with something to grab for support. If your client is only in need of a side rail to prevent him from falling out of bed, you could put chairs up against the bed with their backs against the mattress. Tie the chairs together and tie them to the bed. The same rules and procedures apply for any type of bed.

- Keep the bed dry and clean—change linen when necessary.
- Keep the linen wrinkle-free. Wrinkles are not only uncomfortable, but restrict the client's circulation and can cause painful decubitus ulcers (bed sores). These are open wounds that often slow the client's recovery. Decubiti can form very quickly and are difficult to heal.

- Make the bed to suit your particular client.
- Keep the bed free of food particles and crumbs.

Guidelines—*Bed Making*

- Use the linen the client has available. If you do not have enough, report this to your supervisor.
- Try to make the bed according to the custom of the house. If you must change the custom, explain your reasons to the client and his family.
- Do not use a torn piece of linen. It may tear even more and could be dangerous.
- Never use a pin on any item of linen.
- Do not shake the bed linen. Shaking spreads harmful microorganisms to everything and everyone in the room, including you.
- Never allow any linen to touch your uniform.
- Dirty used linen should never be put on the floor.
- Put dirty linen in the place agreed upon by you and the client's family.
- Some clients use fitted bottom sheets. Others use flat sheets with which the homemaker/home health aide makes mitered corners. The mitered corners keep the sheets firm and smooth and makes the bed neat and attractive.
- The bottom sheet must be firm, smooth, and wrinkle-free. This is very important for the client's comfort.
- By fanfolding the top of the bed, you make it easy for the client to get in and out of his bed.
- The draw sheet is about half the size of a regular sheet. When draw sheets are not available, a large sheet can be folded in half widthwise (with small and large hems together) and used. The fold must always be placed toward the head of the bed and the hems toward the foot of the

bed. You could also use a tablecloth. If you must protect the bed, a plastic tablecloth under the draw sheet makes an excellent protective sheet. Never use plastic from a garment bag or garbage bag.

▪ The plastic draw sheet and disposable bed protectors protect the mattress. Plastics should never touch a client's skin. When using a plastic draw sheet, be sure to cover it entirely with a cloth draw sheet.

▪ Some clients do not use a draw sheet. Instead, small disposable bed protectors are placed on the bed under the client as necessary. These are often expensive. Check with your supervisor before you suggest this to the family.

▪ To save linen and washing, a used clean top sheet may be used as a draw sheet or bottom sheet.

▪ A client who does not use his bed a great deal may not have to have the linen changed every day. Evaluate the linen, the home, the client, and the entire situation before you change the bed.

▪ Always use good body mechanics, no matter what kind of bed your client is in.

▪ "Bottom of the bed" refers to the mattress pad, if used; the bottom sheet; and the draw sheets.

▪ "Top of the bed" refers to the top sheet; the blanket, if used; and the bedspread.

▪ Remember that you save time and energy by first making as much of the bed as possible on one side before going to the other side.

Three Basic Beds

There are three basic ways to make a bed:

1. The closed bed. This bed is usually made when it will remain empty for a while. You can make it with a bedspread or using only a sheet and blanket.

2. The open bed. This bed is used when it will be occupied within a short period of time.

3. The occupied bed. This bed is made with the client in the bed.

*P*ROCEDURE

Making the Closed Bed

1. Assemble your equipment:
> Mattress cover, if used
> Bottom sheet
> Cotton and plastic draw sheet (or disposable bed protector)
> Top sheet
> Blanket
> Bedspread
> Pillowcase
> Pillow
> Pillow protector, if used
> Chair

2. Wash your hands.

3. Place a chair near the bed.

4. Put the pillow on the chair.

5. Stack the bed-making items on the chair in the order in which you will use them: first things to be used on top, last things to be used on the bottom.

6. If you have a hospital bed, adjust the bed to the highest horizontal position and lock the bed in place. If not, move the bed so you have room to practice good body mechanics.

7. Pull the mattress to the head of the bed until it touches the headboard.

8. Place the mattress pad on the mattress, even with the head of the mattress.

9. Fold the bottom sheet lengthwise and place it on the bed:
   a. Place the center fold of the sheet at the center of the mattress from head to foot (Figure 7.1).
   b. Put the small hem at the foot of the bed, even with the edge of the mattress.
   c. Place the large hem at the head of the bed with about 18 inches left to tuck in. Always do this while practicing good body mechanics. Bend your legs, not your back.
10. Open the sheet. It should now hang evenly over each side of the bed.
11. Tuck the sheet in tightly at the head of the bed. Lift the mattress with the hand closest to the foot of the bed and tuck with the other hand. This is good body mechanics.
12. To make a mitered corner:
   a. Pick up the edge of the sheet at the side of the bed 12 inches from the head of the mattress (Figure 7.2).
   b. Place the triangle (the folded corner) on top of the mattress (Figure 7.3).
   c. Tuck the hanging portion of the sheet under the mattress (Figure 7.4).

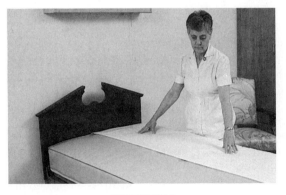

FIGURE 7.1

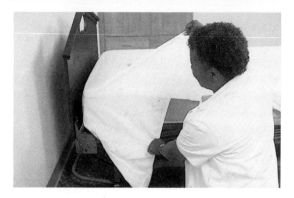

FIGURE 7.2

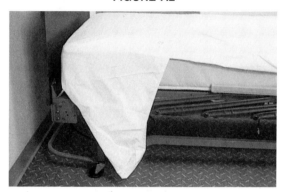

FIGURE 7.3

FIGURE 7.4

123

   d. While you hold the fold at the edge of the mattress, bring the triangle down over the side of the mattress.

   e. Tuck the sheet under the mattress from head to foot (Figure 7.5).

13. Stand and work entirely on one side of the bed until that side is finished.

14. Place the plastic draw sheet 14 inches (two open handspans) down from the head of the bed. Tuck it in (Figure 7.6).

15. Cover the plastic draw sheet with the cotton draw sheet and tuck it in (Figure 7.7).

16. Fold the top sheet lengthwise and place it on the bed:

   a. Place the center fold on the center of the bed from the head to the foot.

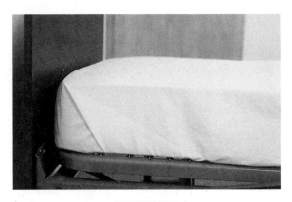

FIGURE 7.5

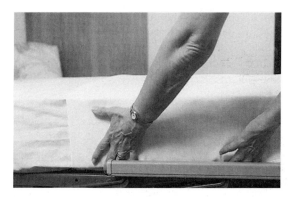

FIGURE 7.6

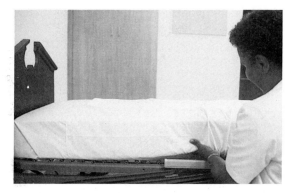

FIGURE 7.7

b. Place the large hem at the head of the bed, even with the top edge of the mattress.

c. Open the sheet, with the rough edge of the hem up.

d. Tightly tuck the sheet under the foot of the bed.

    e. Make a mitered corner at the foot of the bed.

    f. Do not tuck the sheet in at the side of the bed.

17. Fold the blanket lengthwise and place on the bed.

    a. Place the center fold of the blanket on the center of the bed from head to foot.

    b. Place the upper hem 6 inches from the top edge of the mattress.

    c. Open the blanket.

    d. Tuck it under the foot tightly.

    e. Make a mitered corner at the foot of the bed.

    f. Do not tuck in at the side of the bed.

18. Fold the bedspread lengthwise and place it on the bed.

19. Now move to the other side of the bed. Start with the bottom sheet.

    a. Straighten the sheet to get rid of all wrinkles. This should be done three times, first near the head, then the middle, and then at the foot of the bed.

    b. Miter the top corner.

    c. Pull the sheet tight so it is wrinkle-free. Roll the sheet up in your hands so it is near the bed and pull slightly down and tuck in. Do this near the head, the middle, and the foot of the bed.

    d. Pull the plastic draw sheet tight and tuck it in.

    e. Pull the cotton draw sheet tight and tuck it in.

    f. Straighten out the top sheet, making the mitered corner at the foot of the bed.

    g. Miter the corner of the blanket.

    h. Miter the corner of the bedspread (Figure 7.8).

20. To make the cuff:

    a. Fold the top hem of the spread under the top hem of the blanket.

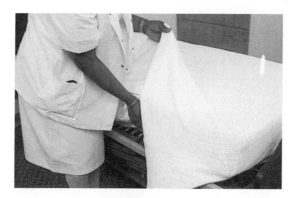

FIGURE 7.8

FIGURE 7.9

b. Fold the top hem of the sheet back over the edge of the
spread and the blanket to form a cuff. The hemmed side
of the sheet must be on the underside, so that it does not
come in contact with the client (Figure 7.9).

21. To put the pillowcase on a pillow:

  a. Hold the pillowcase at the center of the end seam.

b. With your hand outside the case, turn the case back over your hand.

c. Grasp the pillow through the case at the center of the end of the pillow.

d. Bring the case down over the pillow (Figure 7.10).

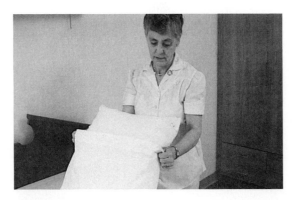

FIGURE 7.10

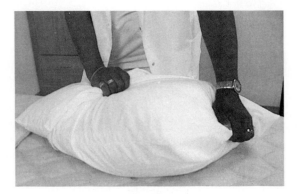

FIGURE 7.11

   e. Fit the corner of the pillow into the seamless corner of the case (Figure 7.11).

   f. Fold the extra material from the side seam under the pillow.

   g. Place the pillow on the bed with the open end away from the door.

22. Adjust the bed to its lowest horizontal position if the client has a hospital bed.

Procedure

Making the Open, Fanfolded, Empty Bed

1. Make a closed bed.

2. Grasp the cuff of the bedding in both hands.

3. Pull it to the foot of the bed (Figure 7.12).

4. Fold the bedding back on itself toward the head of the bed. The edge of the cuff must meet the fold.

5. Smooth the sheets on each side neatly into the folds you have made.

6. Wash your hands.

FIGURE 7.12

*G*uidelines—*The Occupied Bed*

Divide the bed in two parts—the side the client is lying on and the side you are making. By doing this, the weight of the client is never on the side where you are working.

- Always keep the side rail up on the client's side.
- Usually, the occupied bed is made after giving the client a bed bath. The client should be covered with the bath blanket while you are making the bed.
- The sheets must be placed on the bed so the rough seam edges are kept facing the mattress and away from the client's skin.
- Some clients prefer the pillow to be moved with them from side to side as the bed is being made. Some clients will ask you to remove the pillow while making the bed. Either way is acceptable unless there is a medical contraindication (reason for not doing something). Your supervisor will tell you if a particular bed position must be maintained.
- Remember to talk to your client while you are making the bed. Continually notice his condition during the procedure.

*P*ROCEDURE

Making the Occupied Bed When Side Rails Are Present

1. Assemble your equipment near the bed, in the order in which you will use them. A chair is useful for this purpose.
   Two large sheets
   One plastic draw sheet, if used

One cotton draw sheet, if used
Disposable bed protectors, if used
One bath blanket, if available
Pillowcase(s)
One blanket
One bedspread
Container for dirty laundry

2. Wash your hands.

3. Ask any visitors to step out of the room, if appropriate.

4. Tell the client you are going to make his bed.

5. If you are working on a hospital bed, lower the backrest and knee rest until the bed is flat, if that is allowed. Raise the bed to its highest horizontal position and lock in place.

6. Loosen all the sheets around the entire bed.

7. Take the bedspread and blanket off the bed, and fold them over the back of the chair. Leave the client covered only with the top sheet.

8. If using a bath blanket, cover the client with this by placing it over the top sheet. Ask the client to hold the bath blanket. If he is unable to do this, tuck the top edges of the bath blanket under the client's shoulders. Without exposing him, remove the top sheet from under the bath blanket. Fold the top sheet and place over the back of a chair.

9. If the mattress has slipped out of place, move it to its proper position touching the headboard. Remember to use proper body mechanics. If you cannot move the mattress, get assistance.

10. Raise the side rail on the opposite side from where you will be working, and lock in place.

11. Ask the client to turn onto his side toward the side rail. Help the client to turn if necessary. If the client cannot turn, have him stay on his back but move as far as possible toward the side rail. Be careful as to the placing of the client's hands. Adjust the pillow to suit the client's needs. Check it for items such as dentures and eyeglasses.

12. Fold the cotton draw sheet toward the client and tuck it against his back. Protect him from any soiled matter on the bedding (Figure 7.13).

13. Raise the plastic draw sheet (if it is clean) over the bath blanket and client.

14. Roll the bottom sheet toward the client and tuck it against his back. This strips your side of the bed down to the mattress (Figure 7.14).

15. Take the large clean sheet and fold it in half lengthwise. Do not permit the sheet to touch the floor or your uniform.

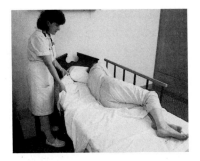

FIGURE 7.13

FIGURE 7.14

16. Place it on the bed, still folded, with the fold running along the middle of the mattress. The small hem end of the sheet should be even with the foot edge of the mattress. Fold the top half of the sheet toward the client. (This is for the other side of the bed.) Tuck the folds against the client's back, below the plastic draw sheet.

17. Tuck the sheet around the head of the mattress by gently raising the mattress with the hand closest to the foot of the bed and tucking with the other hand.

18. Miter the corner at the head of the mattress. Tuck in the clean bottom sheet on your side from head to foot of the mattress.

19. Pull the plastic draw sheet toward you, over the clean bottom sheet, and tuck it in.

20. Place the clean cotton draw sheet over the plastic sheet, folded in half. Keep the fold near the client. Fold the top half toward the client, tucking the folds under his back, as you did with the bottom sheet. Tuck the free edge of the draw sheet under the mattress.

21. Ask the client, or help him, to roll over the "hump" onto the clean sheets toward you.

22. Raise the side rail on your side of the bed, and lock into place.

23. Go to the opposite side of the bed and lower the side rail.

24. Remove the old bottom sheet and cotton draw sheet from the bed. Put them into the container for soiled linen. Pull the fresh bottom sheet toward the edge of the bed. Tuck it under the mattress at the head of the bed and make a mitered corner. Then pull the bottom sheet under the mattress from the head to the foot. Do this by rolling the sheet up in your hand toward the mattress and pull it as you tuck it under.

25. One at a time, pull and tuck each draw sheet under the mattress (Figure 7.15).

26. Have the client turn on his back.

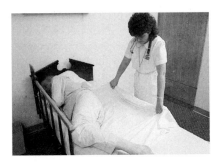

FIGURE 7.15

27. Change the pillowcase, and place the pillow under the client's head. If necessary, assist the client to place the pillow under his head.

28. To put the pillowcase on a pillow:

    a. Hold the pillowcase at the center of the end seam.

    b. With your hand outside the case, turn the case back over your hand.

    c. Grasp the pillow through the case at the center of the end of the pillow.

    d. Bring the case down over the pillow.

    e. Fit the corner of the pillow into the seamless corner of the case.

    f. Fold the extra material from the side seam under the pillow.

    g. Place the pillow on the bed with the open end away from the door.

29. Spread the clean top sheet over the bath blanket with the wide hem at the top. The middle of the sheet should run along the middle of the bed. The wide hem should be even with the head edge of the mattress. Ask the client to hold the hem of the clean sheet, if he can, while you remove the

bath blanket, moving toward the foot of the bed. Do not expose the client.

30. Tuck the clean top sheet under the mattress at the foot of the bed. Make sure you leave enough room for the client to move his feet freely. Miter the corner of the sheet if the client likes this.

31. Spread the blanket over the top sheet. Be sure the middle of the blanket runs along the middle of the bed. The blanket should be high enough to cover the client's shoulders.

32. Tuck the blanket in at the foot of the bed if the client likes this. Make a mitered corner with the blanket.

33. Place the spread on the bed as the client prefers. Pull up the side rails.

34. Go to the other side of the bed. Put down the side rails, turn the top covers back and miter the top sheet, then miter the blanket. Be sure the top covers are loose enough that the client is able to move his feet.

35. To make the cuff:

a. Fold the top hem edge of the spread over and under the top hem of the blanket.

b. Fold the top hem of the top sheet back over the edge of the spread and blanket to form a cuff. The rough edge of the hem of the sheet must be turned down so the client does not come in contact with it.

36. Raise the backrest and knee rest to suit the client if this is allowed.

37. Lower the entire bed to its lowest horizontal position.

38. Put the side rails in place.

39. Make sure the client is comfortable.

40. Put all used linen in the proper place.

41. Wash your hands.

42. Chart any observations you made during this procedure.

Safety

It is important to remember that, by your actions, you are teaching family members. As they observe you practicing safety, they will be made aware of its importance.

It is your responsibility to protect your client and be continually aware of his safety. Make yourself aware of potential hazardous situations and their remedies in each home where you work.

It is also your responsibility to protect yourself. Be careful! Be aware! Be alert!

More accidents occur in the home than in any other place. There are several reasons for this:

- We are careless.
- We do not have safety inspections in homes as we do in commercial buildings.
- We are not aware of the potential hazards that exist in homes.

General Safety Rules You Should Follow

- Discuss emergency communication with your supervisor. If no telephone is available, determine the best route of communicating.
- Report to your supervisor any unsafe conditions where you are working.
- When you see something on the floor that does not belong there, pick it up. If you see spilled liquid, wipe it up.
- Avoid slippery floors.

- If slippery floors cannot be avoided, walk on them carefully.

- Remove scatter rugs. If you cannot remove them, tack them down.

- Be sure to set the brakes on the wheelchair when a client is getting in or out.

- Use side rails on the bed if there is a chance the client will fall out.

- Do not work in poor light.

- Do not use any piece of equipment unless you are sure you know how it works.

- Keep the telephone numbers of the police, rescue squad, fire department, and poison control center near each telephone.

- Read labels. If a container does not have one, do not use the contents.

- Know how to get out of the house in case of fire.

- Be aware of what accidents are most prevalent at different ages.

- Do not attempt a task if you have any doubt that you can do it.

- Do not reach into a garbage can or trash basket. You may hurt yourself on sharp objects.

Safety Precautions for Children

- Small children should never be left unattended.

- Articles used in the child's care should be kept out of reach of a toddler when they are not being used, especially needles, water, safety pins, medications, matches, electrical equipment, syringes, and thermometers.

- Toys should never be left carelessly on the floor. Pick them up because they could cause someone to fall. Clean up spills and messes such as food, urine, and feces immediately.

- The sides of a child's crib should be up at all times except when someone is giving direct care to the child.

- Doors to stairways and the kitchen should be closed and locked.

- Venetian blind cords should be kept out of the reach of children.

- Be sure there are no small toys or objects in the bed/crib that could be swallowed.

- Be sure there are no large objects in the bed or crib that the child could stand on. The child might fall out of bed as a result.

- Keep all poisonous substances in a high place behind locked doors.

Safety Precautions for the Aged

Abilities change as we age. Unfortunately, many people do not realize this fact. Therefore, they attempt tasks that they can no longer do safely. You should be aware of the capabilities of your particular client.

- Be sure there is adequate lighting for every task.

- Be alert to sensory changes that may or may not have taken place.

- Protect your client from falling. Recovery from falls takes a long time in elderly people.

- Protect your client from burns. Temperature sensation becomes less accurate as we age. Run cold water through a faucet after you run hot water so if your client touches the faucet, he will not burn himself. Test the bath water yourself.

- If a confused client tells you he is going to do something that you know to be harmful, take him seriously and protect him.

Electricity

- Make sure all electrical equipment you use is in good condition.

- Be sure the cords are not frayed and that you are using the proper tool for the job.

- Do not put electrical cords under rugs. They can become frayed and can go unnoticed under a rug. This is a perfect place for a fire to start.

- Be sure your hands are dry before you use any electrical equipment.

- Do not change fuses or touch circuit breakers unless you are sure you know what you are doing.

- Do not run all household appliances at the same time in an effort to save time because this could blow a fuse or throw off a circuit breaker that would cause all electricity to go off.

Smoking

Many clients smoke. Many visitors smoke. If a client permits smoking in his home—unless it is not allowed due to a medical reason or the presence of oxygen—you will be asked to tolerate it. If you are uncomfortable in a house with cigarette smoke, discuss this with your supervisor.

- Be sure ashtrays are provided and that they are used.

- Never empty warm ashtrays into plastic bags, plastic wastebaskets, or containers. When you empty ashtrays, be sure the contents are cool. Wet the ashes if you are in doubt.

- A client who has been given a sedative should not smoke.

- A confused client should not smoke.

- A client in bed should not smoke unattended.

- Check chairs, upholstery, and blankets for ashes or cigarettes if your client is smoking.

- If a client has hand tremors, light his cigarette and assist him as he smokes.

Safety in the Kitchen

- Keep a fire extinguisher in the kitchen.
- Do not leave grease on the stove. Clean it up.
- If you have a grease fire, do not put water on it. Use a chemical-type fire extinguisher or baking soda to smother it.
- Do not leave cooking pots unattended.

- Have good lighting in the kitchen.

- Be alert when carrying hot liquid.

- Keep paper towels, napkins, and potholders away from the burner.

- Keep the kitchen floor clean and free of clutter and spills.

- Store knives so that blades are protected.

- Electric cooking does not produce a visible flame, so be sure to check that the dial is at the setting you want or at OFF.

- If you or the client has a pacemaker, stay out of the kitchen when a microwave oven is working.

Safety in the Bathroom

- Is the toilet secure to the floor? Is the seat secure to the toilet?

- Can your client get up and down safely? Can he sit without additional support?

- Are the hot and cold water faucets correctly marked?

- Is the tub very deep, and can your client get in and out safely?

- Does your client get weak while bathing?

- Is there ventilation in the bathroom?

- Are the floor tiles slippery when wet? Is there a secure bathmat on the floor?

- If there are grab bars, are they secure in the wall? Towel bars were not designed to support weight. Special bars are necessary!

■ If you must use electrical equipment such as hair dryers or shavers, be sure your hands, body, and feet are dry.

Proper Storage

Dispose of articles in well-ventilated containers. Do not keep used rags in closed containers. They can catch fire by a process called spontaneous combustion. This means they will burn as a result of their own heat. Get rid of the rags before this happens!

Do not store flammable liquids near any source of heat. Flammable liquids are those that can burn. Keep them in the garage but away from cars. Use flammable liquids in a well-ventilated area. This reduces the risk of fire and the risk of illness due to the fumes.

Do not keep piles and piles of newspapers. Make arrangements for them to be given to a recycling plant.

FIRE PREVENTION

Fire safety means three things:

1. Preventing fires
2. Doing the right things if fire should occur
3. Protecting your client and yourself (Figure 7.16)

Fires start because of:

■ Smoking and matches
■ Improper rubbish disposal
■ Misuse of electricity
■ Improper cooking techniques

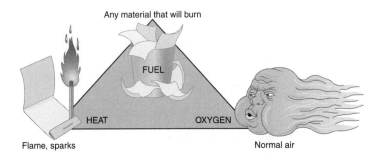

FIGURE 7.16 By removing one of the needed elements, you can prevent a fire.

- Defects in heating systems
- Improper ventilation
- Spontaneous combustion

Making a Fire Plan

As you meet your client and learn the layout of the home, ask yourself the following questions:

- Where are the exits from this house located in case of fire?
- How would I remove the client from this house in case of fire?
- If the client is bedridden, how would I remove him from the fire scene?
- Are there fire extinguishers in this house—one for grease fires and one for other types of fires?
- Are there smoke detectors in this house? Do they work?

- Does the family have a fire evacuation plan?
- Are there special precautions, indicated by the town fire department, which should be taken so they are aware of small children, bed-bound residents, or people dependent upon oxygen or ventilators?

What To Do in Case of Fire

Seal off the fire! If the fire is behind a closed door, do not open it (Figure 7.17a)! Take another route out of the building to safety. If you must go through a smoke-filled room, put a cloth (a wet one if you can get it) over your mouth and nose and one over those of your client. Crawl along the floor to safety or keep your client as low to the ground as possible (Figure 7.17b). Keeping in mind the word RACE will help you remember the steps to take in case of a fire (Figure 7.18).

- Get your client out of the house.
- Call the fire department from a neighbor's house. Do not reenter the house for any reason.
- Keep your client warm and comfortable.
- Stay with your client.

*P*OISONS

Children frequently swallow things that are not meant to be swallowed. This is considered poisoning. Clients often forget that they took their medication and take additional doses of it. This, too, is considered poisoning. A confused client may take one medication when he really wanted

(a)

(b)

FIGURE 7.17 (a) Feel the door BEFORE you open it. If it is hot, the fire is close. Stay in the room. (b) Heat and smoke rise. Crawling increases your ability to reach safety.

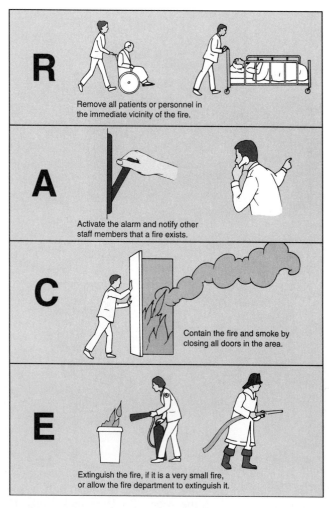

FIGURE 7.18 In case of a fire, remember the word RACE.

another one. This also is considered poisoning. Prevention is the best treatment for poisoning.

- Keep all poisons and medications locked away from children and confused clients.

- Never keep food products near poisons or cleaning products.

- Make it a habit to read labels each time you pick up any container.

- Call the poison control center for assistance if you have any suspicion a poisonous substance has been swallowed or an overdose of medication has been taken. Keep the phone number close to the phone.

- There are instructions for antidotes on the bottles of many potentially dangerous substances; unfortunately, these antidotes are not always correct. Do not use them. Call the poison control center and follow their instructions.

OXYGEN SAFETY

Clients may have oxygen prescribed to them for many different reasons. They may be instructed to use the oxygen in different ways, but the safety rules are always the same.

- There is *never* any smoking in the room where the oxygen tank is kept. This is true if the tank is open or shut.

- Do not use electrical appliances such as heating pads, hair dryers, or electric shavers near oxygen. Keep the appliances unplugged while the oxygen is running. If a plug were pulled from the outlet while the oxygen is running, a spark could cause an explosion.

- Remove cigarettes, matches, and ashtrays from the room.

- Do not use candles or open flames in the room.

- Oil, alcohol, or talcum powder should not be used to rub the client while the oxygen is running.

- Avoid combing a client's hair while he is receiving oxygen. A spark of electricity from his hair can set off an explosion.

- Wool blankets, nylon, and some synthetic fabrics can cause static electricity (an electric spark sent into the air). Remove these fabrics from the client's room. Use cotton items when possible.

- Check the equipment regularly for leaks and proper functioning.

- Ask for careful instructions as to which valves you may touch and which valves should not be moved.

- All oxygen tanks are painted green.

*R*ESTRAINTS

A restraint is a device, prescribed by a physician, used to confine a client and prevent injury to that client or others. Every client has the right to a safe environment and to have his dignity and his rights as a person maintained. Tying a human being to chairs and beds does not support these rights. Restraint devices, while appearing to protect an individual, may really be violating his rights and could, on some occasions, be identified as a form of abuse.

At times, a client may need to be restrained. This should always be for his protection and not the convenience of the caretaker. A client should not be restrained without a physician's order. Your supervisor will demonstrate the proper way to apply the restraint. You will be expected to remove the restraint, reposition the client, and offer the client toileting, exercise, and food and water at least every 2 hours. It is important that the family maintain this routine after you have left the house. If, for any reason, you think the family is not adhering to the restraint release schedule, notify your supervisor immediately.

A restraint should be chosen to be the least-restrictive possible and to be used for the shortest length of time. Before using a restraint, be sure that alternative measures have been tried and proved futile.

- Can someone sit with the client to provide comfort, distraction, and direction?
- Has the medication regimen been reviewed to be sure that the medications are not contributing to the confusion?
- Can diversional activities be used, such as music, television, reading, and visitors?
- Can positional devices be used as reminders to clients instead of actual restraints (Figure 7.19)?

Examples of restraints are seen in Figure 7.20. When applying any of them:

- Be sure the restraint is not too tight.
- Be sure the client can still call for assistance.
- Be sure the tie can be untied quickly in case of an emergency.
- Be sure the family supports the restraint release schedule.

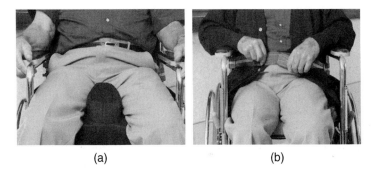

(a)   (b)

FIGURE 7.19 Restraint alternatives: (a) saddle cushion, which prevents sliding forward; (b) self-releasing safety belt.

Improvising to Meet Client Needs

There are times when you will want to make your client more comfortable or to provide him with items that will help him become more independent. Many of these items will not be used for long and therefore the family does not wish to buy them. Suggest to him that you improvise and make some of the needed items.

Backrest

A backrest is used in a client's bed to prop him up when he eats, to take part in his care; and to allow him to visit with people, read, or watch TV. When a client is propped up, it is important to remember that:

- He should be able to support himself in that position and not fall or slip out of bed or into an uncomfortable position.
- He should be able to call for help to change position.

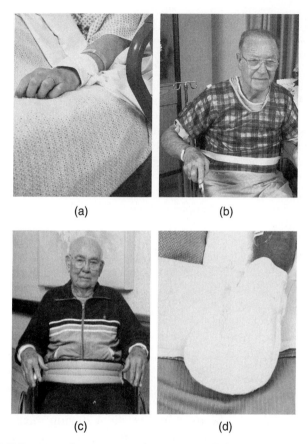

(a)

(b)

(c)

(d)

FIGURE 7.20 Soft protective devices (a) soft limb tie; (b) safety vest; (c) pelvic support; (d) soft cloth mitten.

- He should be comfortable in that position, and the position should be permitted by his physician.
- You will be able to secure the backrest so that it does not slip in the bed.

*P*ROCEDURE

Making a Backrest

1. Gather the equipment you will need:

    A clean sturdy cardboard box about 24 inches by 24 inches by 18 inches

    A pair of scissors or sharp knife

    String, tape, or cord to secure the ends

2. Position the box on a flat surface with the wide side toward you.

3. Cut the right and left seams from the top to the bottom. The box will now be open and the front will be lying flat (Figure 7.21a).

4. Make a cut (score) through the inside layer of the cardboard on the side flaps as shown in Figure 7.21b.

5. Fold the ends toward the middle of the box along the scoring lines (Figure 7.21c).

6. Fold the front of the box (the part that has been laying flat) up to cover the triangles (Figure 7.21d).

7. Fold the top down and tie or tape in place (Figure 7.21e).

Bed Table

A bed table can be used by the client during meal time, during personal care, and for recreation activities such as cards or reading. Having a light, easy-to-use bed table available encourages the client to be more independent. A table at the side of the bed, much like the ones in the hospital, can be improvised by standing an adjustable ironing board near the bed, adjusting the height, and locking it in place.

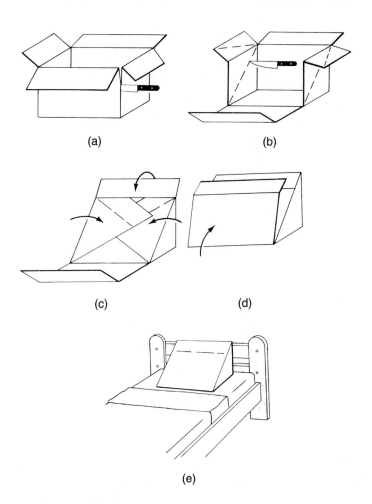

(a)

(b)

(c)

(d)

(e)

FIGURE 7.21 Making a backrest

PROCEDURE

Making a Bed Table

1. Gather the equipment you will need:

   A clean sturdy cardboard box about 10 inches by 12 inches by 24 inches

   A sharp knife or pair of scissors

   A pencil

2. Cut off the four top flaps of the box along the seams (Figure 7.22a).

3. Draw a curved opening on both wide sides of the box. Be sure the opening is large enough to fit over the client's legs. Be sure there is enough cardboard left on the side, at least 2 inches, to support the weight of the items you will put on the tray.

4. Cut out the opening along the lines you have drawn (Figure 7.22b).

5. Cut small openings in the side near the top for handholds.

6. Cover the table with adhesive-backed plastic or wallpaper to protect it and to make it more attractive (Figure 7.22c).

Bed Cradle

A bed cradle is used under the blankets and sheets and over the client's legs so that the covers do not touch the skin. This relieves the knees, the legs, and the feet of the pressure of the covers. Use the same procedure to make a bed cradle as you would to make a bed table. Be sure, however, that the box you choose is big enough to provide space for the client to move his legs.

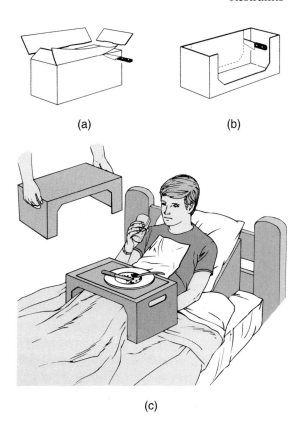

(a) (b)

(c)

FIGURE 7.22 Making a bed table

Footboard

A footboard is used to support the covers so that they do not touch the client's toes and to provide a place where the client can rest his foot. If the possibility of foot drop exists, this is a necessary piece of equipment.

PROCEDURE

Making a Footboard

1. Gather the equipment you will need:

A piece of wood that is just about as long as the bed is wide and high enough to keep the covers at least 2 inches off the client's feet

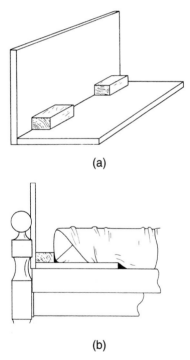

(a)

(b)

FIGURE 7.23

   Two blocks of wood for added support
   Sandpaper, nails or screws, hammer or screwdriver

2. Sand the edges of the boards so that they are smooth and will not cause splinters or tear the bed covers.

3. Secure the two pieces of wood at right angles to each other with screws and glue (Figure 7.23a).

4. Position the support on the bed under the bed covers (Figure 7.23b).

5. Instruct the client and family as to the function of the support.

CHAPTER 8

Planning, Purchasing, and Serving Food

BASIC NUTRITION

Food gives us energy to carry out the day's activities and is necessary to rebuild body tissue. Eating is also a social activity. There are often many family and personal preferences and practices associated with food. Do not assume that each family is the same.

Nutrients are substances that our bodies need to repair, maintain, and grow new cells. Each nutrient comes from many sources. It does not matter from which sources you get the nutrient as long as you get it in sufficient supply. When a person is unable to get the proper amount of a nutrient from his food, he will take supplements.

Dietary requirements are different at different stages of life. Children need more protein and calories than older persons need, but older persons need more of other nutrients. All foods have been divided into basic food groups: milk, yogurt, and cheese; vegetables; meat, poultry, fish, eggs, dry beans, and nuts; breads, cereals, rice, and pasta; fruit; and oils, fats, and sweets. The food groups

159

are presented in a pyramid that indicates the recommended daily servings of each group (Figure 8.1). If you eat the correct number of servings from each food group, you will get the correct amount of all nutrients (Figure 8.2). Although diet will often be as important to the health of your client as his medication or exercise regimen, the client and his family may not understand this. Discuss with your supervisor ways to teach the family the importance of food and the proper diet while incorporating family and cultural preferences. If you do not understand some practices, you may discuss them with the client or a family member in a respectful and nonjudgmental manner.

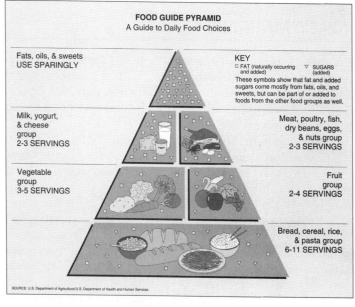

FOOD GUIDE PYRAMID
A Guide to Daily Food Choices

Fats, oils, & sweets
USE SPARINGLY

KEY
□ FAT (naturally occurring and added)   ▽ SUGARS (added)
These symbols show that fat and added sugars come mostly from fats, oils, and sweets, but can be part of or added to foods from the other food groups as well.

Milk, yogurt, & cheese group
2-3 SERVINGS

Meat, poultry, fish, dry beans, eggs, & nuts group
2-3 SERVINGS

Vegetable group
3-5 SERVINGS

Fruit group
2-4 SERVINGS

Bread, cereal, rice, & pasta group
6-11 SERVINGS

SOURCE: U.S. Department of Agriculture/U.S. Department of Health and Human Services

FIGURE 8.1 The food guide pyramid shows the division of foods into the baic food groups.

Nutrients Class	Bodily Functions	Food Sources
CARBOHYDRATES 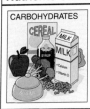	Provides work energy for body activities, and heat energy for maintenance of body temperature.	Cereal grains and their products (bread, breakfast cereals, macaroni products), potatoes, sugar, syrups, fruits, milk, vegetables, nuts.
PROTEINS 	Build and renew body tissues; regulate body functions and supply energy. Complete proteins: maintain life and provide growth. Incomplete proteins: maintain life but do not provide for growth.	Complete proteins: Derived from animal foods—meat, milk, eggs, fish, cheese, poultry. Incomplete proteins: Derived from vegetable foods— soybeans, dry beans, peas, some nuts and whole-grain products.
FATS 	Give work energy for body activities and heat energy for maintenance of body temperature. Carrier of vitamins A and D; provide fatty acids necessary for growth and maintenance of body tissues.	Some foods are chiefly fat, such as lard, vegetable fats and oils, and butter. Many other foods contain smaller proportions of fats— nuts, meats, fish, poultry, cream, whole milk.
MINERALS Calcium 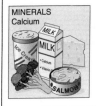	Builds and renews bones, teeth and other tissues; regulates the activity of the muscles, heart, nerves; and controls the clotting of blood.	Milk and milk products except butter; most dark-green vegetables; canned salmon.

FIGURE 8.2   (*continues*)

Nutrients Class	Bodily Functions	Food Sources
Phosphorus 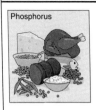	Associated with calcium in some functions to build and renew bones and teeth. Influences the oxidation of foods in the body cells; important in nerve tissue.	Widely distributed in foods; especially cheese, oat cereals, whole-wheat products, dry beans and peas, meat, fish, poultry, nuts.
Iron 	Builds and renews hemoglobin, the red pigment in blood which carries oxygen from the lungs to the cells.	Eggs, meat, especially liver and kidney; deep-yellow and dark-green vegetables; potatoes, dried fruits, whole-grain products; enriched flour, bread, breakfast cereals.
Iodine 	Enables the thyroid gland to perform its function of controlling the rate at which foods are oxidized in the cells.	Fish (obtained from the sea), some plant-foods grown in soils containing iodine; table salt fortified with iodine (iodized).
VITAMINS A 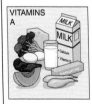	Necessary for normal functioning of the eyes, prevents night blindness. Ensures a healthy condition of the skin, hair, and mucous membranes. Maintains a state of resistance to infections of the eyes, mouth, and respiratory tract.	One form of vitamin A is yellow and one form is colorless. Apricots, cantaloupe, milk, cheese, eggs, meat organs (especially liver and kidney), fortified margarine, butter, fish-liver oils, dark-green and deep-yellow vegetables.

FIGURE 8.2 (*continued*)

Nutrients Class	Bodily Functions	Food Sources
B Complex B₁ (Thiamine) 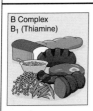	Maintains a healthy condition of the nerves. Fosters a good appetite. Helps the body cells use carbohydrates	Whole-grain and enriched grain products; meats (especially pork, liver and kidney). Dry beans and peas.
B₂ (Riboflavin) 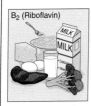	Keeps the skin, mouth, and eyes in a healthy condition. Acts with other nutrients to form enzymes and control oxidation in cells.	Milk, cheese, eggs, meat (especially liver and kidney), whole-grain and enriched-grain products, dark-green vegetables.
Niacin 	Influences the oxidation of carbohydrates and proteins in the body cells.	Liver, meat, fish, poultry, eggs, peanuts; dark-green vegetables whole-grain and enriched-cereal products.
B₁₂ 	Regulates specific processes in digestion. Helps maintain normal functions of muscles nerves, heart, blood—general body metabolism.	Liver, other organ meats, cheese, eggs, milk, leafy green vegetables.

FIGURE 8.2   (*continued*)

Nutrients Class	Bodly Functions	Food Sources
C (Ascorbic Acid)	Acts as a cement between body cells, and helps them work together to carry out their special functions. Maintains a sound condition of bones, teeth, and gums. Not stored in the body.	Fresh, raw citrus fruits and vegetables— oranges, grape- fruit, cantaloupe, strawberries, tomatoes, raw onions, cabbage, green and sweet red peppers, dark-green vegetables.
 D	Enables the growing body to use calcium and phosphorus in a normal way to build bones and teeth.	Provided by vitamin D fortification of certain foods, such as milk and margarine. Also fish— liver oils and eggs. Sunshine is also a source of vitamin D.
 Water	Regulates body processes. Aids in regulating body temperature. Carries nutrients to body cells and carries waste products away from them. Helps to lubricate joints. Water has no food value, although most water contains mineral elements. More immediately necessary to life than food— second only to oxygen.	Drinking water and other beverages; all foods except those made up of a single nutrient, such as sugar and some fats. Milk, milk drinks, vegetables, fruit juices. Ice cream, watermelon, strawberries, lettuce, tomatoes, cereals, other dry products.

FIGURE 8.2   (*continued*)

PERSONAL PREFERENCE

Everybody knows of foods he likes and those he dislikes or will not eat. Sometimes, a client will not eat a food for a cultural reason, a religious reason, or a reason that is unexplainable. You must respect these preferences and plan meals and diets taking these personal wishes into consideration. Be observant as to what your client eats. Also note when he eats which foods.

PLANNING, SHOPPING FOR, AND SERVING A MEAL

Mealtime is important. It should be a pleasant change in a client's day. The atmosphere, the place, and the way the food is served is important in stimulating an appetite. Try to serve a client in a room that is free from unpleasant odors and is comfortable for the client. Keep the room at a comfortable temperature and with a minimum of noise. It is often helpful to let the client decide what foods he wishes to eat and when he prefers to eat.

You may find it necessary to purchase food for the client. First, develop a menu of what foods will be prepared. Be sure the menu is planned from the client's diet and preferences. It is important to keep in mind the client's ability to chew and swallow as you prepare food. Take into consideration the recommended servings from the food pyramid. Check the ingredients the client has on hand. Then make a shopping list. A list will help avoid unnecessary trips to the store for forgotten ingredients. It will also prevent duplicate buying of foods already on hand and, if grouped by types of food, avoid extra steps in the market. When planning a meal, remember:

- *Variety*. A well-balanced diet consists of nutrients from many different kinds of food.
- *Texture*. Unless the client is on a special diet and the texture of the food is controlled, try to choose different types of texture within each meal served.
- *Flavors*. Keep the strong-flavored foods as the spotlight and milder-tasting foods as the background in a meal. Season the food as the client prefers and his diet permits.
- *Temperature*. Cook the food at the correct temperature. Ask the client at what temperature he prefers his food. Not everyone enjoys food very hot or very cold. Some people like ice. Some do not.
- *Taste*. Cook the meal to the taste of the client. Discuss with the family the spices they like and how they usually season their food.
- *Shape*. Prepare the food with familiar shapes. Some families always slice their tomatoes, some cut them into chunks. Ask what is prefered in this household.
- *Color*. Give each meal eye appeal by keeping the colors compatible. A sprig of parsley, radish roses, olives, or carrot curls may make an interesting dash of color.
- *Cost*. Plan meals that are within your client's budget and do not cause waste.

All the food to be eaten during a day is included in the planning. The food may be eaten at three traditional meals or as snacks throughout the day. Plan meals as close to the client's usual eating habits as possible.

When a client's diet is changed, special care could be taken to try to keep this new diet as close to the diet of the other family members as possible. For example, food for a client on a salt-free diet should be separated from the other family members' food before salt is added, but the food may be the same.

Food habits can also be influenced by the religious beliefs or ethnic background of the client. In some Jewish households, a kosher kitchen may be kept. This means that utensils and equipment used for meat products are kept separately from those used for dairy products. Meat and dairy products may not be eaten at the same meal. The degree to which a client keeps a kosher home should be discussed with the family.

Other ethnic groups may not eat pork, shellfish, or beef. Vegetarians eat no animal meat or by-products. Be alert that these foods or foods made from them are not included in any prepared foods you may purchase.

People who have strong bonds with their ethnic background may not keep to a prescribed diet but eat foods that are more familiar to them. Encourage the client to stay on his therapeutic diet, and notify your supervisor. Most of the time your client's therapeutic diet can be adapted to his ethnic preferences.

Food Allergies

Some clients may have food allergies. Eating foods to which a person is allergic can cause mild skin irritations or severely affect his ability to breathe. Be sure to honor all of a person's allergies. Do not take it upon yourself to introduce any food, even in small amounts. Sometimes, children will have food restrictions if one of their parents is highly allergic to a substance.

Purchasing Food Wisely

When purchasing packaged food, read the labels. The listing of ingredients on labels is critical to a person on a special diet.

Labels provide information on the amount in the container. On some labels, the number of servings and the amount of the serving is listed. Often, the labels contain the calories per serving of the products. The label may also list the kind of nutrients in the food and the amount of the nutrient (Figure 8.3).

Products that contain more than one ingredient, such as spaghetti in meat sauce, must list all the ingredients used in making the product. The ingredient that is found in the greatest amount is listed first.

Shopping for Your Client

Before you go shopping for your client, be sure your supervisor knows that you are leaving the home.

Before you go shopping:

- Prepare a list and discuss it with the client.
- Discuss the size of the purchase, money available, likes and dislikes, and favorite stores.
- Be sure your client will be safe while you are out.

After you shop:

- Save all receipts.
- Carefully write down how much money you were given, how much you spent, and how much change you brought back.

Nutrition Facts

Serving Size 1 cup (49g)
Servings Per Container about 10

Amount Per Serving	Cereal	Cereal with 1/2 cup Skim Milk
Calories	170	210
Calories from Fat	5	5
	% Daily Value**	
Total Fat 0.5g*	1%	1%
Saturated Fat 0g	0%	0%
Polyunsaturated Fat 0g		
Monounsaturated Fat 0g		
Cholesterol 0mg	0%	0%
Sodium 0mg	0%	3%
Potassium 200mg	6%	11%
Total Carbohydrate 41g	14%	16%
Dietary Fiber 5g	21%	21%
Insoluble Fiber 5g		
Sugars 0g		
Other Carbohydrate 36g		
Protein 5g		
Vitamin A	0%	4%
Vitamin C	0%	2%
Calcium	2%	15%
Iron	8%	8%
Thiamin	8%	10%
Riboflavin	2%	10%
Niacin	15%	15%

FIGURE 8.3 Learning to read labels will help you plan meals and budget money.

Unit Pricing

Unit pricing tells the customer what the cost is by a particular quantity. This can be determined by weight (for example, a box of cereal might read 72 cents per pound) or by pieces (for example, a bag of soap bars might read 25 cents per bar). This information is given in addition to the amount you will be charged for the product at the checkout counter.

The unit price can be displayed by:

- ▪ A poster that tells all the prices for the food in this section of the store.
- ▪ A label on the edge of the shelf where the food is displayed.
- ▪ A price sticker that is put on each item.

Convenience foods (those foods with some of the preparation already done) generally cost more than those you make yourself. But if only one or two people are eating the food, the ingredients for the homemade process might spoil before they are completely used. The decision as to which is most practical must be made individually by the client. You can share your opinion, but the client must make the final decision.

Purchasing larger quantities of an item is generally cheaper than buying small quantities. But if the item is rarely used or if storage is difficult, it may have to be discarded before it is finished. Discuss this with your client before you go to the store so you will not have to make this decision in the supermarket.

Good Buys

Menus should be planned with seasonal foods in mind. The cost will be less and the selection greater.

In selecting foods, be aware that the best quality is not always necessary. In choosing tomatoes for a salad, the most attractive and usually the most costly would be desirable. In selecting tomatoes for tomato sauce, a less expensive product with perhaps a blemish on the skin might be considered a better buy. When buying foods that are high in protein, you can reduce the cost by:

- Using poultry when it is cheaper than meat.
- Considering cuts of meat that may cost more per pound but give more servings per person.
- Learning to prepare less-tender cuts of meat in casseroles or pot roasts.
- Serving eggs or egg substitutes.
- Substituting dried bean and pea dishes for higher-cost meats.
- Using fillers such as bread crumbs or pasta to make a meat dish serve more people.

Storing Food

Proper storage prevents the loss of nutrients and possible food poisoning. Some people do not have sole use of a refrigerator or a stove. If your client does not have good storage or cooking facilities, discuss this with your supervisor.

General Storage Hints

- Do not buy more food than you can safely store.
- Keep refrigerators operating properly by defrosting when needed.
- Check the expiration date on food before purchasing it. Choose the food with the longest time before expiration.

- Rotate food at home by using the most recently purchased food last.

- Dry ingredients such as flour, sugar, cereal, and pasta products should be stored in tightly covered containers.

Tips for Specific Foods

- *Meats*. Refrigerate all meats. Ground meat and variety meats spoil more quickly than others, so use them soon after purchase.

- *Fruits and vegetables*. Keep most fresh fruits and vegetables in the refrigerator in plastic bags, tightly covered containers, or the crisper.

- *Bread*. If wrapped properly, bread can be frozen to keep it most efficiently for a long time.

- *Milk*. Instant nonfat dry milk can be used in many of the same ways as whole milk and can be stored for much longer periods without refrigeration.

- *Canned foods*. Store in a cool, dry place.

- *Frozen foods*. Keep in freezer at 0°F temperature.

Preparing a Meal

When preparing foods, be aware of the amount of energy you are using. By doing this, you will save time and money, and indicate your concern for the client's resources.

- Use the oven to prepare more than one food at a time.

- Do not preheat the oven longer than necessary.

- Put the pot on the correct-size burner. The burner should be as close to the size of the pan as possible. Using too big a burner wastes fuel.

- Cover pots when they are cooking.
- Make one-dish meals.
- Make enough food for more than one meal and reheat the remaining servings.
- If you are using an electric range, turn off the heat a few minutes before the food is ready.
- Use the correct appliance for the job. Use small toaster ovens for small jobs and the big oven for big jobs.

Methods of Cooking

- *Bake or roast*: to cook with dry heat in a confined space, such as an oven.
- *Boil*: to cook in a liquid that is hot enough for bubbles to break on the surface.
- *Braise*: a long, slow cooking method that makes use of moist heat in a tightly covered vessel at a temperature just below boiling. The cooking liquid should just barely cover the food to be braised. Braising is a good way to cook tough meats and vegetables because the long cooking time breaks down their fibers.
- *Broil*: to cook directly under or above a source of heat.
- *Fry*: to cook food in fat or oil. When only a small amount of fat is used, the process is called pan frying or sautéing. When larger amounts of fat are used—enough to cover the food—the process is called deep frying or deep fat frying.
- *Poach*: a method of cooking used to preserve the delicate texture and prevent the toughening of

foods. The food is barely covered by water or some other liquid. Depending on the type of food being cooked, the liquid may be either boiling or at the boiling point.

▪ *Steam*: a method of cooking in which the food is exposed to the steam of boiling water. The food must be above the liquid, never in it. The container is kept closed during cooking to let the steam accumulate. Steaming keeps a high proportion of the original flavor and texture of the foods because the nutrients are not dissolved in the cooking liquid, as is the case with boiling or poaching.

▪ *Stew*: a process of long, slow cooking of food in liquid in a covered pot with seasoning. Good for tougher cuts of meat.

PREPARING A CLIENT FOR A MEAL

Serve the client in an orderly and friendly fashion. Prepare small portions, especially if the client has a poor appetite. A great deal of food will only cause him to be uncomfortable. Serve the meal as the client wants it. Some people want their soup first; some want their salad first. Accommodate the client, unless there is a health reason why you may not. The place people eat is very important. Allow the client to choose the place.

An important part of serving a client a meal are the observations made about the client at mealtime:

▪ How is the client's appetite?
▪ Does he eat foods on his diet?

- What foods does the client avoid?
- Is there any discomfort associated with eating?
- Does the client drink fluids?
- Does the client eat several big meals, or does he eat smaller meals all day long?
- Who serves the client when you are not there?

Serving a Meal

A poor appetite does not mean that the body's need for food is lowered. The sick person's body is in a weakened condition. The client needs as much food as ever—if not more—to return to health. The sight and aroma of food often make a person hungry. If a client asks for a particular food (and if he is permitted to have it), serve it to him.

- Tell the client you will be serving him a meal.
- Most people enjoy company during mealtime. Visitors and family members should be encouraged to remain with the client, and even eat with the client, if that is appropriate.
- Before or after the meal, offer the client the bedpan or urinal. Remember to offer a washcloth to wash his hands too.
- After the meal, offer the client oral hygiene.

DIETS

The type of diet will be determined by the client's doctor. The therapeutic diet will be planned to incorporate the client's likes and dislikes, his ethnic background, and his budget (Table 8.1).

TABLE 8.1 *T*YPES OF DIETS GIVEN TO PATIENTS

Type of Diet	Description	Common Purpose	Foods Often Recommended	Foods to Avoid
Normal regular	Provides all essentials of good-nourishment in normal forms	For clients who do not need special diets		
Soft (mechanical)	Same foods as on normal diet, but chopped or strained	For clients who have difficulty chewing or swallowing		
Bland	Foods mild in flavor and easy to digest; omits spicy foods	Avoids irritation of the digestive tract, as with ulcer and colitis clients	Puddings, creamed dishes, milk, eggs, plain potatoes	Fried foods, raw vegetables or fruit, whole-grain products
Low-residue	Foods low in bulk: omits foods difficult to digest	Spares the lower digestive tract; for clients with rectal diseases		Whole-grain products, uncooked fruits and vegetables
High-calorie	Foods high in protein, minerals, and vitamins	For under weight or malnourished clients	Eggnog, ice cream, frequent snacks, peanut butter, milk	
Low-calorie	Foods low in cream, butter, and fats; cereals; low-fat desserts	For clients who should lose weight	Skim milk, fresh fruit and vegetables, lean meat, fish	Fried foods, sauces, gravies, rich desserts
Low-fat	Limited amounts of butter, cream,	For clients who have difficulty	Veal, poultry, fish, skim milk, fresh fruits,	Bacon, butter, cheese, fried foods, liver,

TABLE 8.1 *(continued)*

Type of Diet	Description	Common Purpose	Foods Often Recommended	Foods to Avoid
	fats, and eggs	digesting fats and may have gall bladder, cardio-vascular, and liver disturbances	and vegetables	whole milk, ice cream, chocolate
Low-cholesterol	Low in eggs whole milk, cheese, and meats	Helps regulate the amount of cholesterol in the blood	Fruits, vegetables, cereals, grains, nuts, vegetable oil	Brains, organ meats
Diabetic	Balance of carbohydrates, protein, and fats, devised according to the needs of individual clients	For diabetic clients: matches food intake with the insulin and nutritional requirements	Fresh fruits, and vegetables, low-sugar products	High-sugar foods, alcohol, carbonated beverages
High-protein	Meals with high-protein foods, such as meat, fish, cheese, milk, and eggs	Assists in the growth and repair of tissues wasted by disease	Milk, meat, eggs, cheese, fish	
Low-sodium (salt)	Limited amount of foods containing sodium; no salt allowed at the table	For clients whose circulation would be impaired by fluid retention; for clients with certain heart or kidney conditions	Puffed wheat/rice or shredded wheat, fruits, fruit juices	Canned vegetables, ham, luncheon meats, frank-furters, most cheeses
Salt-free	Completely without salt		Most fresh or frozen vegetables	

CHEMOTHERAPY AND RADIATION

Many people who are receiving chemotherapy and radiation therapy change their eating habits due to periods of nausea, vomiting, appetite loss, and/or constipation or diarrhea.

- Decrease intake of red meats; many people prefer fish, chicken, turkey, and other nonmeat foods that are high in protein.
- Use plastic utensils, as some people complain of a bitter taste from metal utensils.
- Maintain adequate fluid intake of cool, clear liquids.
- Eat small, frequent meals; chew food well; eat warm, not hot, food.
- Decrease intake of sweets and fried or fatty foods; this will decrease nausea and decrease intake of empty calories.
- Remain in a sitting position for 2 hours after meals.
- Eat non–gas-producing foods.
- Discuss the fiber intake with your supervisor.
- Provide a pleasant, quiet atmosphere.
- Vary the diet.
- If the client has difficulty eating by himself or being neat as he eats, protect his clothes without making him feel like an infant.

SAFETY FACTORS WHEN FEEDING A CLIENT

Be sure a client is able to swallow before you put food in his mouth. Some clients will be able to swallow one food and not another. Pay special attention to the temperature of food. If a food is hot, tell the client and then offer him a small amount. If the food is cold, do the same. Keep food on a table away from the client's bed so that the client can change position without spilling the food. If a client is blind, name each mouthful before you offer it to him.

- Allow clients to feed themselves as much as possible; give assistance only as needed.
- Do not rush the feeding; sit if possible.
- Be gentle with forks and spoons; straws may help in feeding liquids.
- Keep the conversation pleasant and make the meal a highlight of the day.
- Feed the foods separately rather than mixed together.
- When offering a glass or cup, first touch it to the lips.
- Record the intake and output.
- Record your observations about the client when you were feeding him.

CHAPTER 9

Basic Body Movement and Positions

BODY MECHANICS

Body mechanics refers to the way of standing and moving one's body so as to prevent injury, avoid fatigue, and make the best use of strength. The muscles that flex (bend) the joints are the strongest. In your arms, you have the greatest power and control when you are lifting with your palms facing up. In your legs, your hip flexors and your knee flexors are strongest. This is why you bend your hips and knees slightly when using good body mechanics. This puts the muscles in the best position to do heavy work. Your strongest muscles are not in your back, so do not expect your back to do heavy work. This is a major safety factor for both you and your client.

The base of support determines how stable your balance will be. That is because by separating your feet, you make your base of support larger and your balance more stable.

The center of gravity of any object is the point at which, when held, you will have the greatest control over

181

the object with the least amount of effort. A person's center of gravity is located around the pelvic area (Figure 9.1). When moving or assisting a client, support him through his center of gravity. By holding a client close to his center of gravity and your center of gravity, you will have the greatest amount of control with the least amount of effort.

Balancing is keeping your center of gravity with your base of support. When you must lift heavy objects, spread your feet apart and bend your knees. This will lower your center of gravity, increase stability, and broaden your base of support. When a person gets up from a sitting position, he must bend forward enough so that this center of gravity is over his base of support.

FIGURE 9.1 Be aware of your center of gravity and your base of support as you work.

*G*uidelines—*Good Body Mechanics*

- When an action requires physical effort, try to use as many groups of muscles as possible. For example, use both hands, rather than one hand, to pick up a heavy piece of equipment.
- Use good posture. Keep your body aligned properly. Keep your back straight. Have your knees bent. Keep your weight evenly balanced on both feet.
- Check your feet when you are going to lift something. They should be at least 12 inches apart. This will give you a broad base of support and good balance.
- If you think you may not be able to lift the load or if it seems too large or heavy, get help.
- Lift smoothly to avoid strain. Always count "one, two, three" with the person with whom you are working. Do this with both the client and with other helpers.
- If you have to move or lift a heavy object or person, use a lumbar support. A support can be obtained from your agency, or you may prefer to purchase one of your own so it is always available to you.
- When you want to change the direction of movement:
  a. Pivot (turn) with your feet.
  b. Turn with short steps.
  c. Turn your whole body without twisting your neck and back.
- Get close to the load that is being lifted.
- When you have to move a heavy object, it is better to push it, pull it, or roll it rather than lift and carry it.
- Use your arms to support the object. The muscles of your legs actually do the job of lifting, not the muscles of your back (Figure 9.2).
- The muscles that bend your elbow are stronger than the ones that straighten it out—your greatest lift power is in pulling.

(a)   (b)

FIGURE 9.2 (a) Use your longest and strongest muscles. (b) Use your center of gravity and base of support as you lift and move objects.

- When you are doing work, such as giving a back rub, making a corner on a bed, or exercising a client, work with the direction of your efforts, not against them.

- When working with a client in a hospital bed (bathing, dressing, exercising, etc.), raise the bed to a comfortable position for you. Also, move the client close to the side of the bed where you are working.

- When working with a client in a bed that does not raise up, if you must stand, put one foot up on the lowered side rail or on a footstool to relieve the pressure on your lower back. Remember the same rules of a broad base of support (use the strongest muscles for the work and keep your center of gravity close to your work) apply when you are working with a regular bed.

- Avoid twisting your body (or your client's body) as much as you can.

Client's Daily Level of Ability

Check the client's daily ability level before you ask him to perform an activity. Observe the client's activity tolerance each day. Note if it decreases or increases. Activities performed one day may not be possible the next.

- Can the client hear and understand you?
- Can the client follow directions?
- How much can the client do alone?
- How does the client look?
- What are his vital signs?
- Will pain be a factor in this activity?
- Are joint motions limited?
- Does the client tire easily?

Guidelines—*Assisting Clients*

- Expect the client to do as much as possible.
- Help only when needed.
- Work at the client's level and speed.
- Direct activity in short, simple sentences instead of asking the client. For example, say "It is time to stand, Mrs. N" instead of "Do you want to stand up, Mrs. N?"
- Plan ahead. Gather all equipment and put it in place before you begin the activity.
- Know your own capabilities.
- Praise the client for following directions. If he does not do something correctly, stop the activity and redirect him

until the correct activity is done. That way, the client will get used to doing the activity the correct way only.

▪ Your body language (your tone of voice, facial expression, the way you touch, etc.) will be received more strongly than the meaning of the words you use. Make sure your nonverbal messages fit the words you use.

▪ Touch is an important sense. You will be giving contact care to your client. If you are comfortable with this, he will be, too.

▪ Always use smooth, steady motions with clients. Avoid sudden, jerking movements.

Positioning a Client in Bed

The client's body should be straight and properly supported. The correct positioning of the client's body is referred to as body alignment or bed positioning. Arrangement or adjustment of the client's body is made so that all parts of the body are in their proper positions in relation to each other. Proper body alignment can be seen as proper standing posture. When people lie in bed, it is often necessary to use pillows and rolled-up towels to keep this alignment. Some conditions and injuries, as well as special client care treatments, make it difficult or even dangerous for a client to be in a certain position. You will be told about any special positions that your client requires. If a client is not properly positioned during the first part of his illness, it can create problems that must be taken care of before rehabilitation can begin.

A client who is unable to move needs to have his position changed every 2 hours to:

▪ Minimize the possibility of muscle tightness
▪ Reduce the chance of skin breakdown

- Maintain proper body alignment
- Make the client comfortable
- Avoid delaying rehabilitation

Clients who need physical therapy or any other types of assistance usually have some type of disability. They may have a weakness or an injury on one side. Refer to it as the involved side. This means it is involved in the treatment. Refer to the other side as the uninvolved side.

If your client understands the concept of right and left, refer to his limbs in those terms. At times, you will have to touch the arm or leg you want him to move. You may also have to demonstrate the activity first.

The term *functional* describes the usefulness of something. It may be an activity or a body part. An activity such as folding clothes, making salad, or combing one's hair is a functional activity because it produces a desired result. Nonfunctional body parts will not perform a useful activity.

- A rolled-up washcloth makes an excellent support for the hand.
- If an arm or leg is swollen, try to keep the part higher than the heart. Gravity will help the extra fluid drain from the limb.
- Any open skin will heal more quickly if pressure is reduced and air is allowed to circulate around it.
- Position and support only nonfunctional parts of the body. The rest should be left free to move. This will help the blood to circulate.

Moving Clients in Bed

For good positioning, the client must be up at the head of the bed. If your client can stand, even briefly, have him sit over the edge of the bed. Help him to stand and move his buttocks up toward the head of the bed. Repeat the process until he is in a good position to lie back down, with his head at the top of the bed.

For those clients who cannot move themselves, a pull sheet can help you move the client in bed more easily. A regular extra sheet folded over many times and placed under the client can be used as a pull sheet. The cotton draw sheet can also be used as a pull sheet. When moving the client, roll up the pull sheet tightly on each side next to the client's body. Grip the rolled portion underhand to slide the client into the desired position. By using the pull sheet, you avoid friction and irritation to the client's skin that touches the bedding.

Positioning a Client Who Has a Weak Side on His Back

- ▪ Place a:
    - **a.** Small comfortable pillow under the client's head
    - **b.** Small hand towel folded under the shoulder blade of the weak side
    - **c.** Bath towel folded under the hip on the weak side
    - **d.** Washcloth rolled up in the hand on the weak side
    - **e.** Weak arm and elbow on a pillow positioned higher than the heart
    - **f.** Small pillow under the calf of the weak leg, with the heel hanging off the mattress edge (Figure 9.3).
- ▪ Loosen the top sheet so pressure is removed from the toes.

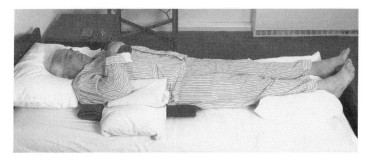

FIGURE 9.3 Be sure the client is both safe and comfortable as you place the towels and pillows.

Positioning a Client on His Uninvolved Side

- Place a small pillow under the head. Keep the head in alignment with the spine.
- Roll a large pillow lengthwise and tuck it in at the client's back to prevent him from rolling and to give him support.
- Place a:
  - **a.** Pillow in front to keep the arm the same height as the shoulder joint
  - **b.** Medium pillow between the client's knees (the top knee may be slightly bent or both may be bent)
  - **c.** Small pillow between the ankles and feet (Figure 9.4)
- Place a:
  - **a.** Small pillow under the head
  - **b.** Large pillow under the involved arm to keep it level with the shoulder joint
  - **c.** Large pillow at the stomach area (if the client wishes) for the client to roll onto

FIGURE 9.4 Remember, the client also has a center of gravity and must be in proper alignment when he is in bed.

Positioning a Client on His Involved Side

The same principles of positioning are used as listed previously, plus:

- The client's comfort will be the key to how and where support should be used.
- Change the client's position more frequently than when he is positioned on the uninvolved side.
- Disability can be accompanied by a lessened sense of pain and pressure. Check the involved side for signs of pressure and skin irritation.

PROCEDURE

Moving a Client Up in Bed with His Help

1. Wash your hands.
2. Tell the client you are going to help him move up in the bed.
3. Lock the wheels on the bed, if they are present.

4. Raise the whole bed to a height that is best for you.

5. Remove the pillow. Put the pillow on a chair or at the foot of the bed.

6. Put the side rail in the up position on the far side of the bed.

7. Put one hand under the client's shoulder. Put your other hand under the client's buttocks.

8. Tell the client to bend his knees and brace his feet firmly on the mattress.

9. Tell the client to put his hands on the mattress to help push.

10. Have your feet 12 inches apart. The foot closest to the head of the bed should be pointed in that direction.

11. Bend your knees. Keep your back straight.

12. Facing the client and turned slightly toward the head of the bed, bend your body from your hips (Figure 9.5).

13. At the signal "one, two, three," have the client pull with his hands toward the head of the bed and push with his feet against the mattress.

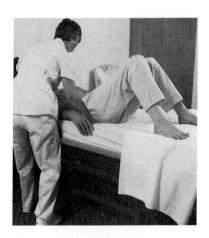

FIGURE 9.5

14. At the same time, help him to move toward the head of the bed by sliding him with your hands and arms.

15. Put the pillow back in place. Reposition the client correctly.

16. Make the client comfortable. Lower the bed to the lowest horizontal position, if possible.

17. Wash your hands.

18. Chart your observations of the client during this procedure.

PROCEDURE

Moving a Client Up in Bed, Two People

1. Ask another person to work with you.

2. Wash your hands.

3. Tell the client you and your partner are going to move him up in bed. Say this even if he appears to be unconscious.

4. Remove the pillow from the bed. Place it on a chair.

5. Lock the wheels on the bed, if they are present.

6. Raise the whole bed, if possible, to a height that is good for you.

7. Stand on one side of the bed. The person assisting will stand on the opposite side.

8. Both of you should stand slightly turned toward the head of the bed. Your feet should be about 12 to 14 inches apart. The foot closest to the head of the bed should be pointed in that direction. Bend your knees. Keep your back straight.

9. Use of a draw, pull, or turning sheet is always preferred for moving a client up in bed. This avoids friction between the client's skin and bedding. It will prevent irritation of the skin.

10. You will be sliding the client's body when you move him up in bed. Roll the draw sheet up to the client's body and grab underhand. Shift the weight of your body from your back leg to your front leg up near the head of the bed. By keeping your back and arms "locked" in position when you shift your weight, your legs will help you use your body weight to your advantage and pull the client up.

11. Explain step 10 to both your assistant and the client. Count to three as pre-arranged. You and your partner will move together to slide the client gently toward the head of the bed (Figure 9.6).

12. Replace the pillow. Position the client correctly. Raise the side rails (if necessary). Replace the bed to the original horizontal position.

13. Wash your hands.

14. Chart any observations you may have made while doing this procedure.

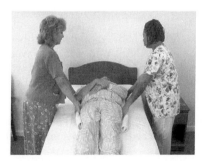

FIGURE 9.6

Procedure

Moving a Client Up in Bed, One Person

1. Wash your hands.

2. Tell the client you are going to move him up in bed. Say this even if he appears unconscious.

3. Ask the visitors to leave, if appropriate.

4. Remove the pillow from the bed. Place it on a chair.

5. Lock the wheels on the bed, if they are present.

6. Raise the whole bed, if possible, to a height that is comfortable for you.

7. Stand at the head of the bed. One foot should be in close to the bed, the other slightly behind.

8. Reach over the top of the draw sheet. Roll the edge and grab it.

9. On a count of three, "lock" your arms and back into one unbendable unit and shift your weight to your back leg. The client will slide easily to the top of the bed with the sheet. Make sure you do this slowly and use good body mechanics (Figure 9.7).

10. Replace the pillow. Position the client correctly. Raise the side rails. Replace the bed to its original horizontal position.

11. Wash your hands.

12. Chart your observation of the client during the procedure.

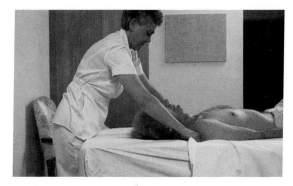

FIGURE 9.7 Use the sheet and good body mechanics to move the client.

Procedure

Moving a Client to One Side of the Bed on His Back

1. Wash your hands.
2. Tell the client you are going to move him to one side of the bed on his back without turning him. Explain that this is a safety measure so that when he is turned to his side, he'll be in the center of the bed.
3. Lock the wheels on the bed, if they are present.
4. Raise the whole bed to the highest position that is best for you.
5. Lower the backrest and footrest, if this is allowed.
6. Put the side rail in the up position on the far side of the bed.
7. Loosen the top sheets, but do not expose the client.

8. Place your feet in good position—one in close to the bed and one back. Slide both your arms under the client's back to his far shoulder, then slide the client's shoulders toward you by rocking your weight to your back foot (Figure 9.8).

9. Keep your knees bent and your back straight as you slide the client.

10. Slide both your arms as far as you can under the client's buttocks, and slide his buttocks toward you the same way.

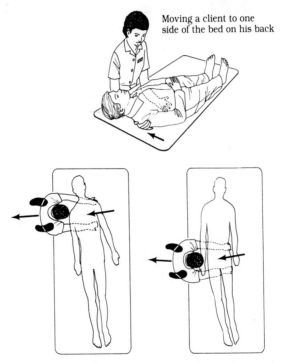

Moving a client to one side of the bed on his back

FIGURE 9.8 As a safety measure, do this before turning the client so that when he is turned to his side, he'll be in the center of the bed.

Use a pull (turning) sheet whenever possible for helpless clients.

11. Place both your arms under the client's feet and slide them toward you.

12. Replace and adjust the pillow, if necessary.

13. Remake the top of the bed.

14. Make the client comfortable. Lower the bed to its lowest horizontal position.

15. Wash your hands.

16. Chart your observations of the client during this procedure.

PROCEDURE

Rolling the Client (Log Rolling)

1. Wash your hands.

2. Tell the client you are going to roll him to his side as if he were a log.

3. Lock the wheels on the bed, if they are present.

4. Raise the whole bed to the best height for you.

5. Raise the side rail on the far side of the bed.

6. Remove the pillow from under the client's head, if allowed.

7. Move the client to your side of the bed as in the previous procedure (Moving a Client to One Side of the Bed on His Back).

8. Raise the side rail closest to the client, and go to the other side of the bed and lower that rail.

9. By holding the client at his hip and shoulder, roll the client toward you onto his side. Turn him gently (Figure 9.9).

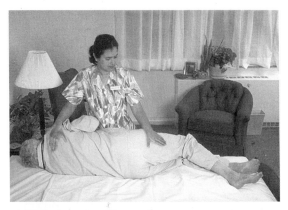

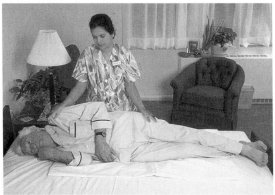

FIGURE 9.9

10. Place the client in a good bed position, and remake the top covers of the bed.
11. Wash your hands.
12. Chart your observations of the client during this procedure.

PROCEDURE

Raising the Client's Head and Shoulders

1. Never pull on a client's arm to lift him up. If assistance is required, slide your arm under the shoulder blade to lift, or raise the head of the bed, if possible.

2. If a client has some strength in one or both arms, "plant" your feet in the proper position, hold your arm out steady, and let the client pull up on you. That way you remain stationary while the client does the work. You then have one hand free to adjust the pillow, and so on (Figure 9.10).

3. Remember, good body mechanics are important to your success.

FIGURE 9.10 Client's hand should be under your armpit and placed on your shoulder or across his waist.

CHAPTER 10

Skin Care

Basic skin care

Good skin care is one of your prime responsibilities. It is much easier to prevent skin deterioration than to heal a decubitus ulcer. The skin must be inspected daily for changes, reddened areas, tender places, sore areas, or areas of breakdown. It is important to recognize the client who is at risk for skin breakdown and protect him from the danger of the formation of decubiti. Besides being very observant of your client's skin condition, you must be able to provide a safe environment for your client.

Many conditions working together affect the health of your client and the condition of your client's skin.

- Disease process

- Exercise and mobility

- Medication

- Health habits

- Nutrition

- Financial resources

- Assistance in his home when you are not with him

High-Risk Factors

The primary cause of skin breakdown is pressure on body parts, especially the bony prominences. These are places where the bones are close to the skin. Pressure on these areas decreases the circulation, leading to decubitus ulcer formation. These areas are the shoulder blades, elbows, knees, heels, ankles, and backbone. Because these are the areas covered by thin layers of skin that receive a smaller blood supply than other areas, they are at high risk for decubiti.

Obese clients tend to develop decubiti where skin surfaces rub together, causing friction in such areas as under the breasts, between the folds of the buttocks, and between the thighs.

Shearing occurs when the skin moves one way and the bone and tissue under the skin move another. When this happens, the skin is pinched, the tiny blood vessels are pinched, and the blood supply to the skin is decreased. This leads to skin damage. Cornstarch placed directly on the sheets decreases friction and allows the client to move more easily.

Skin Care of the Elderly

The elderly are especially susceptible to skin problems. With aging there is a gradual loss of skin tone. This includes loss of the natural oils, leading to dry, itchy, scaly, or rough skin. As the skin loses its underlayer of fat, the skin becomes thin, fragile, and unable to sense or maintain temperature accurately. There is also a decrease in circulation to the skin and in the ability to sense and react to temperature changes. Protecting a client from heat and cold becomes one of your responsibilities.

Decreasing Pressure to Body Areas

- Use an air cushion under the base of the spine or leg.
- Use sheepskin placed against the skin. Wash and dry frequently.
- An egg-crate mattress placed over the regular mattress and under the sheet will decrease the pressure on the back and permit air to circulate.
- An air mattress or a water-filled mattress redistributes the weight of a patient and is placed over the regular mattress and under a loosely fitting sheet (Figure 10.1a–e). Do not use safety pins to anchor the mattress. If your client has a special mattress, be sure to ask how you should care for the equipment.
- Sheepskin booties and elbow pads can be used.
- Bed cradles are used under blankets and sheets and over the client's legs so that the covers do not touch the client's skin (Figure 10.2).

General Observations

Observe the condition of the skin each time you visit. Note the temperature, cleanliness, and dryness. If there is a difference between two extremities, report this immediately. Observe for bruises and scratches. A bruise could indicate a reaction to a medication, a change in diet, a change in the client's ability to complete some tasks, a safety issue, or abuse. Try to determine when the bruise appeared, note how big it is, how long it lasts, and if it becomes worse or improves. Document all observations and discuss them with your supervisor immediately.

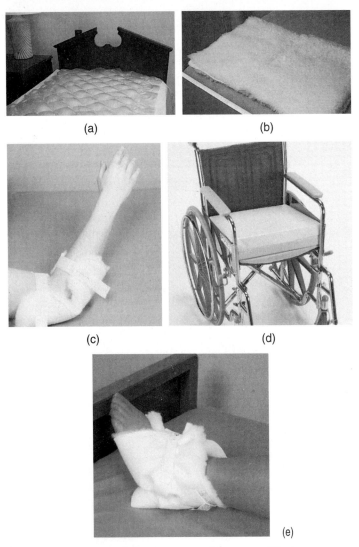

FIGURE 10.1 Special mattresses: (a) water-filled mattress; (b) sheepskin pad; (c) elbow protector; (d) wheelchair cushion; (e) heel protector.

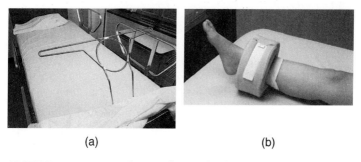

(a)   (b)

FIGURE 10.2 Secure the cradle to the bed so that neither the covers nor the cradle touch the client's toes and feet.

*G*uidelines—*Basic Skin Care*

- Care for the skin gently. Protect your client and his skin from all injuries.

- Protect your client from exposure to the sun and the elements, such as wind, cold, or rain. If your client insists on sitting in the sun, encourage him to use a protective lotion with a sunscreen in it and to wear a hat that protects his face.

- Keep the client's body as clean and dry as possible. It is important to keep his perineum clean and dry, but a complete bath on a daily basis is often unnecessary. Use a mild soap to wash the client, and be sure to dry each body area thoroughly. Do not use perfumes, bubble-bath crystals, or bath salts. If itchy skin is a problem, discuss with your supervisor what can be added to the bath water or put on the client's skin.

- If the client is incontinent, keep him clean and dry no matter how often you must wash him and change the bed. If you do not have enough linen in the house, report this to your supervisor. Do not put the client in rubber pants. To protect the bed and to make cleaning the client easier, use a disposable bed protector. Change the bed immediately when it becomes wet, and be sure that the plastic side of the protector never touches the client's skin.

- Use lotion on the skin to prevent contact with any bodily discharges or drainage from a wound. Use powder and cornstarch sparingly, and be sure to wash it all off when you bathe the client. Both tend to cake in body creases.
- Turn the client often, at least every 2 hours. Move the client slowly so as not to cause sheet burns or shearing.
- Pressure from sitting on the rim of a bedpan causes friction when getting on and off the pan, and this can worsen the skin condition. Never leave your client on the bedpan longer than necessary. Avoid spilling urine on the skin. Padding the rim of the bedpan can reduce some pressure. Powdering the rim will also minimize friction.
- Keep linen wrinkle-free and dry at all times.
- Remove crumbs, hairpins, and any other hard objects from the bed promptly.
- Do not let the client lie on catheters or any type of tubing.
- Be alert to the effects that medications have on the skin.
- Do not rub the skin hard. Always rub the skin with lotion and in a circular motion. Rubbing stimulates the circulation of blood to the skin, but hard rubbing can damage skin that is fragile.
- Keep walkways clear of furniture so the client will not bump his toes or legs.
- Encourage good eating habits and the adequate intake of fluids.

DECUBITUS ULCERS (BEDSORES)

Decubitus ulcers—bedsores, or pressure sores—occur where the skin has broken because of pressure. Both external and internal factors affect the skin's breakdown.

External factors may be abrasions, scratches, burns, or chemicals. Internal factors may be swelling, abscesses, or allergic reactions. As part of his disease process, a client may have poor circulation. Pressure on the skin can come from the weight of the body lying in one position too long or from splints, casts, or bandages. Wrinkles in the bed linen can cause a decubitus ulcer. Decubiti are made worse by continued pressure, heat, moisture, and lack of cleanliness. Irritating substances on the skin, such as perspiration, urine, feces, wound drainage, or even soap, tend to make decubiti worse. If a decubitus ulcer is not treated, it will quickly become larger, very painful, and even infected.

Report the first sign of decubiti to your supervisor so that steps can be taken to prevent further damage.

Signs of Decubiti

The signs of a decubitus are a warm area of skin, redness, tenderness, discomfort, and a feeling of burning. After this, the skin often gets gray in color. This means that the blood supply to the area is greatly decreased. If the condition is allowed to continue, a blister will form, and finally the skin will actually break and a wound will appear (Figure 10.3). When the skin is broken, a decubitus ulcer has formed.

Care of a Decubitus Ulcer

- Specific treatment for a decubitus ulcer is prescribed by a doctor. The wound, however, must be kept clean and the rules of asepsis must be followed.
- The client must be positioned so that pressure is removed from the decubitus.

(a)

Inflammation or redness of the skin which does not return to normal after 15 minutes of removal of pressure. Edema is present. It involves the epidermis. Skin may or may not be broken.

(b)

Skin blister or shallow skin ulcer. Involves the epidermis and dermis. Looks like a shallow crater. Area is red, warm, and may or may not have drainage.

(c)

Full-thickness skin loss, exposing subcutaneous tissue; may extend into next layer. Edema, inflammation, and necrosis present. Drainage present, which may or may not have an odor.

(d)

Full-thickness ulcer. Muscle and/or bone can be seen. Infection and necrosis is present. Drainage present, which may or may not have an odor.

FIGURE 10.3 Stages of skin breakdown.

- Often a simple nonsterile dressing is used to cover it. If tape is used, alternate the site so the tape doesn't cause irritation. Be very gentle when removing the tape.
- If the client is incontinent, and urine and feces continue to drain into the wound, discuss alternatives with your supervisor.
- Teach the family to follow the plan of care when you are not in the home.
- Document/report all your observations clearly and in a timely manner.

*F*OOT CARE

Feet are often the site of many problems because of decreased circulation, infection, poor nutrition, and poor care.

Chronic diseases such as diabetes, arthritis, chronic obstructive pulmonary disease (COPD), and hypertension often cause foot problems because of lack of circulation, poor nutrition, and decreased physical ability to care for the feet.

Clients may not notice changes in their feet. Be observant and report the following changes:

- Pain either while resting or during exercise
- Changes in sensation on skin or in the feet, either tingling, "pins and needles," or lack of feeling
- Change in color, such as to blue or dark red
- Decreased temperature sensation or sensitivity to cold
- Increased fluid—edema or swelling

- Dry, cracked skin
- Presence of open areas, such as ulcers or blisters
- Toenails that are thick and curling into the toes
- Absence of toenails

Basic Foot Care

1. Inspect the feet each day for changes before you wash them.

2. Wash and dry feet daily. Feet should be washed with mild soap in warm water and dried well, especially between toes. Soaking is not desirable or needed. If the skin is dry, a lubricant or cream can be applied. Do not apply any over-the-counter medications.

3. Do not cut nails, corns, or bunions. If they require attention, call your supervisor.

4. Shoes should fit well and give support. They should be appropriate for the time of year and the activity. Going barefooted is not advised, as this decreases support and permits injuries to toes and feet. Socks or stockings should be worn. Certain socks are the best because they "breathe" and absorb perspiration. Socks and stockings should be the proper size: Those that are too big cause irritation and those that are too small constrict circulation. Do not use garters or rubber bands to hold up socks or stockings.

5. Check the temperature of bath water. If a client has decreased temperature sensation, he will not be able to notice that the water is too hot. The client should not use heating pads to keep warm but rather cotton socks and down slippers inside and

insulated boots out of doors. Walk in well-lit and clear areas. In warm weather, keep feet protected from hot sand, boardwalks, objects on the beach, and the sun.

6. Diet is important for the health of the entire body. A client should consult a nutritionist for specific foods that will affect his feet.

If you notice the following problems, call your supervisor immediately.

Problem	Immediate Action
Swollen legs and feet	Elevate the legs and feet on a chair or couch and report this.
Pain	Stop exercise or activity, rest, and call your supervisor.
Open areas	Do not put on socks or bandage with tape. Cover with clean dressing and call your supervisor.
Temperature variations (hot and cold)	Cover lightly with blanket and report to your supervisor. Do not use a hot water bottle or ice.

*R*ADIATION THERAPY

Radiation therapy is the use of a specialized type of energy ray to stop the growth of cancer cells by destroying the cells' ability to grow and reproduce. Radiation is used at various times in the treatment of cancer.

During the first visit to the radiation center, lines are drawn on the skin to indicate the target for the radiation. It is important not to wash off these marks. The skin within these marks may appear red or burned. Should the skin break, contact your supervisor immediately.

- Care for the skin gently with cool water. Do not wash the area with soaps or lotions.
- Protect the radiation site from sunlight.
- Cover it with loose-fitting clothing that will not scratch or irritate it.
- Use only electric razors. Check with your supervisor as to the type of shaving cream to be used, and make sure it is specific for electric razors.
- Do not use hair-removal chemicals or lotions.

CHEMOTHERAPY

Chemotherapy is a general term used to describe the use of drugs to treat cancer. There are many differences in the way drugs are given, how often they are given, and how each person responds.

Chemotherapy works by destroying cancer cells' ability to reproduce. Unfortunately, normal cells also pick up some of the chemicals, which causes some side effects.

- If the client's mouth and throat are dry, offer moist foods and drink fluids. Eating cold, soft foods often helps. Bland foods will not cause further irritation.
- Use a soft-bristle toothbrush followed by a nonirritating mouthwash for mouthcare.

- Keep lips moist and lubricated.
- Discuss a dental consult with your supervisor.
- Hair follicles frequently are affected by drugs. Often the hair grows back when the drugs are stopped. Men may wear hairpieces. Some women wear turbans or hats. It is important to keep the scalp clean and free of irritations during this time. If the client's hair falls out, use a wig or hat to protect the skin.
- Contact your supervisor if the itching becomes severe or if the skin is broken due to itching or a rash.

CHAPTER 11

Personal Care

ORAL HYGIENE

Oral hygiene is part of every client's care, whether he is conscious or unconscious, eating or not eating, self-sufficient or partially dependent. It gives a feeling of well-being and decreases mouth odor.

Oral hygiene includes the cleansing of the mouth, gums, and teeth or dentures. This procedure should be done twice a day and after meals, whenever possible.

PROCEDURE

Oral Hygiene

Be sure that your client is able to spit out water before you allow him to take it.

1. Assemble your equipment:
   Fresh water
   Cup
   Straw, if necessary
   Toothbrush and toothpaste
   Emesis basin, sink, or small basin
   Face towel and disposable gloves
   Mouthwash (optional)

2. Wash your hands.

3. Ask visitors to step out of the room, if appropriate.

4. Explain the procedure to the client.

5. Have the client sit up or assist him to the sink. (If the client goes to the sink, omit any steps that are unnecessary.)

6. Spread the towel across the client's chest to protect him. Put on gloves.

7. Offer the client water to rinse his mouth.

8. Hold the emesis basin under the client's chin so he can spit out the water.

9. Put toothpaste on the wet toothbrush.

10. Offer the toothbrush to the client if he is able to brush his own teeth. If he is unable, you must do it. Use a gentle motion, starting above the gum line and going down the teeth. Repeat this until you have brushed all the teeth.

11. Offer the client water to rinse his mouth.

12. Offer the client mouthwash if he likes it.

13. Make the client comfortable.

14. Clean and put away the equipment. Remove your gloves.

15. Wash your hands.

16. Make a notation on the client's chart that you have completed this procedure. Also note anything you observed about the client during this procedure.

Clients who wear dentures (false teeth) also require oral hygiene. Pieces of food must be removed from gums and the tongue. The gums must also be stimulated to ensure good circulation. Gums should be stimulated with a soft toothbrush whenever dentures are removed. Dentures need not be cleaned each time they are removed if the client removes them several times a day. They can, however, be soaked in a cleansing solution each time. They should be brushed thoroughly at least once every 12 hours.

Dentures are expensive and difficult to replace. Always put them in a carefully marked denture cup. Do not wrap them up in tissue, put them under a pillow, or leave them on a night table. They could be thrown out by accident.

PROCEDURE

Oral Hygiene for Clients Who Wear Dentures

1. Assemble your equipment:
   Tissues
   Denture cup
   Small basin or emesis basin
   Toothbrush or denture brush
   Denture-soaking solution
   Towel and disposable gloves
   Denture toothpaste
   Mouthwash (optional)
2. Wash your hands.
3. Ask visitors to step out of the room, if appropriate.
4. Tell the client you wish to clean his dentures.
5. Spread the towel across the client's chest to protect his bedclothes. Put on gloves.
6. Ask the client to remove his dentures. Have tissue in the emesis basin ready to receive the dentures. Help the client if he cannot remove them himself.
7. Take the dentures to the sink in the basin. Hold them securely.
8. Line the sink with a paper towel or washcloth so that if the dentures slip out of your hand, they will be cushioned as they fall. Fill the sink with water.

9. Apply toothpaste or denture cleanser to the dentures. With the dentures in the palm of your hand, brush them until they are clean. Do not use kitchen cleanser or abrasive cleansers.

10. Rinse the dentures thoroughly under cool water.

11. Fill the denture cup with denture soaking solution, cool water, or some mouthwash and water. Place the dentures in the cup, and cover it.

12. Help the client rinse his mouth with water and/or mouthwash.

13. Have the client replace the dentures in his mouth if that is what he wants. Be sure the dentures are moist before replacing them. Ask the client if he uses denture adhesive.

14. Leave the labeled denture cup with the clean solution where the client can easily place the dentures if he takes them out between cleanings.

15. Clean your equipment and replace it in the proper place.

16. Remove gloves and wash your hands.

17. Make a notation on the client's chart that you have completed this procedure.

Also note anything you have observed about the client during this procedure.

Note: It is a safety precaution to label a denture cup so that no one throws the dentures out accidentally.

*T*HE UNCONSCIOUS CLIENT

Be very careful not to overlook mouth care of your client if he is unconscious. Oral hygiene will prevent the oral tissues from cracking and bleeding.

PROCEDURE

Oral Hygiene for the Unconscious Client

Do not put water into the client's mouth.

1. Assemble your equipment:
   Towel and disposable gloves
   Small basin or emesis basin
   Special disposable mouth care kit—if such a kit is not
       available, you will need a tongue depressor, padded
       with several gauze squares (be sure they are securely
       fastened to the tongue depressor) and a lubricant, such
       as glycerine or a solution of glycerine and lemon juice

2. Wash your hands.

3. Ask visitors to step out of the room, if appropriate.

4. Tell the client what you are going to do. Even though the
   client seems to be unconscious, he may still be able to
   hear you.

5. Stand at the side of the bed, and turn the client's face
   toward you. Put on gloves.

6. Support the client's face on a pillow covered by a towel.

7. Put a small basin on the towel under the client's chin.

8. Place the mouth care equipment near you so you do not
   have to move.

9. Wipe the client's entire mouth (roof, tongue, and inside
   the lips and cheeks) with the swab or the tongue
   depressor dipped in solution. Do not put your fingers
   in the client's mouth. He may close his mouth and
   injure you.

10. Put the used swabs in the basin. The swabs will leave a coating of glycerine solution on the entire mouth and tongue. This will protect and lubricate the oral tissues.

11. Dry the client's face with a towel.

12. Using a clean applicator, put a small amount of lubricant on the client's lips.

13. Make the client safe and comfortable.

14. Clean your equipment, and put it in the proper place.

15. Remove your gloves, and wash your hands.

16. Make a notation on the client's chart that you have completed this procedure. Note your observations of the client during the procedure.

ASSISTING A CLIENT TO DRESS AND UNDRESS

- Allow a client to choose his own clothes. If a client is in his bed most of the day, be sure the bedclothes are not wrinkled. If a client spends most of the day out of bed, encourage him to dress in street clothes.

- If a client has a method of dressing himself that suits him and is safe, allow him to continue using his personal method.

- Do not expose the client unnecessarily as you assist him.

- An injured or inflexible (rigid) arm or leg is first into the garment and last out.

PROCEDURE

Assisting a Client to Dress and Undress

1. Assemble your equipment:
   Clean clothes

2. Wash your hands.

3. Ask visitors to leave the room, if appropriate.

4. If the client is able to sit on the edge of the bed, assist him into this position. Avoid exposing him. If the client must remain in bed, assist him into a flat position on his back.

5. Put on underwear and trousers or pajamas. If a leg is injured, place it into underwear or pajamas first, followed by the other leg.

6. Ask the client to stand up, if possible, and pull the pants to his waist. If the client is in bed, have him lift his buttocks and you pull up his pants.

7. To put on an over-the-head type of shirt (or other garment), place an injured arm into the shirt first. Then put the neck of the shirt over the client's head. Finally, guide the other arm into the shirt.

8. To put on a button-type shirt, place the sleeve over an injured arm first. Bring the shirt to the back of the client and guide the other arm into the sleeve.

9. Assist the client with socks or stockings. Do not use round garters, because they decrease circulation.

10. Assist the client with shoes. Be sure they fit well and give support. Look for any blisters or red areas on the feet.

11. Make the client comfortable.

12. Wash your hands.

13. Make a notation on the client's chart that you have completed this procedure. Also note anything you have observed about the client during this procedure.

*H*ELPING A CLIENT TO BATHE

Bathing:

- Takes waste products off the skin.
- Cools and refreshes the client.
- Stimulates the skin and improves circulation.
- Requires movement of the muscles.
- Provides a good opportunity for the homemaker/ home health aide to observe the client.
- Provides an opportunity to talk with the client.

Clients may not need to have a complete bath each day. The frequency of your client's bath will depend on climate, need, skin condition, and the client's diagnosis. The client may prefer to have a partial bath at times to conserve energy. Most people are used to bathing themselves privately. Some clients are embarrassed by having another person do this for them. Keep clients covered, bathe them in a professional and reassuring manner.

- Usually, the complete bath is given as part of morning care. However, if your client enjoys his bath at another time of day, try to follow his request.
- Take everything to the bedside before you start the bath.
- Always cover the client with a bath blanket, a thin blanket, big towel, or terry cloth bathrobe.

- Use good body mechanics. Keep your feet separated, stand firmly, bend your knees, and keep your back straight.
- When you are using soap, keep it in the soap dish, not the basin of water.
- Use lotions and creams that the client usually uses.
- Check the client's bedclothes for personal items before putting them in the laundry.
- Talk to the client as you bathe him.
- Keep the client's body in proper alignment.
- Change the water as often as you need to so that you have warm, clean water at all times.
- Assist the client with establishing a bathing routine to save his energy.
- Allow the client to bathe as much of his body as he can safely reach.

The Partial Bath

- Bring a basin to the bed, or assist the client to the bathroom.
- Take a chair into the bathroom or have the client sit on the toilet covered by a towel.

PROCEDURE

The Complete Bed Bath

1. Assemble your equipment:
   Soap in a soap dish
   Washcloth and disposable gloves

Several bath towels
Wash basin
Powder, deodorant
Clean gown or pajamas
Bath blanket
Orange stick for nail care if used by your agency
Lotion for back rub
Comb and hairbrush

2. Wash your hands.

3. Ask visitors to step out of the room, if appropriate.

4. Tell the client you are going to give him a complete bed bath.

5. Offer the bedpan or urinal.

6. Assist the client with oral hygiene.

7. Take the bedspread and regular blanket off the bed. Fold them loosely over the back of a chair, leaving the client covered with the top sheet.

8. Place the bath blanket over the top sheet. Ask the client to hold the blanket in place.

9. Remove the top sheet from underneath without uncovering (exposing) the client. Fold the sheet loosely over the back of the chair if it is to be used again; if not, put it in the laundry bag.

10. Lower the headrest and knee rest of the bed, if possible and if permitted. The client should be in a flat position, as flat as is comfortable for him.

11. Raise the bed to its highest horizontal position, if possible.

12. Remove the client's nightclothes and jewelry. Keep the client covered with the bath blanket. Place the gown in the laundry bag, and put the jewelry in a safe place.

13. Fill the wash basin two-thirds full of water. Ask your client how he likes the water—hot, warm, or cool. Test it with your whole hand. Then let him test it with the inside of his hand.

14. Help the client to move to the side of the bed closest to you. Use good body mechanics. Put on gloves.

15. Put a towel across the client's chest and make a mitten with the washcloth (Figure 11.1). Wash the client's eyes from the nose to the outside of the face. Be careful not to get soap in his eyes. Rinse and dry by patting gently with the bath towel.

16. Put a towel lengthwise under the client's arm farthest from you. This will keep the bed from getting wet. Support the arm with the palm of your hand under his elbow. Then wash his shoulder, armpit (axilla), and arm. Use long, firm strokes. Rinse and dry the area well.

17. Place the basin of water on the towel. Put the client's hand into the water and let it soak. Be sure to support the arm and the basin. Wash, rinse, and dry the hand well. Place it under the bath blanket.

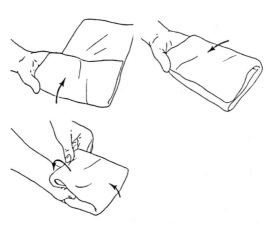

FIGURE 11.1

18. Wash, rinse, and dry the arm, hand, axilla, and shoulder closest to you in the same way.

19. Clean the client's fingernails with an orange stick, if used by your agency.

20. Place a towel across the client's chest. Fold the bath blanket down to the client's abdomen. Wash and rinse the client's ears, neck, and chest. Take note of the condition of the skin under the female client's breasts. Dry the area thoroughly.

21. Cover the client's entire chest with the towel. Fold the bath blanket down to the pubic area. Wash the client's abdomen. Be sure to wash the umbilicus (navel) and in any creases of the skin. Dry the client's abdomen. Then pull the bath blanket up over the abdomen and chest and remove the towels.

22. Empty the dirty water. Rinse the basin and refill it.

23. Fold the bath blanket back from the client's leg farthest from you.

24. Put a towel lengthwise under that leg and foot.

25. Bend the knee and wash, rinse, and dry the leg and foot. Support the leg if the client is unable to do so. Take hold of the heel for more support when flexing the knee.

26. If the client can easily bend his knee, put the wash basin on the towel. Then put the client's foot directly into the basin to wash it. Support his leg and the basin. Protect the ankle area from too much pressure on the basin.

27. Observe the toenails and the skin between the toes for general appearance and condition. Look especially for redness and cracking of the skin. Take away the basin. Dry the client's leg and foot and between the toes. Cover the leg and foot with the bath blanket and remove the towel.

28. Repeat the entire procedure for the leg and foot closest to you. Empty the basin, rinse it, and refill it with clean water.

29. Ask the client to turn on his side with his back toward you. If he needs help in turning, assist him.

30. Put the towel lengthwise on the bottom sheet near the client's back. Wash, rinse, and dry the back of the neck, back, and buttocks with long, firm, circular strokes. Give the client a back rub with warm lotion. The client's back should be rubbed for at least a minute and a half. Give special attention to bony areas (for example, shoulder blades, hips, and elbows). Look for red areas. Dry the client's back, remove the towel, and turn him on his back.

31. Offer the client a soapy washcloth to wash his genital area. Give him a clean, wet washcloth to rinse himself well. Give him a dry towel for drying himself. If he is unable to do this for himself, it is your responsibility to wash the client's genital area. Provide for privacy at all times.

32. Put a clean gown or pajamas on the client. Note: Usually, the client's hair is combed and the bed is changed; however, this depends on the needs of your client.

33. Arrange the bed so that your client is comfortable and safe.

34. Clean your equipment, and put it in its proper place.

35. Remove gloves and wash your hands.

36. Make a notation on the client's chart that you have completed this procedure. Note your observations of the client during this procedure.

The Tub Bath and Shower

Several of your clients will want a tub bath. Some houses do not have showers. Some clients are used to taking baths rather than showers. Some baths are prescribed for therapeutic reasons. Remember, you must have specific instructions from your supervisor to give a client a tub bath, and you, as the homemaker/home health aide, must be sure that you can carry out this procedure.

PROCEDURE

The Tub Bath

1. Assemble your equipment:
    Bath towels
    Nonskid bathmat on the bathroom floor
    Washcloths and disposable gloves
    Soap
    Nonskid bathmat to be used in the tub
    Chair for client to sit on, or use the commode
    Clean gown or pajamas
    Equipment to wash the tub before and after your
       client's bath

2. Check the tub. Wash it if necessary.

3. Wash your hands.

4. Ask visitors to leave the room, if appropriate.

5. Tell the client that you would like to assist him with his tub bath.

6. Assist the client to the bathroom.

7. For safety, remove all electric appliances from the bathroom. Check grab bars. Check to see that there is proper ventilation.

8. Fill the bathtub half full with water. Ask your client how he likes the bath water—warm, hot, or cool. Run cold water through the faucet last so it will be cool if the client should touch it. Test the water for temperature. Have the client test the water.

9. Assist the client in getting undressed and into the bathtub.

10. Let the client stay in the bathtub as long as permitted, according to your instructions. Give him privacy as is safely permitted.

11. Help the client wash himself as needed. Wear gloves.

12. Empty the tub. It is easier to get out of an empty tub than a full one.

13. Put one towel across the chair or the commode. Have the client sit on this.

14. Allow the client to dry as much of his body as he can. Assist him with putting on clean bedclothes or street clothes.
15. Assist the client out of the bathroom to his bed or chair. Make him comfortable.
16. Return to the bathroom. Clean the tub and bathroom as necessary.
17. Remove all used linen and put them in the proper place.
18. Wash your hands.
19. Make a notation on the client's chart that you have completed this procedure. Also note anything you have observed about the client during this procedure.

*B*ACK RUBS

Rubbing a client's back refreshes him, relaxes his muscles, and stimulates circulation. Because of pressure caused by the bedclothes and lack of movement to stimulate circulation, the skin of a client who spends a great deal of time in bed needs special attention.

Back rubs are usually given as part of morning care after the client's bath. They are also given in the evening before a client goes to sleep and during the day whenever a client changes position or requires this procedure.

*P*ROCEDURE

Giving a Client a Back Rub

1. Assemble your equipment:
   Towels and disposable gloves
   Lotion of the client's choice
   Basin of warm water (optional)

2. Wash your hands.

3. Ask visitors to leave the room, if appropriate.

4. Tell the client you are going to give him a back rub.

5. Raise the bed to its highest horizontal position, if possible. Ask the client to turn on his side or abdomen so that you can easily reach his back. Have him positioned as close to the side of the bed where you are working as possible.

6. If the client's bed has side rails, keep the side rail up on the far side of the bed, but lower it on the side of the bed where you are working.

7. Warm the lotion by placing it in a basin of warm water. Put on gloves.

8. Expose the client's back and buttocks. Do not overexpose him.

9. Pour a small amount of lotion into the palm of your hand.

10. Rub your hands together, using friction to warm the lotion.

11. Apply lotion to the entire back with the palms of your hands. Use firm long strokes from the buttocks to the shoulders and the back of the neck and shoulders.

12. Use proper body mechanics. Keep your knees slightly bent and your back straight.

13. Exert firm pressure as you stroke upward from the buttocks toward the shoulders. Use gentle pressure as you move your hands down the back. Do not lift up your hands as you massage.

14. Use a circular motion on each bony area. This rhythmic rubbing motion should be continued for 1 to 3 minutes (Figure 11.2).

15. Dry the client's back by patting it with a towel.

16. Assist the client in putting on a gown or pajamas.

17. Reposition the client. Make him comfortable.

18. Arrange the top sheet of the bed neatly.

19. Arrange the bed so that your client is safe and comfortable.

20. Put your equipment back in its proper place.

21. Remove gloves and wash your hands.

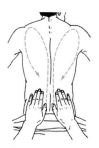 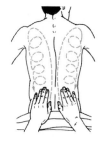 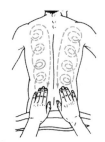

FIGURE 11.2

22. Make a notation on the client's chart that you have completed this procedure. Also note anything you have observed about the client during this procedure.

HAIR CARE

It is important to keep your client's hair neat and clean. This prevents scalp and hair breakdown, improves the client's appearance, improves circulation to the scalp, and improves the client's general feeling about himself.

- Keep the client free of drafts.
- Never cut a client's hair.
- Never color a client's hair.
- Never give a client a permanent.
- Never use a hot comb or curling iron on a client's hair.
- Style the client's hair as he or she is accustomed to have it.

PROCEDURE

Giving a Shampoo in Bed

1. Assemble your equipment:
   Client's comb and brush
   Client's shampoo
   Conditioner (optional)
   Several containers of warm to hot water, as client prefers
   Chair
   Pitcher
   Large basin or pail to collect dirty water
   Bed protectors
   Several large bath towels
   Wash cloth and disposable gloves
   Water trough or 1½ yards of 60-in. wide plastic to
      make one
   Cotton balls (optional)
   Bath blanket
   Waterproof pillow (optional)
   Electric blow dryer (optional)
   Curlers (optional)

2. Wash your hands.

3. Ask visitors to leave the room, if appropriate.

4. Tell the client that you are going to shampoo his hair
   in bed.

5. Raise the bed to the highest horizontal position, if possible.
   Lower the headrest and the side rail on the side you are
   working, if possible. Ask the client what water temperature
   he prefers.

6. Place a chair at the side of the bed near the client's head.
   The chair should be lower than the mattress. Put on gloves.

7. Inspect the client's hair for knots and lice. If the client's hair
   has knots, carefully comb them out. If the client has lice,

stop the procedure and report this to your supervisor. Lice are tiny black insects that live on hair and scalp.

8. Place a towel on the chair. Place the large basin or pail on the towel.

9. (Optional) Remove the pillow from under the client's head. Cover the pillow with a waterproof case. Have the pillow under the small of the client's back so when he lies on it his head is tilted backward.

10. Put the bath blanket on the client. Fanfold the top sheets to the foot of the bed without exposing the client.

11. Ask the client to move across the bed so that his head is close to where you are standing.

12. Place the bed protectors on the mattress under the client's head.

13. Put small amounts of cotton in the client's ears for protection.

14. Place the shampoo trough under the client's head. A trough can be made by rolling up the sides of the plastic sheet. This makes a channel for the water to run into the pail. Three sides must be rolled to make the channel. The top edge should be rolled around a rolled bath towel. Place the edge with the rolled towel in it under the client's neck and head. Have the open edge hanging into the pail on the chair (Figure 11.3).

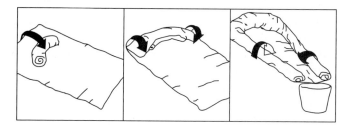

FIGURE 11.3

15. Loosen the pajamas so the client is comfortable and no clothing is in the trough.

16. Ask the client to hold the washcloth over his eyes

17. Pour some water over the client's hair. Use a pitcher or a cup. Repeat until the hair is completely wet.

18. Apply shampoo and, using both hands, wash the hair and massage the scalp with your fingertips. Avoid using your fingernails because they could scratch the client's scalp.

19. Rinse the shampoo off by pouring water over the hair. Have the client turn from side to side. Repeat this until the hair is free of soap.

20. If the client uses a conditioner, apply it after reading the directions.

21. Dry the client's forehead and ears.

22. Remove the cotton from the client's ears.

23. Raise the client's head, and wrap it in a bath towel.

24. Rub the client's hair with a towel to dry it as much as possible.

25. Remove the equipment from the bedside. Be sure the client is in a safe, comfortable position before you leave.

26. Comb the client's hair as he is accustomed to having it done. You may leave a towel spread over the pillow under the client's head as his hair dries or you may set the client's hair. If an electric blow dryer is available, use it on cool.

27. Remove the bath blanket and, at the same time, bring up the top sheets to cover the client.

28. If possible, lower the bed to its lowest horizontal position and raise the side rails.

29. Make the client comfortable.

30. Clean your equipment, and put it in its proper place.

31. Remove gloves and wash your hands.

32. Make a notation on the client's chart that you have completed this procedure. Also note anything that you have observed about the client during this procedure.

Combing a Client's Hair

If the client wears glasses, ask him to remove them. Comb and brush the hair in the style requested by the client. If the hair is long and knots easily, suggest braids. Comb the hair into age-appropriate styles. Use the hair products the client is accustomed to using. Inspect the hair for knots and lice. If there are knots, comb them out slowly and gently. Comb each section of hair separately using a downward motion and working up toward the head. Turn the client's head gently so that you can reach all areas of the head. Lice are little black insects that live on the scalp and the hair. If you notice lice, stop combing and notify your supervisor.

*P*ROCEDURE

Combing a Client's Hair

1. Assemble your equipment on the bedside table:
Towel
Comb or brush
Any hair preparation the client usually uses
Hand mirror, if available

2. Wash your hands.

3. Ask visitors to leave the room, if appropriate.

4. Tell the client you are going to brush or comb his hair.

5. If possible, comb the client's hair after the bath and before you make the bed. Some clients prefer to have their hair combed while sitting in a chair.

6. Lay a towel across the pillow, under the client's head. If the client can sit up in bed, drape the towel around his shoulders.

7. If the client wears glasses, ask him to take them off before you begin, unless this makes the client uncomfortable. Be sure to put the glasses in a safe place.

8. Part the hair down the middle to make it easier to comb.

9. Brush or comb the client's hair carefully, gently, and thoroughly in his usual style.

10. For the client who cannot sit up, separate the hair into small sections. Then comb each section separately, using a downward motion, starting at the loose end and working up toward the head. Ask the client to turn his head from side to side. Or turn it for him so that you can reach the entire head.

11. Arrange the client's hair the way he wants it.

12. If the client has long hair, suggest braiding it to keep it from getting tangled.

13. Be sure you brush the back of the head.

14. Remove the towel when you are finished.

15. Let the client use the mirror.

16. Make the client comfortable.

17. Wash your hands.

18. Make a notation on the client's chart that you have completed this procedure. Also note anything you have observed about the client during this procedure.

SHAVING A CLIENT'S BEARD

A regular morning activity for most men is shaving the beard. A client is often well enough to shave himself. In this case, you will give him the help that is necessary, such as being sure he has the equipment he needs. Sometimes, however, clients are unable to shave themselves. In such cases, you will do it. Before shaving any client's face, be sure you have been instructed to do so by your supervisor. Certain clients may not be permitted to shave or be shaved.

Shaving can be done using only an electric razor or a safety razor. Electric razors should never be used if the client is receiving oxygen.

PROCEDURE

Shaving a Client's Beard

1. Assemble your equipment at the bedside:
    Basin of water, very warm to hot
    Shaving cream
    Safety razor
    Face towel and disposable gloves
    Mirror
    Tissues
    Aftershave lotion (optional)
    Face powder (optional)
    Washcloth

2. Wash your hands.

3. Ask visitors to leave the room, if appropriate.

4. Tell the client that you are going to shave his beard.

5. Adjust a light so that it shines on the client's face but not in his eyes.

6. Raise the head of the bed if possible and if allowed. Put on gloves.

7. Spread the face towel under the client's chin. If the client has dentures, be sure they are in his mouth.

8. Put some warm water on the client's face, or use a damp warm washcloth to soften his beard.

9. If using a razor, apply shaving cream generously to the face.

10. With the fingers of one hand, hold the skin taut (tight) as you shave in the direction that the hair grows. Start under the sideburns and work downward over the cheeks. Continue carefully over the chin. Work upward on the neck under the chin. Use short, firm strokes.

11. If using a razor, rinse it often in the basin of water.

12. Areas under the nose and around the lips are sensitive. Take special care in these areas.

13. If you nick the client's skin, wash the area and report this to your supervisor. Do not put any medication on the area.

14. If you used a razor, wash off the remaining shaving cream when you have finished.

15. Apply aftershave lotion or powder as the client prefers.

16. Make the client comfortable.

17. Clean your equipment, and put it in its proper place.

18. Remove gloves and wash your hands.

19. Make a notation on the client's chart that you have completed this procedure. Also note anything you have observed about the client during this procedure.

TOILETING

Toileting is usually an activity that is private and one that is not openly discussed. The clients you care for will now have to perform this activity with varying amounts of assistance. They may be embarrassed. You may be embarrassed. Your role is to assist the client with this important and normal bodily function in a way that is acceptable to him and safe to both of you. There are often special words associated with elimination. Knowing these words may make the communication between you and your client easier. Try to keep to the schedule and way the client usually toilets, because this will help when you are not there.

Elimination of body waste is important if the body is to maintain its health and function. Report the following:

- Frequency of elimination
- Color
- Odor
- Any pain with elimination
- Ability to control elimination
- Any foreign material, such as blood or mucous

For clients who are unable to get out of bed to use the bathroom, a urinal and a bedpan are required (Figure 11.4a and b). The urinal is a container into which the male client urinates. The bedpan is a pan into which he defecates (moves his bowels). The female client uses the bedpan for urination and defecation. There are times, however, when a female urinal must be used. Always cover the bedpan and remove it from the client's bedside to the

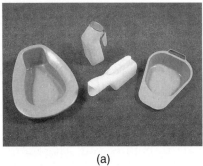

(a)

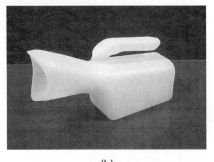

(b)

FIGURE 11.4 (a) Two different types of bedpans and male and female urinals (b) female urinal

bathroom as quickly as possible after use. Measure the volume and collect a specimen if required.

Some clients are able to get out of bed but unable to walk to the bathroom. These clients can use a portable commode that is brought to the house.

PROCEDURE

Offering the Bedpan

1. Assemble your equipment:
   Bedpan and cover, or fracture bedpan and cover
   Toilet tissue
   Wash basin with water or wet washcloth
   Soap
   Talcum powder or cornstarch
   Hand towel and disposable gloves

2. Wash your hands.

3. Ask visitors to leave the room, if appropriate. You may, however, wish to demonstrate this procedure to the family members.

4. Ask the client if he would like to use the bedpan. Put on gloves.

5. Warm the bedpan by running warm water inside it and along the rim. Dry the outside of the bedpan with paper towels and put talcum powder or corn starch on the part that will touch the client. If the client is going to move his bowels and a specimen is not needed, place several sheets of toilet tissue or a slight bit of water in the bedpan. This will make cleaning it easier.

6. Raise the bed to the highest horizontal position, if possible.

7. Lower the side rail on the side where you are standing, if possible.

8. Fold back the top sheets so that they are out of the way.

9. Raise the client's gown, but keep the lower part of his body covered with the top sheets.

10. Ask the client to bend his knees and put his feet flat on the mattress. Then ask the client to raise his hips. If necessary, help the client to raise his buttocks by slipping your hand

under the lower part of his back. Place the bedpan in position with the seat of the bedpan under the buttocks (Figure 11.5).

11. Sometimes the client is unable to lift his buttocks to get on or off the bedpan. In this case, turn the client on his side with his back to you. Put the bedpan against the buttocks. Then turn the client back onto the bedpan (Figure 11.6).

12. Replace the covers over the client.

13. Raise the backrest and knee rest, if allowed, so the client is in a sitting position.

14. Put toilet tissue where the client can reach it easily.

15. Ask the client to signal when he is finished.

16. Raise the side rails to the up position.

17. Leave the room to give the client privacy. Remove gloves and wash your hands if you are going to do another task.

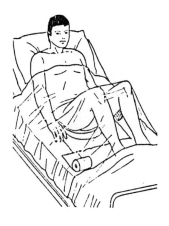

FIGURE 11.5

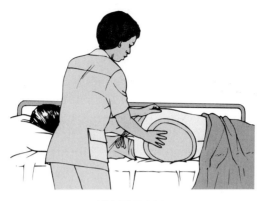

FIGURE 11.6

18. When the client signals, return to the room.

19. Wash your hands and put on gloves.

20. Help the client to raise his hips so you can remove the bedpan.

21. Help the client if he is unable to clean himself. Turn the client on his side. Clean the anal area with toilet tissue.

22. Raise the side rails, if possible. Cover the bedpan immediately. You can use a disposable pad or a paper towel if no cover is available.

23. Take the bedpan to the client's bathroom. Remove gloves and wash your hands.

24. Return to the client. Offer the client the opportunity to wash his hands in the basin of water.

25. Make the client comfortable.

26. Put on gloves and note the excreta (feces or urine) for amount, odor, and color.

27. If a specimen or sample is required, collect it at this time. Measure the urine, if necessary.

28. Empty the bedpan into the client's toilet.

29. Clean the bedpan and put it in the proper place. Cold water is always used to clean the bedpan. You may also use a toilet brush, if available.

30. Remove gloves and wash your hands.

31. Make a notation on the client's chart that the client has used the bedpan. Also note anything you have observed about the client during this procedure.

*P*ROCEDURE

Offering the Urinal

1. Assemble your equipment:
    Urinal and cover
    Basin of water or wet washcloth
    Soap
    Towels
    Disposable gloves

2. Wash your hands.

3. Ask visitors to leave the room, if appropriate. You may, however, wish to demonstrate this procedure to family members.

4. Ask the client if he wishes to use the urinal. Put on gloves.

5. Give the client the urinal. If the client is unable to put the urinal in place, put his penis into the opening as far as it goes. If the client is unable to hold it in place, you will have to do so. Raise the head of the bed if the client prefers, if possible.

6. Ask the client to signal when he is finished.

7. Leave the room to give the client privacy. Remove gloves and wash your hands.

8. When the client signals, return to the room. Wash your hands and put on gloves.
9. Take the urinal. Be careful not to spill it. Cover it and take it to the client's bathroom. Remove gloves and wash your hands.
10. Return to the client. Put on gloves. Help him wash his hands in the basin of water with a wet washcloth. Remove gloves and wash your hands.
11. Make the client comfortable.
12. Put on gloves. Check the urine for color, odor, and amount.
13. Measure the urine, if that is necessary. Collect a specimen or sample at this time, if necessary.
14. Empty the urinal into the toilet. Rinse the urinal with cold water.
15. Clean it as is your agency policy, and return it to the proper place.
16. Remove gloves and wash your hands.
17. Make a notation on the client's chart that he has used the urinal. Also note anything you have observed about the client during this procedure.

PROCEDURE

Assisting the Client With a Portable Commode

1. Assemble your equipment:
   Portable bedside commode
   Toilet tissue
   Basin of water or wet washcloth
   Soap
   Towel and gloves

2. Wash your hands.

3. Ask visitors to leave the room, if appropriate. However, you may want to demonstrate the procedure to family members.

4. Tell the client you are going to assist him onto the commode (Figure 11.7). Put on gloves.

5. Put the commode next to the client's bed in a safe position for him to which he can transfer.

6. Using proper body mechanics and transfer techniques, assist the client onto the commode.

7. If you do not have to collect a specimen, leave a small amount of water in the bottom of the pail. This will make cleaning it easier.

8. If the client is safe, leave the room to give him privacy.

9. Remove gloves and wash your hands if you are going to do another task.

10. When the client signals you that he is finished, return and wash your hands. Put on gloves.

FIGURE 11.7

11. Offer the client toilet tissue to clean himself. If he is unable to do so, it is your responsibility to clean him. Remove gloves and wash your hands.

12. Assist the client back to his bed.

13. Offer the client a basin of water or the wet washcloth to wash his hands.

14. Make the client comfortable. Put on gloves.

15. Remove the pail from the commode. Cover it and carry it to the bathroom.

16. Check the excreta (feces or urine) for color, amount, and odor.

17. Measure output if that is ordered. If a specimen or sample is required, collect it at this time.

18. Empty the pail into the toilet, and clean it according to your agency policy.

19. Put the pail back into the commode.

20. Remove gloves and wash your hands.

21. Make a notation on the client's chart that he has used the commode. Also note anything that you observed about the client during this procedure.

Perineal Care

Perineal care or peri-care is the gentle cleansing of the perineal area or perineum. This may be necessary following the birth of a child, following surgery, or when a female client does not take a full bath but wishes to clean the genital area. This procedure is done to promote healing, prevent infection, and refresh the client. The use of a squeeze bottle—or peribottle—is encouraged rather than cleansing the area with a washcloth. The bottle directs a stream of water so that it removes waste or drainage without damaging the skin. The use of the bottle also enables clients to clean themselves even if they cannot reach the area with their hands.

PROCEDURE

Care of the Perineal Area

1. Assemble your equipment:
   2 peribottles or squeeze bottles
   Mild soap
   Clean dressings or peripads and undergarments
   Towels and gloves
   Garbage bag for soiled dressings
   Warm water

2. Wash your hands.

3. Ask visitors to leave the room, if appropriate.

4. Tell the client what you are going to do and what you expect. Put on gloves.

5. Remove old peripads or dressings and discard in a paper or plastic bag. Note the drainage, color, amount, and odor.

6. Assist client onto commode, toilet, or bedpan.

7. Fill one bottle with warm soapy water and the other with warm clean water.

8. Place the bottle filled with soapy water parallel to the perineum. Let the water drain over the perineum. Move the bottle so that the whole perineal area is cleansed. Do this for at least 2 minutes. You may have to refill the bottle.

9. Rinse the perineum with plain warm water.

10. Assist the client to stand up or to get off the bedpan.

11. Pat the area dry.

12. Assist the client with clean dressings and undergarments. Make the client comfortable.

13. Clean the equipment and commode.

14. Remove gloves and wash your hands.

15. Make a notation on the client's chart that you have completed this procedure. Also note anything you observed about the client during this procedure.

*P*OSTPARTUM CARE

The first several weeks after childbirth are considered the postpartum period. This is the time when a woman is getting used to being a mother for the first time or getting used to this baby. She is bonding with the child. Her body is changing rapidly. Women also experience emotional changes as their role changes, as their hormones change, and as their bodies return to their prepregnancy state.

- Women usually experience some mood swings as a result of the hormonal changes and the fact that the woman is assessing her new role and planning how to adjust. Some women are weepy. Some are euphoric and have a great deal of energy.
- Women may want friends around or they may want to be alone. If the client wants to be alone, gently tell friends and family that perhaps they should call before coming to visit or they should come and stay for short periods of time.

Families react to the addition of a new child in many ways. Families have cultural practices that dictate how they react to the new mother. Some families react differently when the child is a girl or when the child is a boy. Some families lavish gifts and attention on the child. Some lavish gifts and attention on the mother. Some do neither.

Husbands or significant others either become fathers for the first time or learn to balance emotions for one more child. It takes time to learn the role of father. Refer to role models the man may have had as he grew up. He will be able to identify those behaviors he liked as a child and those he did not, and be able to pattern his behavior to support his child. Learning to relate to a woman who has become a mother also takes time. Encourage the new mother and father to talk about their needs and feelings with each other. If they need professional assistance, contact your supervisor for a referral.

Children learn to adjust to a new sibling. The presence of a new brother or sister can affect each child differently. Respect each child's way of adjusting to the new family member. If you have any questions about the meaning of behaviors, discuss it with your supervisor. Do not compare one child with another.

- Some children assume extra responsibility.
- Some children return to very childish behaviors, such as talking baby talk, sucking their thumbs, or even wetting their beds.
- Some children may refuse to go to school, leave their house, or leave their parents.
- Some children ignore the new baby.
- Some children are anxious to take part in the care of the new baby.

Physical Changes

Getting used to a body that is changing continuously is difficult for some women. It takes about 6 weeks until the internal organs return to prenatal status. It may take

6 months for the woman to lose weight and regain her prenatal appearance. Support her as she tries to exercise, change diet, and become familiar with her changing needs.

During the first 2 to 3 days, a reddish, bloody discharge from the vagina is to be expected. This is called lochia. About the fourth day, this discharge changes to yellowish and continues for another week. Usually, all discharge stops about the twenty-first day. The woman should wear whatever peripads she wishes. It is usually recommended that they be deodorant-free. Tampons are not worn. Dispose of the used pads as you would any dressing in a paper or plastic bag. Be sure to observe standard precautions. The perineum should be cleaned and washed with warm soapy water after each bowel movement and voiding. The peripads should be changed at that time, too.

Usually, the woman looses the fluid she accumulates during pregnancy between the second and fifth day postpartum. Encourage her to drink fluids to prevent dehydration. It is important that bowel function be regular during this time. Because the perineal area may be sore, bowel movements may be uncomfortable. A diet that has sufficient fiber and fluid usually prevents most discomfort.

Diet

A balanced diet helps with maintaining a feeling of well-being, regulating bowel and bladder function, and helping the body return to prenatal status. If the woman is nursing, additional calories and fluids will be required. This is not the time to start crash diets or decrease fluids in an attempt to lose weight.

Contraception

Sexual relations following the birth of a child are a very personal activity. Sometimes, there is a change in the pattern of sexual activity. This change will be discussed between the client and her partner. If questions or concerns remain, she should be encouraged to discuss these with her physician.

- Pregnancy can occur shortly after the birth of a child.
- Pregnancy can occur while a woman is nursing a child.
- Pregnancy can also occur before normal menstrual periods have resumed.
- Contraception or abstinence is recommended if another pregnancy is to be avoided.

Breast Care

The decision to breast-feed a baby is a personal one. Respect her decision and support her. Sometimes, even when a woman decides not to breast-feed, her breasts fill with milk. Encourage her to call her physician if this happens. Breasts should always be supported with a good bra until they return to prenatal size. They should be kept clean at all times.

You will be asked to support the client during this time of change. The way in which you respond to her emotional needs and her physical changes will signal to the client and her family whether her actions are normal and acceptable. Every family reacts to childbirth differently. You will be asked to reinforce the family's culture and their customs in dealing with the new baby and the new mother. If you do not understand some of the actions, ask your supervisor to explain them. If you feel that some actions are not safe or are contrary to your assignment, discuss them with your supervisor immediately. You may suggest changes in a routine or an action that in your experience has worked. Do not be offended if the family chooses not to adopt your suggestions. There are often many ways to accomplish the same goal, and each family must set up a system that is comfortable for them when you leave.

Document the normal activities of the household including:

- Activity level
- Lochia: amount, color, odor
- Sleep patterns of the client
- Bowel and bladder function
- Emotional status
- Family dynamics
- Diet and fluid intake

Call your supervisor if:

- The client experiences temperature and/or chills.
- There is any discomfort, pain, or discoloration of limbs or abdomen.
- There is any difficulty breathing or speaking, or general anxiety.
- The lochia is excessive and/or foul-smelling.
- The client has difficulty urinating or voiding is painful.
- There is a sudden change in the client.

CHAPTER 12

Rehabilitation of the Client

*R*EHABILITATION

Rehabilitation is the process of relearning how to function, in the best possible way, as an independent person despite a disability. Sometimes, a client will use a brace or support for an injured body part. The way in which you assist the client will communicate to him if you really believe he will succeed or if you feel his attempts are useless. Be alert to your verbal and nonverbal communications.

Factors taken into consideration when a rehabilitation program is started are:

- How much active motion does the client have?

- How much passive motion does the client have?

- Symptoms of all medical diagnoses that may affect function.

- Sensory deficits in vision, hearing, speech, touch, balance, or proprioception (knowledge of limb position in space with eyes covered).

- Attitude. Is he depressed, euphoric, angry, cooperative, resentful, or frustrated? Does he want to try to do things for himself?

- Ability. What can he do for himself?

- Previous level of function. Which limb is dominant (used for most activities)? What did he do before he became disabled? If a person did not have the desire to do something before an illness, he may not be motivated to do it afterward.

- Priorities. A priority is something the client wants to do. Often, the priority is something that we might not feel is important, but achieving it makes the client feel less handicapped.

- Equipment. What is the client using now, and what does he need to help him function?

- Environmental barrier. Those things in the client's home that make it difficult for him to care for himself: a second-floor bathroom when a client cannot climb stairs, throw rugs that can trip him, narrow doorways that prevent him from moving from room to room in a wheelchair.

- Support system. The people involved in the care of a client. Are there family members or friends who will assist him to regain functional independence?

*W*ORKING WITH A PHYSICAL THERAPIST

A physical therapist is a person who, in conjunction with a physician, establishes a routine of exercises to improve or maintain function.

Joints are where two or more bones meet to form a movable area of the skeletal frame. Muscles move the bones.

If muscles are not used, they can shorten and tighten. This makes the joint motion painful and limited. Muscle shortening can happen in a short time. Therefore, it is important that clients are helped to use their muscles.

Flexibility of the neck is very important to maintain good posture and good balance and to allow the client to take part in daily activities (Figure 12.1).

You may be instructed by your supervisor to place your hands in a different position than indicated in the photo. This is acceptable, provided the patient's head is supported and the rules of safety and good body mechanics are observed (Figure 12.2).

Range-of-Motion (ROM) Exercises

There are four types of range-of-motion (ROM) exercises. Each is ordered for a specific purpose.

Type	Client	Helper
Passive		Takes client through ROM Client does not help
Active/assist	Active motion	Helps to make motion easier; moves body part farther than client can
Active	Done totally by client	
Resistive	Active motion	Makes exercise harder by providing resistance to motion but allows completion of motion

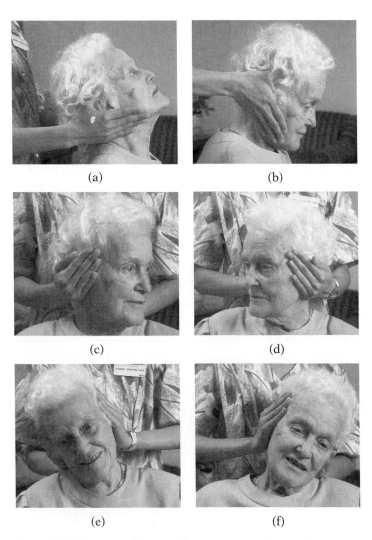

(a)

(b)

(c)

(d)

(e)

(f)

FIGURE 12.1 Assist clients with proper exercises to keep muscles flexible.

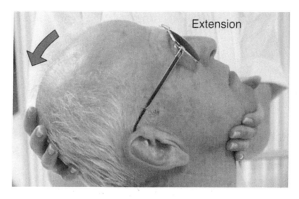

FIGURE 12.2 Depending on the client's condition and comfort, alternate hand positions may be used.

Assisting with ROM

- Do not start ROM exercises until you have received specific instructions for your particular client.

- Never take a client beyond the point of pain or force a body part. Report client pain to your supervisor.

- Report to the supervisor if the client does not do the exercises when you are not in the house.

- Report to the supervisor if the client is finding the exercises harder to do rather than easier.

- Use the flat part of your hand and fingers to hold the client's body parts. Do not grip with your fingertips. Some people are sensitive to pressure. Some people are ticklish.

- If you forget what to do, think of your own body and how it works.

- Talk to the client. Explain what is being done and why. If the person does not appear to understand, the tone of your voice and touch of your hands can help you communicate.

- Do each exercise as you have been instructed in a slow, steady movement.
- Follow a logical sequence during the exercises so that each joint and muscle is exercised. For example, start at the head and work down to the feet.
- Include the family or caregivers in the activity so they can learn and continue the exercises when you are not there.

PROCEDURE

Range-of-Motion Exercises

1. Wash your hands.
2. Explain to the client that you are going to help him exercise his muscles and joints.
3. Ask visitors to leave, if appropriate.
4. Offer the client the bedpan or urinal.
5. Drape the client for modesty.
6. Raise the bed to the highest horizontal position, if possible.
7. Lower the side rail on the side you are working, if possible. Move the client close to you.
8. Proceed with the exercises as you have been instructed (Figure 12.3a–u).
9. Make the client comfortable.
10. Wash your hands.
11. Chart that you have completed the exercises. Also note anything you observed about the client during the procedure.

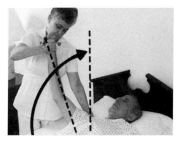

(a) Shoulder flexion

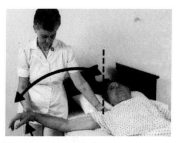

(b) Shoulder abduction and adduction

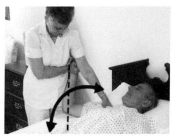

(c) Shoulder internal and external rotation

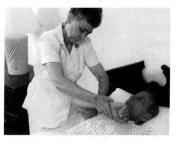

(d1) Shoulder horizontal abduction

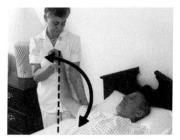

(d2) Shoulder horizontal adduction

(e) Elbow flexion and extension

FIGURE 12.3 Range-of-motion exercises.

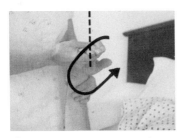

(f) Forearm pronation and supination

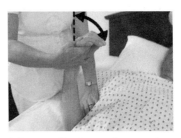

(g) Wrist flexion and extension (Bend up and down.)

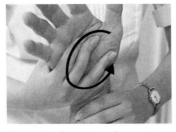

(h) Wrist flexion and extension (Bend back and forth and in a circle.)

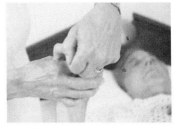

(i1) Finger flexion (Make a fist.)

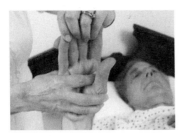

(i2) Finger extension (Straighten together.)

(j1) Finger flexion (Touch tip of each finger to its base.)

FIGURE 12.3 Range-of-motion exercises. *(continued)*

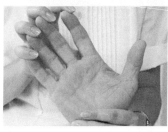

(j2) Finger flexion (Straighten each finger in turn.)

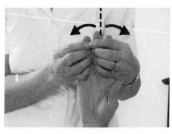

(k1) Finger adduction (With fingers straight, squeeze together.)

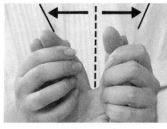

(k2) Finger abduction (Spread apart.)

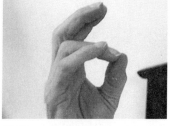

(l) Finger/thumb opposition (Touch thumb to each finger, open hand each time.)

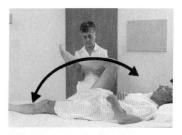

(m) Hip/knee flexion and extension (Bend knee up, toward chest, then lower with straightening knee.)

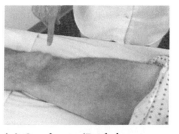

(n) Quad sets (Push knee hard into the bed to straighten, with tightened thigh muscles, for count of five. Repeat with rolled towel under knee.)

FIGURE 12.3 Range-of-motion exercises. *(continued)*

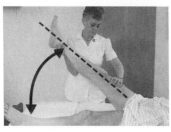

(o) Straight leg raising (Keep knee straight.)

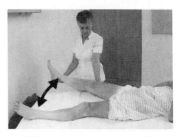

(p) Hip abduction and adduction (With leg flat on bed and knee pointing to ceiling, slide leg out to side then slide back to touch other leg.)

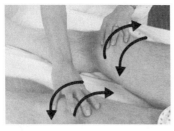

(q) Hip internal and external rotation (Turn both legs so knees face outward; then turn in to face each other.)

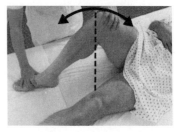

(r) Hip internal and external rotation variation (Do each leg separately.)

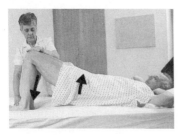

(s) Bridging (Push on bed to raise hips, hold for count of five, relax.)

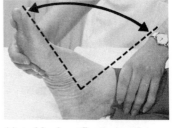

(t) Ankle dorsiflexion and extension (Bend ankles up, down, and from side to side.)

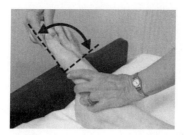

(u) Toe flexion and extension
(Bend and straighten toes.)

FIGURE 12.3 Range-of-motion exercises. *(continued)*

Choosing a Chair for a Client

- The chair should provide good support to the client's back.
- A reclining chair is difficult to get out of, especially when the client is tired.
- The type of chair that gives the client the most safety and independence is best.
- The types of chairs available must be considered.
- A dining room chair or straight-back chair provides a great deal of support.
- A chair with arms so that the client is able to sit with his feet resting on the floor or to place his feet on the floor comfortably without straining is best. Otherwise, he will not be able to get up safely.
- A wheelchair can provide good support, while allowing the client freedom to move around the house.
- Always have the brakes locked on a wheelchair when helping the client to stand up or sit down.

- Never leave a confused client restrained in a wheelchair with his feet on the foot pedals.

PROCEDURE

Helping a Client to Sit Up

1. Wash your hands.
2. Ask visitors to step out of the room, if appropriate.
3. Tell the client what you are going to do.
4. Roll the client on his side, facing you. Bend his knees.
5. Reach one arm over to hold him in back of his knees.
6. Place your other arm under the neck and shoulder area (Figure 12.4a).
7. Position your feet with a wide base of support and your center of gravity close to the bed.
8. On the count of "one, two, three," shift your weight to your back leg. While you are doing this, swing the client's legs over the edge of the bed while pulling his shoulders to a sitting position (Figure 12.4b).

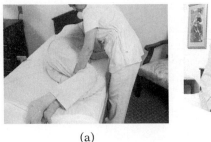
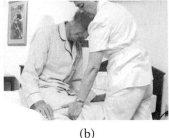

(a)   (b)

FIGURE 12.4

9. Remain in front of the client with both your hands on him for support. Do not leave him until you are sure he is stable.

10. Proceed with the remainder of the transfer. (For a client who requires only a little assistance, the procedure remains the same. Direct the client through the steps above and support him when necessary. Be sure to remain with him in the sitting position until he is stable.)

Transferring a Client

- Know yourself. Know your capabilities. Always stay within your capabilities. If you feel confident, your client will sense this and have confidence in you, too.

- Observe the client's abilities and do not help him more than necessary. A guarding belt (any leather belt buckled around the midsection) can help you with a large client and give you better control over his center of gravity (Figure 12.5).

FIGURE 12.5 Assisting a client wearing a guarding belt.

- Before a person can move from bed to another place, he must come to a sitting position with his legs over the side of the bed. Be sure the bed is secure before the client attempts to stand.

- Stand on the client's weaker side to provide extra stability.

- Taking care of business (TCOB) means concentrating on what you are doing and being aware of what is going on around you. Dizzy spells or loud noises can cause lapses in concentration that could cause a client to fall or lose his balance. If you are TCOB, you will usually be able to prevent serious injury to the client and yourself.

- Some clients are too weak or too heavy to be transferred by another person. In such cases a mechanical lift is used. An example of one is shown in Figure 12.6.

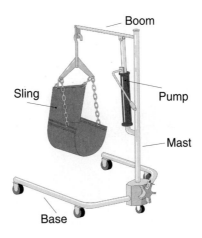

FIGURE 12.6 A mechanical lift.

Helping a Client to Stand and Sit

The procedure to help a client stand up can be used with clients who need a great deal of assistance and those who need very little. By using the same sequence of actions each time, you teach the person how to stand up by himself. Remain in good position to guard him as he stands.

Keep your directions short. Memorize the following sequence so you can repeat the instructions to the client each time you help him.

PROCEDURE

Helping a Client to Stand

1. "Move to the front of your chair or bed. Put your hands on the arms of the chair." This client is sitting over the edge of the chair or bed. Place one of your knees between his knees. Your feet should be in good position and you should be close to the chair or bed. If the client has a weak knee, brace it with your knee (Figure 12.7a).

2. "Put one foot in under you." This should be the strongest leg. Bend your knees and lean onto your forward foot to place the same side arm around the client's waist and place your other hand at the other side of the client's waist. You have now encircled the client and are holding him at his center of gravity.

3. "On the count of three, push down with your arms, lean forward, stand up." Remember to count to three. It allows you both to know when to start the motion and work as a team. Hold the client closely. The more assistance needed, the closer you hold the client. On the count of three, rock your weight to your back foot (Figure 12.7b).

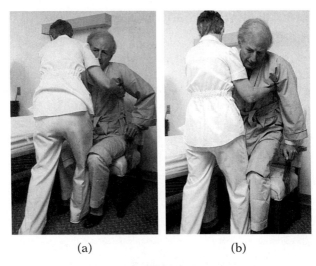

(a)   (b)

FIGURE 12.7

PROCEDURE

Helping a Client to Sit

Your body mechanics and positioning are the same as in helping the client to stand. Just reverse the directions.

1. Be sure that the wheels on the bed or chair are locked.
2. Remind the client to feel the bed or chair with the back of his legs.
3. Direct the client to reach back for the arms of the chair or the bed.
4. You support and direct the activity as he sits down.

Pʀocᴇᴅuʀᴇ

Pivot Transfer from Bed to Chair

1. Prepare the equipment. Place the wheelchair at a 45° angle to the bed. Place the chair so that the client will move toward his stronger side.

2. If you are transferring the client to a wheelchair, lock the wheels of the chair. If the bed has wheels, lock these wheels, too.

3. Wash your hands.

4. Tell the client what you are going to do.

5. Bring the client to a sitting position, with his legs over the edge of the bed.

6. Place slippers or shoes on his feet.

7. Explain the procedure to the client:
   a. He will come to a standing position.
   b. He will then reach for the arm of the chair, pivot, and sit (Figure 12.8a).

(a)   (b)

FIGURE 12.8

    c. You will remain in good support position and guide him.

    d. You will keep your foot near the client's foot for extra support (Figure 12.8b).

8. When you are sure that the client understands the procedure, perform the transfer. You will use good body mechanics to support him and prevent injury to yourself.

9. Secure the client in the chair. Make him comfortable. Leave him in a safe place.

10. Wash your hands.

11. Chart any observations you may have made during this procedure.

PROCEDURE

Transfer from Chair to Bed

Your body mechanics and positioning are the same as in helping the client into the chair. Just reverse the directions.

1. Wash your hands.

2. Prepare the bed.

3. Place the chair at a 45° angle to the bed so the client moves toward his stronger side.

4. If you are transferring the client from a wheelchair, lock the wheels of the chair. If the bed has wheels, lock these wheels, too.

5. Get into a good position using a firm base of support and proper body mechanics.

6. Direct the client to come to a standing position.

7. Direct the client to reach for the bed and pivot. Help and guide him.

8. Make the client comfortable. Reposition the side rails.
9. Wash your hands.
10. Chart any observations you may have made during this procedure.

Assistive Walking Devices

Canes, crutches, and walkers are used by people to help support themselves while walking (Figure 12.9). Use of this equipment may be permanent or temporary. The equipment is prescribed by a physician and fitted by a nurse or a physical therapist. A client may use different pieces of

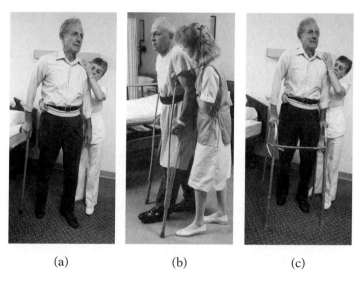

(a)   (b)   (c)

FIGURE 12.9 Clients using assistive devices for walking: (a) cane; (b) crutches; (c) walker.

equipment at different times. Do not change the equipment or the way in which the client has been instructed to use it.

The individualized fit of an assistive walking device decreases the possibility of accidents. If a piece of equipment is borrowed, check it for fit and make sure that it is safe before it is used.

*G*uidelines—*Using Assistive Walking Devices*

- Canes, crutches, and walkers must always be used with rubber tips on the ends.
- Tips should not be worn, wet, or torn.
- Screws and bolts should be tightened securely in place. If one is lost, replace it. Do not use the device without the proper screws in place.
- Wooden canes and crutches should be smooth and without cracks.
- Metal canes, crutches, and walkers should not have any sharp edges and should be straight.
- To go up stairs: Advance the strongest leg to the next step. Bring the cane or crutches and then the weaker leg to the step.
- To go down stairs: Advance the cane or crutches to the lower step, followed by the weaker leg and then the stronger one.
- The hand piece of each device should be level with the hip so that there is a slight bend at the elbow when the client is standing.
- All equipment is used after the client has come to a standing position.
- Do not let clients come to a standing position by pulling up on walkers or canes.

- Clothing should fit well and not block the client's view of the floor.
- Shoes should be flat, with non-skid soles.

Using a Cane

There are several types of canes (Figure 12.10). The client walking with the cane will:

1. Place the cane about 12 inches in front on his stronger side (Figure 12.11).
2. Bring the weaker leg forward so that it is even with the cane (Figure 12.12).
3. Bring the stronger leg forward, just ahead of the cane (Figure 12.13).

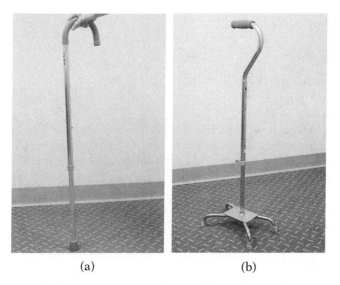

(a)   (b)

FIGURE 12.10 Two types of canes: (a) single-tipped cane; (b) quad-cane.

FIGURE 12.11   *FIGURE 12.12*   *FIGURE 12.13*

Crutches

Crutches are used when the client is unable to put complete weight on one or both legs. Crutches may be made of wood or aluminum.

While using crutches, the client puts his body's weight on his hands and arms, not on the top of the crutch under his arms. Sometimes, clients will have to exercise their upper arms before they begin using crutches.

The physical therapist, nurse, or physician will teach the client how to use the crutches and which gait to use (Table 12.1).

Walker

A walker is used when a person requires support because of greater imbalance or weakness (Figure 12.9c). The walker

TABLE 12.1 *C*RUTCH WALKING

Gait	Features	Steps
Three-point gait	One leg, non–weight-bearing	
Swing through (Figure 12.14)	Strong upper arms Some weight-bearing	1. Place crutches 8 to 12 inches in front of body. 2. Swing body past crutches.
Swing to crutch	Strong upper arms Some weight-bearing	1. Place crutches 8 to 12 inches in front of body while bearing weight on strong leg. 2. Swing body to crutches.
Standard three-point gait (Figure 12.15)	One leg, non–weight-bearing Strong upper arms Client can balance well	1. Place crutches 8 to 12 inches in front of body along with weaker leg. 2. Bring strong leg forward in front of crutches.
Two-point gait (Figure 12.16)	Weight-bearing on both feet Client can balance well	1. Bring right foot and left crutch 8 to 12 inches forward. 2. Bring left foot and right crutch 8 to 12 inches forward.
Four-point gait (Figure 12.17)	Weight-bearing on both feet Stable gait, slow	1. Bring right crutch 8 to 12 inches forward. 2. Bring left foot in front of crutch. 3. Bring left crutch in front of left foot. 4. Bring right foot in front of left foot.

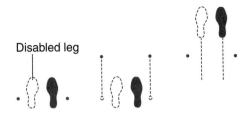

Disabled leg

FIGURE 12.14 Swing through gait. Put both crutches some distance in advance with weight on stronger leg.

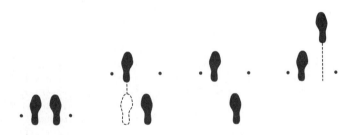

FIGURE 12.15 Standard three-point gait. Advance both of the crutches and the weak foot. Balance weight on both crutches, then advance the stronger foot.

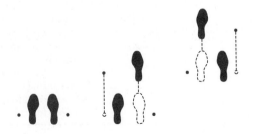

FIGURE 12.16 Two-point gait. Advance right foot and left crutch. Then advance left foot and right crutch simultaneously.

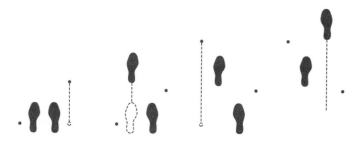

FIGURE 12.17 Four-point gait. Put right crutch forward and advance left foot. Then put left crutch forward and advance right foot.

is safe to push down on only when all four legs are on the ground in a level position. If the walker is being moved, the client's feet should be stationary. If the walker is stationary, then the client can move his feet. The walker should be picked up and moved, not slid along the ground.

PROCEDURE

Going from a Standing Position to a Sitting Position Using Assistive Devices

1. Check to see that the chair is secure and safe. Brace it against a wall if possible.

2. The client will walk toward the chair and get close to it.

3. Direct the client to turn his back to the chair and feel it with the back of his legs.

4. Direct the client to let go of the assistive device and to reach for the arms of the and slowly lower himself into the chair. (*Note:* The client may need reassurance.)

5. Guide and support him as needed. Remain in front of the client and in good position to assist him.

6. Always use good body mechanics.

*W*ORKING WITH A SPEECH-LANGUAGE PATHOLOGIST

The speech-language pathologist is the professional who evaluates the need for therapy and who plans the therapy program.

There is more to communication than just speaking. Communication also means the ability to understand speech, to read, to write, and to gesture.

A client may need speech and language therapy if he has a disorder that affects the parts of the brain, face, lips, tongue, or throat that are used to form words.

Aphasia

Injury to the brain may cause a loss of speech or language abilities, which is called aphasia. An aphasic person may have difficulty in all areas of communication. It may be hard for him to speak, understand speech, read, or write. Aphasia may be mild, moderate, or severe. The kind of aphasia is determined by where the brain injury occurs and how much damage is done to the parts of the brain. Aphasia does not mean that the person is unable to make judgments or think. Aphasia means only that a person cannot communicate with words.

There are two types of aphasia: expressive and receptive. A client with expressive aphasia has difficulty expressing his thoughts and sometimes communicating in writing. A client may say things involuntarily. He may have difficulty:

- Naming people and things
- Saying "yes" and "no" at the right time
- Spelling words
- Counting
- Telling time

Everyone has had the experience of having the name of a person or a thing "right on the tip of the tongue." The feeling of knowing what you want to say but not being able to think of the right word is what an expressively aphasic person experiences all day long.

A person with receptive aphasia has trouble receiving, or understanding, what he is hearing, seeing, or touching. For example, he can hear words clearly, but they do not have any meaning for him. It is as if he were listening to a foreign language. He might have the same problem when he looks at words. Some aphasic people even have trouble understanding the use of common objects. They might pick up a comb and not know what to do with it.

A person with receptive aphasia may have:

- No interest in watching television or listening to the radio
- No interest in reading the newspaper
- No ability to follow directions
- No ability to answer questions appropriately

The behavior of the aphasic person may seem rude or confusing at times. But think about how you might act if you could not say what you wanted to say or if you could not understand what people were saying to you. Always remember that the aphasic person is an intelligent adult. He is just as smart as he was before the injury to his brain. He simply cannot communicate easily. He will be most cooperative and least frustrated when you treat him like the adult that he is.

A client with aphasia may:

- Tire very easily
- Laugh or cry frequently
- Use profanity without meaning to
- Repeat the same word over and over

Your role in working with the aphasic client is important. You will probably spend more time with the client than any other person on the home health team. You will have a better chance to get to know the client and to help him adjust to his new schedule of exercises and activities.

There are two specific tasks that the speech-language pathologist will ask you to do. The first will be to help the client practice speech or language activities. These activities are always taught first by the speech-language pathologist. Remember that the aphasic person may have trouble communicating in many different ways and with different degrees of severity. For this reason, it is always the job of the speech-language pathologist to determine which activities best fit the needs of a particular client. The speech or language activities you practice with one client must never be used with another.

If the client has difficulty understanding or using words, you may be taught how to use pictures and printed words to help improve communication. You may be shown how to help your client practice printing or writing. Sometimes, the client may have weakened muscles of the face, lips, or tongue. The speech-language pathologist may teach specific exercises to help improve the strength and coordination of muscles or prescribe exercises of writing.

It is important to observe how the client makes his needs known and how well he is able to perform the assigned practice tasks. You will want to note how the client makes his feelings known to you. Does he point? Shake his head? Use words?

- Get the attention of the client before starting to speak.

- Keep instructions and explanations simple. Speak slowly but naturally.

- Encourage the client to use common expressions, such as "hello," "goodbye," and "I want."

- Encourage the client to be as independent as possible. He is an adult; treat him like one.

- Ask direct questions requiring a simple "yes" or "no" answer. Ask "Did you eat lunch?" rather than "What's new?"

- Give the client time to reply.

- Give the client opportunities to hear speech, such as on the radio and television.

- Meals and dressing times are good opportunities to encourage the client's attempts to speak. Let him ask for what he needs. He may say the word correctly sometimes and forget it at another time. This is usual for the aphasic person.

- Encourage the client to use whatever speech ability he has. Counting and singing are good activities. Words such as up-down or push-pull can be used during physical therapy exercises.

- Show the client understanding, but not pity. Help him verbalize his feeling of frustration ("I know it must be difficult for you").

- By your body language, patience, and attitude of acceptance, create an air of relaxation for the client. Avoid directions such as "Relax."

- Sometimes, it will be impossible to understand what the client is saying. At such times, tactfully try to change the subject or say, "Let's forget it now and come back to it later. The words will probably come when you're not trying so hard."

You also may encourage the client to learn the words that go with his personal care. When you are helping the client bathe, dress, or eat, say the name of each utensil or body part. For example, say, "Fork, you eat with a fork," or "Arm, I'm washing your arm." Your client may find that he is able to say some of the words with you. If he does, smile and let him know that he has succeeded. If he does not repeat the words, you must not force him. Remember, he wants to talk, and if he could, he would. Talking to him about these activities in the same way each day will help him to relearn what words mean, even if he cannot say them.

Do not:

- Answer for the client if he is capable of speaking for himself. Include the client in social conversations.

- Confuse the client with too much idle chatter or too many people speaking at once.

- Discuss the client's emotional reactions and problems in his presence.

- Interrupt the client or finish sentences for him. He may require extra time to think of the correct word.

- Show your concern about the client's speech, either through words or facial expression. Do not under any circumstances put the client on display or force him to speak. Such remarks as "Say it for them" upset and embarrass the client.

- Ridicule or insist that the client give accurate responses, pronounce correctly, or "talk right."

- Speak to the client as if he were a child, deaf, or retarded. He is not deaf unless a definite hearing loss has been detected. Simplify or rephrase your wording without shouting. Treat him like the adult he is.

One way to have information readily available is a Communication Board. This has information important to the client such as the day of the week, the name of the care-giver, a picture of his family, names of expected visitors, schedule of care of the day, the weather, and other important information (Figure 12.18).

Dealing with Hearing Loss

Some of the people with whom you will work may have some degree of hearing loss. Some are born with a hearing loss. Other people lose their hearing when they are exposed to loud noise over a long period of time. Head injuries or ear infections can also cause loss of hearing. Many people lose some of their ability to hear sounds clearly as they get older.

The person who is hard of hearing may feel that the speech of others is mumbled and unclear. He may have to work harder to understand what is being said. If it becomes too frustrating to try to follow a conversation, the hearing impaired (hard-of-hearing) person may begin to avoid social

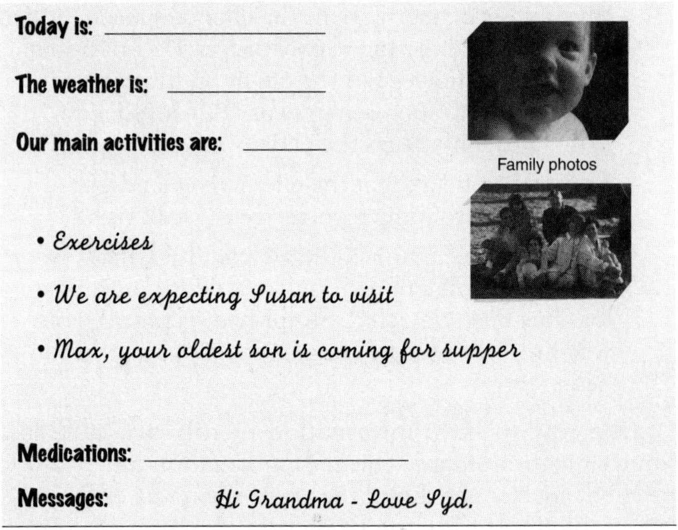

Today is: _____

The weather is: _____

Our main activities are: _____

Family photos

• *Exercises*

• *We are expecting Susan to visit*

• *Max, your oldest son is coming for supper*

Medications: _____

Messages: *Hi Grandma - Love Syd.*

FIGURE 12.18 Communication board.

activities. A hearing aid can often be of great help to the hearing impaired person (Figure 12.19).

Hearing Aid Care

The hearing aid earmold is custom-made to fit the ear. If the earmold does not fit snugly into the ear, there will be a high-pitched whistling noise when the aid is turned on.

The earmold must be kept clean. If earwax or dirt is clogging the earmold, sound will not be able to pass through. The earmold and aid should be wiped with a dry tissue after each wearing. When not in use, the hearing aid should be kept in a safe place away from extreme heat or cold.

FIGURE 12.19 Hearing aids come in various sizes and shapes. (SENSO by Widex, Widex Hearing Aid Company, Inc.)

PROCEDURE

How to Clean the Hearing Aid Earmold

1. Assemble your equipment:
   Pan of warm water and mild liquid detergent
   Pipe cleaner or toothpick
2. Remove the earmold from the body of the hearing aid.
3. Wash the earmold gently with mild soap and water.
4. Carefully remove any earwax using the pipe cleaner or toothpick.
5. Dry thoroughly. Let it dry overnight, or blow air through the opening to be sure all water has come out of the tubing and earmold.

Remember: Wash only the earmold. Never put the body of the hearing aid in water. Never use alcohol or cleaning fluid on the earmold or the aid. Encourage your client to take the hearing aid off or to protect it during rain and snow to prevent it from getting wet.

Batteries Make the Hearing Aid Work

If the hearing aid does not work, the battery may be dead. To insert a new one, match the + on the battery to the + on the hearing aid case. One battery will last about 125 hours, or 10 days. The battery should be removed from the hearing aid whenever the aid is not being worn. This saves the batteries. Extra batteries should be stored in a cool, dry place, such as a dresser drawer.

Precautions:

- Keep the hearing aid away from heat sources, such as radiators and hair dryers.
- Do not get the hearing aid wet.
- Do not drop the hearing aid.
- Do not spray hair spray, perfume, or aftershave lotion on the aid.
- Do not twist the tubing or wires.

If the hearing aid does not work, check to see if:

- The battery is put in correctly and that the case is closed tightly.
- The aid is turned on and the volume is loud enough.
- There is wax in the earmold.
- The tubing or wires are twisted.
- The battery is working.

If all of these things have been checked and the hearing aid still does not work, it should be taken to the hearing aid supplier for repair.

How to Talk to the Hearing-Impaired Person

- Get his attention before you start speaking.
- Talk face to face whenever possible.
- Keep your hands away from your face so they do not block his view of what you are saying.
- Do not chew food when you are speaking.
- Do not exaggerate your words. Speak at a normal rate of speed. You may be asked to speak louder, but do not shout.

The speech-language pathologist may teach you the following exercises to practice with the client. They are often used when the muscles used for speech are weaker. Never practice any exercise with a client that was not taught to him by the speech pathologist.

Name _____ Date _____

Do Each Exercise _____

Lips:

1. Open mouth as wide as possible, stretch, close tightly and pucker, hold.
2. Pucker lips, hold, move lips to the left, hold, move lips to the right, hold.
3. Reach out with lower lip, hold. Reach out with the upper lip, hold.

4. Smile with lips closed, frown. Repeat.

5. Press lips tightly as if you are saying "mm."

6. Say "ma-me-mi-mo-mu" (as clearly and distinctly as you can).

Tongue:

1. Put the tongue in the outer left corner of the mouth, move to the right, and then back again. Work for speed and rhythm of movement.

2. Extend the tongue straight forward, then pull back vigorously with the whole tongue.

3. Open mouth wide, lift tongue tip up to the roof of the mouth, then down. Do not move your jaw; lift your tongue.

4. Say "ta-te-ti-to-tu." Do not move your jaw; lift your tongue.

5. Say "da-de-di-do-du." Do not move your jaw; lift your tongue.

6. Say "la-le-li-lo-lu." Do not move your jaw; lift your tongue.

Throat:

1. Puff up cheeks. Hold air for 5 seconds—then release air as you blow out.

2. Suck in cheeks—then relax.

3. Puff up cheeks with air—move air from one cheek to the other without letting air escape lips. Alternate from one side to the other.

4. Drink liquids whenever possible through a straw.

*W*ORKING WITH AN OCCUPATIONAL THERAPIST

The occupational therapy program focuses on increasing the functional ability of the client within his familiar environment. The trained person who administers this therapy is a registered occupational therapist (OTR) (Figure 12.20).

General areas in which the OTR works with a home-bound client include:

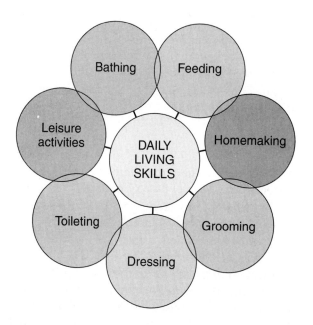

FIGURE 12.20 Helping a client relearn activities of daily living will aid him in his recovery and prepare him for independence.

- Mobilization. Teaching the client techniques that he can use to change position; to reach, grasp, or turn while sitting; or to maintain balance during an activity.

- Activities of daily living (ADLs) Tasks we perform each day—toileting, bathing, dressing, feeding, grooming, homemaking, leisure activities.

- Strength, coordination, and activity tolerance. The ability to do something without tiring quickly.

- Your role in each task will be clearly defined by the OTR.

- If the client finds it difficult and says, "I can't," assist him with part of the routine to help him get started. Example: "You dress your involved arm, and I will help you put on the rest of the shirt." Point out positive changes in the client's activities.

- If the client shows signs of pain, fatigue, or discomfort during the activity, stop the routine and report your observations to the OTR or the nurse supervisor.

- The goal of the client, OTR, and homemaker/home health aide is to help the client become functionally independent, to take care of himself.

- Do not attempt any technique that has not been taught to you and the client by the OTR.

- Make the environment a safe and helpful one for your client (Figures 12.21 and 12.22).

- Discuss the outside world, the change of seasons, what is happening in the community, the specials at the grocery store, and who won the ball game.

- On a day-by-day basis, try to determine the client's daily needs, such as his glasses, tissues, a glass of

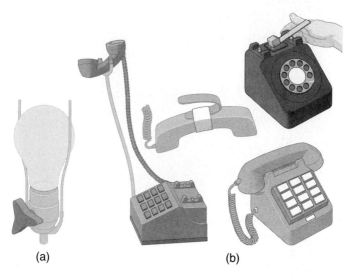

(a)   (b)

FIGURE 12.21 Using adaptive equipment on some everyday devices can help the client return to normalcy. (a) When this piece of adaptive equipment is attached to the lamp switch, the client is able to turn the switch more easily; (b) Use adaptive equipment on everyday devices, such as the telephone.

water, the newspaper, and the TV. As early in his rehabilitation as possible, make these things accessible to him. Let him begin to assume responsibility for using them without your help.

Toileting

Taking care of one's own toileting needs is a basic and personal activity. When a person must rely on another person to help him with this, he often suffers a loss of self-esteem

FIGURE 12.22 Door handles are often difficult to turn. Adaptive equipment allows the client greater ease of use.

or dignity. If he is able to assume responsibility for this part of his personal care, he has taken the first step toward functional independence.

Toileting in Bed

- Tell the client what part of the procedure he will be doing and what you will do.
- Provide a pulling braid. A pulling braid is made from three 4-in. wide strips of sheeting torn lengthwise and braided together. This braid is tied to the bed frame at one end. The other end is knotted and held by the client to assist him in sitting or turning in bed (Figure 12.23).
- Place the bedpan where the client can reach it. Powder it to prevent the client's skin from sticking to it.

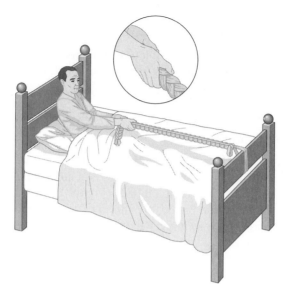

FIGURE 12.23 A client using a pulling braid to sit up in bed.

Toileting on a Commode

- Before he begins, explain to the client what he will be doing.
- Be sure the commode is standing securely.
- Assist the client out of bed as you have been instructed.
- Fasten the toilet paper to the commode. Tie the roll with a string or make a holder by stretching out a wire coat hanger and threading the roll onto it and hooking it to the frame. If you use a wire hanger, bend the ends and hook them over the front and

back of the commode frame. Tape the ends so they do not scratch the client (Figure 12.24).

▪ Place the roll on the client's uninvolved side. If he has general weakness, place it on his dominant (most used) side.

▪ Provide privacy.

Toileting in the Bathroom

▪ Place the commode frame over the toilet as instructed or set the elevated toilet seat in place if the client uses such a device (Figure 12.25). If using the commode frame, an 8-in. by 10-in. sheet of plastic, such as a piece from a garbage or trash bag, can be anchored between the commode seat and frame so it hangs down into the toilet bowl. This will serve as a baffle to prevent urine from splashing out of the toilet bowl. Rinse it off and replace it each time the client uses the toilet.

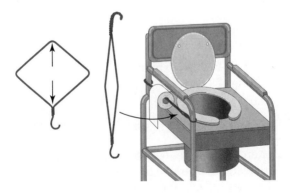

FIGURE 12.24 You can adapt a simple wire coat hanger to make the commode easier for the client to use.

FIGURE 12.25 Various types of adaptive equipment make the commode easier for the client to use.

- Tell the client what he needs to do.
- Allow the client to do as much as he is safely able to do.
- Assist him with getting onto the toilet seat as you have been instructed.
- Provide privacy.

Bathing

Bathing stimulates the body. The person who is bathing himself stimulates his involved extremities as he touches and rubs them. He becomes aware that the extremity "is there," even if he cannot really "feel" it. He may become aware that the involved extremity moves when he is using other parts of his body. As he bathes, he is moving many parts of his body together. He bends, stretches, reaches, grasps, balances, lifts his arms and legs, turns his head, and shifts his eyes.

For the hemiplegic (a person who is paralyzed on one side of his body), it is important that he gives this stimulation to his involved extremities. As he rubs the affected part with the washcloth or towel, sensory nerves lying close to the skin may be aroused. The brain, receiving these sensations, may send a message down the motor pathways that could trigger an automatic response in the involved part.

When you bathe the client, he does not use his own energy output. His body is not being involved with the automatic activity. Therefore, these responses may not be triggered.

*G*uidelines—*Bathing*

- Do not attempt any technique that has not been taught to you and the client by the OTR. A method that was appropriate for a previous client may be inappropriate for your present client.
- Provide a safe environment. Assist the client as necessary.
- Assemble everything the client will need for bathing and dressing. Place them where he can reach them (Figure 12.26).
- Thin washcloths and small face towels may be easier for a weak or arthritic client to handle than thick cloths or large, heavy towels.
- Stabilize wet soap by placing it on a dampened sponge, face cloth, paper towel, or rubber suction disk where it is less likely to slide.
- The hemiplegic should wash his involved arm first. He can drape a well-soaped washcloth over the palm of his involved hand, which should be resting

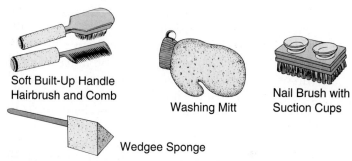

Soft Built-Up Handle
Hairbrush and Comb

Washing Mitt

Nail Brush with
Suction Cups

Wedgee Sponge

FIGURE 12.26 There is adapted equipment available to assist the client in bathing himself.

palm up on his lap. Then he can lean forward and cradle his uninvolved arm in the hand and slide it back and forth to wash it.

- Remind your client to rinse off soap and dry each part of his body as he finishes washing it.

- Place nailbrush, bristles up, in the palm of his involved hand resting on his lap, palm up. Your client can rub his uninvolved fingers across the brush, pushing gently into the palm of the other hand to steady it.

- The client can also use the nailbrush on the fingers of the involved hand. He may lift the hand into the basin to rinse it, using the other hand for assistance if necessary.

- If the client is in bed, raise the bed so that he is able to see his abdomen and legs. In a regular bed, prop him up with pillows.

- Place the washcloth and towel over the bed rail where the client can reach them. If he is in a regular bed, use a chair back or the head of the bed.

- When the client is learning to turn on faucets and run water for himself, make sure he turns on the cold first and then the hot. Run cold water through the faucet last so it will be cool if the client touches it. With some diseases, a client's sense of heat and cold is affected and he cannot judge temperature. Check the water temperature with your hand before the client bathes.

- If your client cannot reach his back, he may use a foam rubber mop or back brush to extend his reach. If not, you should complete this task.

Dressing and Grooming

The client should be encouraged to get dressed for at least part of every day. Even the wheelchair-bound or partially bed-bound person should be assisted to put on clothing other than sleepwear for some part of each day. When the dependent person is up and dressed, it affects not only his feelings of self-esteem but also his family's and friends' perceptions about his health. Let him select what he would like to wear and have him do as much of the actual dressing as possible.

*G*uidelines—*Assisting a Client to Dress*

- Always dress the weak or most involved extremity first.
- Undress the weak or involved extremity last.

- Help the client select clothing that is roomy and will stretch or give when he is putting it on or taking it off. It is easier to put on a garment that opens all the way down the front than one which must be pulled over an involved arm and then pulled over the head.

- Position the client in front of a mirror. The client will become aware through his own eyes that he has missed a button, his collar is turned in, or his pants are pulled to the side.

- Lay out the pieces of clothing where the client can reach them in the order he will put them on.

- If the OTR has suggested the use of any special tools or adapted equipment for dressing, have them near the client's clothing (Figure 12.27). Always use a shoehorn when putting on the client's shoes. He may use a dressing stick, a buttonhook, or a reacher when he begins to dress himself again.

- Follow the same procedure each time the client dresses and undresses.

Laundry

Taking care of one's own laundry is a functional activity. Assist the client with handwashing clothes, but let the client do as much as possible. Folding, sorting, and stacking clean clothes can be done slowly and should be adapted to the client's individual abilities. Obviously, folding socks and shirts is easier than folding sheets, but stacking sheets is easier than stacking socks. Tasks should be shared as the family sees fit.

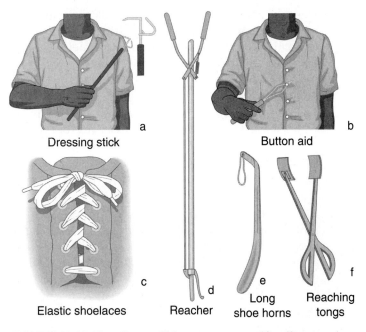

a Dressing stick

b Button aid

c Elastic shoelaces

d Reacher

e Long shoe horns

f Reaching tongs

FIGURE 12.27 The client will become more self-sufficient when he learns to dress himself. Adaptive tools may be necessary.

Meal Preparation

If the client must eventually take part in meal preparation, assist him to assume this responsibility. Offer support where needed. Point out the success he has.

Include the client in all phases of meal planning and preparation. Use a cutting board with two stainless steel nails projecting from it to hold vegetables, fruits, or meats when paring, scraping, and cutting. Supervise as the client begins to place the food onto the nails, and help if he has difficulty turning it or removing it from the spikes.

Use small containers that are easy to handle. Do not fill containers all the way to the top. Use plastic containers instead of glass ones, if available. Let the client assist with the cleanup after the meal—cleaning off the table, cleaning dishes, or drying utensils placed in his lap.

*F*EEDING

The person who has difficulty feeding himself, drops utensils, spills food, or chokes and drools when swallowing often gets discouraged. He may refuse to feed himself or to eat as much as he should. He becomes dependent and loses his sense of self-esteem. Plan mealtimes so that the client can use his available resources and feed himself successfully.

Set up the table or tray so it is convenient and attractive. Give the client utensils and dishes he can handle with a minimum of effort. Use cups and glasses that are light enough for him to lift and silverware that he can grasp securely.

If the client's dominant side is involved and he is still trying to eat with that hand, he may lack sensation and the ability to grasp. You can enlarge the fork or spoon handle by wrapping it with paper towels to about an inch in diameter and tape the paper in place, or slip a foam rubber curler pad over the handle. Enlarging the handle also makes it easier to use the nondominant hand. If a person has never used his left or right hand to feed himself, he may need the enlarged handle when he first tries.

A rigid plastic cup may be easier and safer for the client to handle than a breakable glass. If the cup has a large hand opening, it will enable the client to put his fingers or hand around the cup for security (Figure 12.28).

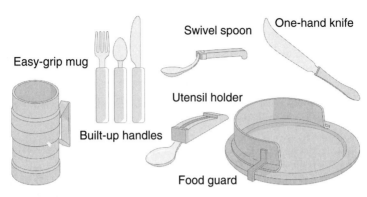

FIGURE 12.28 Utensils and dishes that are easy to handle will help the client at mealtime.

A food guard is a plastic ring that slips over the edge of a plate and creates a bumper for the client to push food against when eating. As food is pushed against an elevated surface, it piles up and spills onto the client's fork or spoon and enables him to get enough on the utensil to feed himself. Plates, bowls, forks, knives, and spoons with specially built-up handles make it easier for the client to grasp and hold onto them while eating.

If a client's grasp is too weak to hold a fork or spoon without dropping it, a feeding cuff may help. It fits over the client's hand. The spoon or fork slips into the pocket and allows the client to lift the utensil without having to grasp it tightly. Cups and glasses with handles open at the bottom can "clip" onto the client's hand, reducing his need to hold tightly while lifting the cup.

Some clients have visual problems. Objects placed to the far right or far left may not be visible to them. You may have to remind them to "look to your left (right)" when they are eating.

Other clients may have sensory deficits. If they lack sensation and the facial muscles are weak on one side, these clients will have difficulty with eating. They cannot swallow easily and they tend to "pocket" food between their cheeks and teeth on the involved side of their face. This can cause them to gag and choke as food builds up. You may have to remind this person to move his tongue to that side of the mouth to dislodge the food.

Place a shaving mirror in front of your client and encourage him to glance at it several times during a meal. This will enable him to use his eyes to make him aware of what occurs when he eats. He may begin to automatically wipe his mouth or to search with his tongue to dislodge stored food or food that remains on his lips.

*L*EISURE ACTIVITIES

Ask the client and his family what activities were pleasurable before the illness. Although you could try to introduce new activities, it is always better to start with familiar ones. Look for signs that the client enjoys or at least acknowledges these activities. The client who used to crochet or knit or sew may wish to relearn these skills. Use aids to help clients reach objects safely (Figure 12.29).

If you have time to play a simple card game with a client, read aloud to him, or turn on the record player for him, it will take his mind off his physical problems and bring him pleasure. Plants and birds, both indoors and outdoors, provide diversion. Pets provide companionship,

FIGURE 12.29 These tongs are helpful when the client needs to reach an item that is too far away.

love, and stimulation to those who enjoy them. Any extra activity that expands the area of interest for a client is both pleasurable and beneficial. Any activity that stimulates interaction is also beneficial and useful.

CHAPTER 13

Measuring and Recording Vital Signs

VITAL SIGNS

Vital signs are those bodily functions that reflect the state of health of the body and that are easily measurable. The term vital signs refers to body temperature, pulse rate, respiratory rate, and blood pressure. It is often written as TPR&BP.

In some cases, the fifth vital sign is pain. This means you will report the status of the client's pain when you report and record the other vital signs.

- Temperature—The balance between the heat produced by the body and heat lost by the body. Normal: 98.6°F or 37°C.
- Pulse—The rate at which the heart is beating. Normal: 60–80 regular beats per minute (bpm).
- Respiration—Process of inhaling and exhaling. Normal: 16–20 regular breaths per minute.
- Blood Pressure—Force of blood pushing against the walls of the arteries. Normal: Under 18 yrs. old—below 120/80 mm of mercury (mm Hg). 18–50 yrs. old—below 140/90 mm Hg.

The decision to check vital signs will be based on the client's present condition, his past history, and his prognosis. Your supervisor will tell you how often this is to be done.

- You should check the vital signs if you observe any change in your client or after a fall. When you call your supervisor to report the change or the fall, report these vital signs. Write down all vital signs immediately after taking them.

- Report all changes.

There was a time when hospitals and doctors did not share information with clients. This is no longer the case. In a person's home, you will be expected to share the vital sign readings with your client. Please do so promptly. If you do not, the client may think you are hiding something from him.

- There are clients who do not wish to know their vital signs. Do not force the information on them.

- You will also work in some homes where, for one reason or another, the client will not be told. Your supervisor will tell you how to handle this situation.

BODY TEMPERATURE

Body temperature is a measurement of the amount of heat in the body. The balance between the heat produced and the heat lost is the body temperature. Normal adult body temperature is 98.6°F or 37°C. There is a normal range in which a person's body temperature may vary and still be considered normal (Figures 13.1 and 13.2).

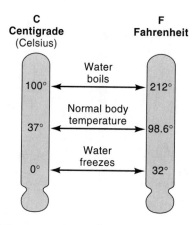

FIGURE 13.1 The two major scales used for measuring temperature.

- Oral: 97.6° to 99°F (36.4° to 37.2°C)
- Rectal: 98.6° to 100°F (37.0° to 37.8°C)
- Axillary (armpit): 96.6° to 98°C (35.9° to 36.7°C)

For recording the client's temperature, three symbols are used:

1. ° degrees
2. F Fahrenheit
3. C Centigrade or Celsius

You will record the client's temperatures according to the method used by your agency. Fahrenheit temperature can be written in two ways:

$$98.6°F \text{ or } 98°F$$

If you are using a centigrade (Celsius) thermometer, the temperature would be written

$$37.3°C \text{ or } 37°C$$

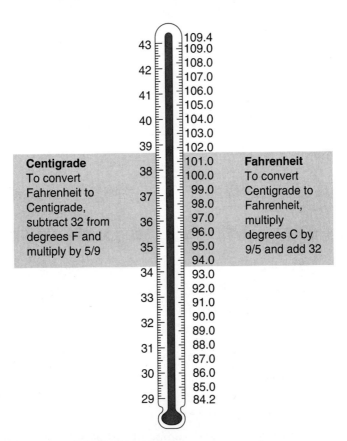

Centigrade
To convert Fahrenheit to Centigrade, subtract 32 from degrees F and multiply by 5/9

Fahrenheit
To convert Centigrade to Fahrenheit, multiply degrees C by 9/5 and add 32

FIGURE 13.2 Temperature conversion.

Write an R with the temperature reading if a rectal temperature was taken. Write an A beside the temperature reading if an axillary temperature was taken.

The body temperature is measured with an instrument called a thermometer. This is a delicate, hollow, glass tube with a liquid sealed inside it. The outside of the glass thermometer is marked with lines, or calibrations, and numbers.

There are several different types of thermometers. They are:

- Glass
- Battery-operated electronic
- Chemically treated paper

Each battery-operated and chemical thermometer is slightly different. Read the instructions carefully before using them.

This section is concerned only with the standard glass thermometer. This is the most common type of thermometer found in the home. There are three types of glass thermometers:

1. *Oral.* This type is used to measure the client's temperature by mouth and is also used in measuring the axillary temperature (under the client's arm, in his armpit area). The bulb is long and thin.
2. *Rectal.* This type is used to measure the client's temperature by inserting the thermometer into the rectum. The bulb is small and round.
3. *Security.* This type has a very strong construction. It is used for taking an infant's rectal temperature. Many agencies use the security or stubby type with a red knob at the stem for rectal temperatures and the one with a green knob at the stem for oral temperatures.

Safety Considerations

- Do not expect a client to talk with a thermometer in his mouth.

- The liquid inside the thermometer is a poison; that is, it may be harmful if it is swallowed or if it comes in contact with the skin for a prolonged period of time.
- Keep each thermometer in a case. Do not leave any loose in a pocket, drawer, or dresser.
- Never clean a glass thermometer with hot water.
- If the client feels that he may be about to sneeze, he should remove the thermometer.

PROCEDURE

Shaking Down a Glass Thermometer

1. Assemble your equipment:
   Thermometer in a container
2. Wash your hands.
3. Before using the thermometer, check to make sure that it is not cracked and that the bulb is not chipped.
4. Hold the thermometer firmly between your fingers and your thumb at the stem end farthest from the bulb. The bulb is the end that is inserted into the client's body.
5. Stand clear of any hard surfaces such as counters and tables to avoid striking and breaking the thermometer while you are shaking it. For practice, you might stand with your arm over a pillow or mattress in case you accidentally drop the thermometer.
6. When you are sure that you have a good hold on the thermometer, shake your hand loosely from the wrist. Do it as if you were shaking water from your fingers.

7. Snap your wrist again and again. This will shake down the mercury to the lowest possible point—below the numbers and lines (calibrations).

8. Always do this before and after using a thermometer.

PROCEDURE

Reading a Fahrenheit Thermometer

1. With your thumb and first two fingers, hold the thermometer at the stem.

2. Hold the thermometer at eye level. Turn the thermometer back and forth between your fingers until you can clearly see the column of mercury inside the thermometer.

3. Notice the scale or calibrations. Each long line stands for 1 degree.

4. There are four short lines between each of the long lines. Each short line stands for two-tenths (0.2) of a degree.

5. Between the long lines that represent 98° and 99°, look for a longer line with an arrow directly beneath it. This special line points out normal body temperature.

6. Look at the end of the mercury. Notice the line or number where the mercury ends. If it is one of the short lines, notice the previous longer line toward the silver tip that goes into the client's mouth. The temperature reading is the degree marked by that long line plus two-, four-, six-, or eight-tenths of a degree. If the mercury ends on the fourth short line after the 97 line, the temperature is 97.8°F (Figure 13.3). If the mercury ends between two lines, use the line closer to the silver tip.

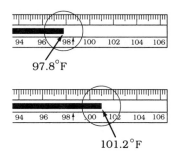

97.8°F

101.2°F

FIGURE 13.3 Accuracy is extremely important. Look at the mercury carefully when reading a thermoeter.

7. Write down the client's temperature right away, using the figure you read on the thermometer. Some agencies will write 97.8°F. Others will write 97°F. Follow the method used by your agency.

PROCEDURE

Reading a Centigrade (Celsius) Thermometer

1. With your thumb and first two fingers, hold the thermometer at the stem.
2. Hold it at eye level. Turn the thermometer back and forth between your fingers until you can clearly see the column of mercury.
3. Notice the scale or calibration. Each long line shows 1 degree.

4. There are nine short lines between each number. These short lines are one-, two-, three-, four-, five-, six-, seven-, eight-, and nine-tenths of a degree. If the mercury ended after the 36° and on the third short line, the temperature would read 36.3°C. If the mercury ended after the long line 37° and on the eighth short line, the temperature would read 37.8°C. If the mercury ends after line 37° on the fifth short line, the temperature would be 37.5°C (Figure 13.4).

5. Write down the client's temperature right away. Some agencies write 37°C. Others will write 37C. Follow the method used by your agency.

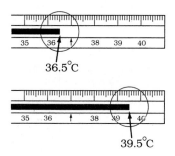

36.5°C

39.5°C

FIGURE 13.4

PROCEDURE

Cleaning a Thermometer

1. Assemble your equipment:

Thermometer	Disposable gloves
Tissue and/or cotton balls	Cool running water
Soap	

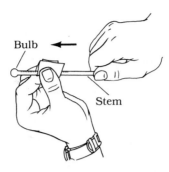

Bulb ◄—

Stem

FIGURE 13.5

2. Wash your hands and put on gloves. Wipe the thermometer off from the stem to the bulb. Throw away the tissue (Figure 13.5).

3. Soap a tissue.

4. Holding the thermometer, rotate the soapy tissue around the thermometer from the stem to the bulb.

5. Holding the thermometer under cool running water, repeat the process.

6. Discard the tissue.

7. Dry the thermometer with a dry tissue. Discard the tissue.

8. Put the thermometer into a case, bulb first.

9. Dispose of gloves and wash your hands.

*P*ROCEDURE

Measuring an Oral Temperature

1. Assemble your equipment:
   Clean oral thermometer in a case   Pad
   Tissue or paper towel   Pencil
   Gloves   Watch

2. Wash your hands.

3. Tell the client that you are going to take his temperature orally.

4. Ask the client if he has recently had hot or cold liquids or if he has smoked. If the answer is yes, wait 10 minutes before taking his temperature.

5. The client should be in bed or sitting in a chair. Do not take a temperature while the client is walking.

6. Take the thermometer out of the container and inspect it for cracks or chips. Do not use it if you see any.

7. Shake the mercury down until it is below the calibrations.

8. Run the thermometer under cool water. This will make the thermometer more pleasant in the client's mouth.

9. Ask the client to lift up his tongue. Place the bulb end of the thermometer under his tongue (Figure 13.6). Ask him to keep his lips gently around the thermometer without biting it. (If the client cannot close his mouth, take the temperature by another method.)

10. Leave the thermometer in place for 8 minutes. (The latest research shows that oral temperature is more accurate when the thermometer remains in the mouth for 8 minutes.

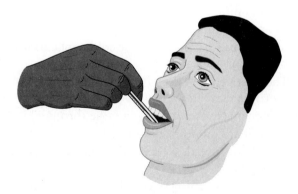

FIGURE 13.6

However, if it is the policy of your agency to let the thermometer stay only 3 to 4 minutes, follow the policy of your agency.)

11. Stay with your client if you feel that he cannot keep his mouth closed. (Wear gloves.)
12. Wash your hands and put on gloves. Take the thermometer out of the client's mouth. Hold the stem end and wipe the thermometer with a tissue from the stem toward the bulb.
13. Read the thermometer.
14. Record the temperature and your observations concerning the client during this procedure.
15. Shake down the mercury thermometer.
16. Clean the thermometer.
17. Make the client comfortable.
18. Remove gloves and wash your hands.

Measuring a Rectal Temperature

Always use a rectal thermometer for taking rectal temperatures. You would automatically take a rectal temperature when:

- The client is an infant or a child who cannot safely use an oral thermometer
- The client is having warm or cold applications on his face or neck
- The client cannot keep his mouth closed around the thermometer
- The client finds it hard to breathe through his nose
- The client's mouth is dry or inflamed
- The client is restless, delirious, unconscious, or confused
- The client is getting oxygen by cannula, catheter, or face mask

- The client has had major surgery in the areas of his face or neck
- The client's face is partially paralyzed, as from a stroke

PROCEDURE

Measuring a Rectal Temperature

1. Assemble your equipment:

Rectal thermometer in a case	Pad
Tissue or paper towel	Pencil
Lubricating jelly	Watch
Disposable gloves	Gloves

2. Wash your hands.
3. Ask visitors to leave the room, if appropriate.
4. Tell the client you are going to measure his temperature rectally.
5. Lower the backrest on the bed.
6. Take the thermometer out of its container. Hold the stem.
7. Inspect the thermometer for cracks or chips. Do not use it if you see any. Put on gloves.
8. Shake down the thermometer.
9. Put a small amount of lubricating jelly on a piece of tissue. Lubricate the bulb of the thermometer with the jelly. This makes the insertion easier and also makes it more comfortable for the client.
10. Ask the client to turn on his side. If he is unable to turn, position him on his side. Turn back the top covers just enough so that you can see the client's buttocks. Avoid overexposing him.
11. With one hand, raise the upper buttock until you see the anus. With the other hand, gently insert the bulb 1 inch through the anus into the rectum (Figure 13.7).

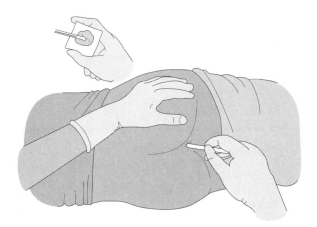

FIGURE 13.7

12. If the client is an infant, remove the diaper. Lay the baby on his back. Raise his legs with one hand. With the other hand, insert the thermometer ½ inch into the rectum. Always hold the thermometer while it is in the child's rectum.

13. Hold the thermometer in place for 3 minutes. Do not leave a client with a rectal thermometer inserted in the rectum, no matter what his condition.

14. Remove the thermometer from the client's rectum. Holding the stem end of the thermometer, wipe it with a tissue from stem to bulb to remove particles of feces.

15. Read the thermometer. Remove gloves and wash hands.

16. Record the temperature and your observations concerning the client during this procedure. (Note this is a rectal temperature by writing R next to the reading.)

17. Make the client comfortable.

18. Put on gloves. Clean the thermometer.

19. Shake down the thermometer.

20. Replace the thermometer in its container.

21. Remove gloves and wash your hands.

PROCEDURE

Measuring an Axillary Temperature

1. Assemble your equipment:

Oral thermometer in a container	Pencil
Tissue or paper towel	Watch
Pad	

2. Wash your hands.

3. Ask visitors to leave the room, if appropriate.

4. Tell the client that you are going to take his temperature by placing a thermometer under his arm.

5. Remove the thermometer from its case and shake down the mercury so that it is below the calibrations.

6. Inspect the thermometer for cracks or chips. Do not use it if you see any.

7. Remove the client's arm from the sleeve. If the axillary region is moist with perspiration, pat it dry with a towel.

8. Place the bulb of the oral thermometer in the center of the armpit in an upright position.

9. Put the client's arm across his chest or abdomen (Figure 13.8).

10. If the client is unconscious or too weak to help, you will have to hold the arm in place.

11. Leave the thermometer in place 10 minutes. Stay with the client.

12. Remove the thermometer. Wipe it off with a tissue from the stem to the bulb.

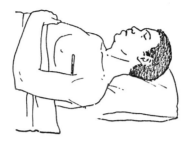

FIGURE 13.8

13. Read the thermometer.
14. Record the temperature and your observations concerning the client during this procedure. (Note that this is an axillary temperature by placing an A next to the reading.)
15. Shake down wthe thermometer.
16. Clean the thermometer.
17. Replace the thermometer in its case.
18. Make the client comfortable.
19. Wash your hands.

Using a Plastic Sheath Over a Thermometer

A plastic thermometer cover, or sheath, may be used to protect the thermometer from the client's secretions and to aid in the cleanup of the thermometer and the reading of the thermometer. The use of a sheath does not mean that you do not have to wash the thermometer after each use; it only makes the washing easier. Be sure to read the directions for each type of sheath because they differ slightly from manufacturer to manufacturer. Also, remember that sheaths for rectal and oral thermometers are different and should not be used interchangeably.

Pulse

The heart pumps the blood in a steady rhythm. The rhythmic expansion and contraction of the arteries, which can be measured to show how fast the heart is beating, is called the pulse. Measuring the pulse is one method of observing how the circulatory system is functioning.

The pulse measures how fast the heart is beating. At certain places on the body, the pulse can be felt easily under your fingers (Figure 13.9). One of the easiest places to feel the pulse is at the wrist. This is called a radial pulse because you are feeling the radial artery (Figure 13.10).

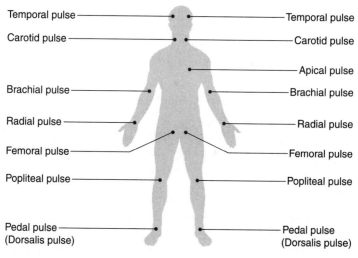

Temporal pulse — Temporal pulse

Carotid pulse — Carotid pulse

Apical pulse

Brachial pulse — Brachial pulse

Radial pulse — Radial pulse

Femoral pulse — Femoral pulse

Popliteal pulse — Popliteal pulse

Pedal pulse (Dorsalis pulse) — Pedal pulse (Dorsalis pulse)

FIGURE 13.9 Pulses can be felt at many places on the body.

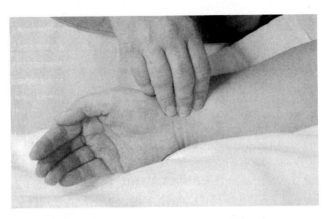

FIGURE 13.10 Measuring the radial pulse.

When taking the pulse report the following:

- *Rate:* the number of pulse beats per minute
- *Rhythm:* the regularity of the pulse beats, that is, whether the length of time between the beats is steady and regular
- *Force:* the strength of the beat (weak or bounding)

You will use a stethoscope to listen to the apical pulse. The apical pulse is the pulse measured at the apex of the heart. The stethoscope makes it possible to listen to various sounds in a client's body. The stethoscope is a tube with one end that picks up sound when it is placed against a part of the body. This end is either bell-shaped and called a bell, or it is round and flat and is called a diaphragm.

The apical-radial deficit is the difference between the pulse count at the apex of the heart and the radial artery.

PROCEDURE

Measuring the Radial Pulse

1. Assemble your equipment:
   Watch with a second hand   Pencil
   Pad

2. Wash your hands.

3. Tell the client that you are going to take his pulse.

4. If the client is standing, ask him to sit down, or have him lie in a comfortable position in bed for 5 minutes before you measure the pulse.

5. The client's hand and arm should be well-supported and resting comfortably.

6. Find the pulse by placing the tips of your middle three fingers on the palm side of the client's wrist, in line with his thumb directly next to the bone. Press lightly until you feel the beat. (If you press too hard, you may stop the flow of blood and then you will not be able to feel a pulse. Never use your thumb. Your thumb has its own pulse and you would be counting your pulse instead of the client's.) When you have found the pulse, notice the rhythm. Note if the beat is steady or irregular. Notice the force of the beat.

7. Look at the position of the second hand on your watch. Start counting the pulse beats (what you feel) until the second hand comes back to the same number on the clock.

   a. Method A: Count the pulse beats for 1 full minute and report the full-minute count. This is always done if the client has an irregular beat.

   b. Method B: Count for 30 seconds, until the second hand is opposite its position when you started. Then multiply the number of beats by 2. This answer is the number you record. For example, if the count for 30 seconds is 35, the count for 60 seconds is 70 beats.

8. Record the pulse rate, rhythm, and force immediately.
9. Make the client comfortable.
10. Wash your hands.

PROCEDURE

Measuring the Apical Pulse

1. Assemble your equipment:

Stethoscope	Pad
Antiseptic swabs	Pencil
Watch with a second hand	

2. Wash your hands.
3. Ask visitors to leave the room, if appropriate.
4. Explain to the client that you are going to take his apical pulse.
5. Clean the earpieces of the stethoscope with antiseptic solution. Put the earpieces facing forward in your ears.
6. Uncover the left side of the client's chest. Avoid overexposing the client.
7. Locate the apex of the client's heart by placing the bell or diaphragm of the stethoscope under the client's left breast. Be sure this is the place you hear the heart beating the loudest (Figure 13.11).
8. Count the heart sounds for a full minute.
9. Write the full-minute count on the note paper. Also record the rhythm and the quality of the sounds and your observations concerning the client during this procedure.
10. Cover the client and make him comfortable.
11. Clean the earpieces of the stethoscope. Return the equipment to its proper place.
12. Wash your hands.

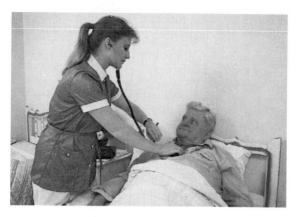

FIGURE 13.11

Respirations

The human body must have a steady supply of air. When you breathe in, air is drawn into the lungs. The waste products from this process are removed from the body as you exhale.

Respiration is the process of inhaling and exhaling. One respiration includes breathing in once and breathing out once. When a person breathes in, his chest expands. When he breathes out, his chest contracts. When you count respirations, you watch a person's chest rise and fall as he breathes. Or you feel his chest rise and fall with your hand. Either way, you need to count respirations without the client knowing it. Besides counting respirations, you will be noticing whether the client breathes easily or is working hard to get his breath. When a person is working hard to get his breath, it is called labored respiration. You must also notice whether his breathing is noisy.

Abnormal Respiration

While you are counting the client's respirations, it is important to observe and make note of anything about his breathing that appears to be abnormal. Different types of abnormal respiration that you should be familiar with are:

- *Stertorous respiration.* The client makes abnormal noises like snoring sounds when he is breathing.
- *Abdominal respiration.* The client breathes using mostly his abdominal muscles.
- *Shallow respiration.* The client breathes using only the upper part of the lungs.
- *Irregular respiration.* The depth of breathing changes and the rate of the rise and fall of the chest is not steady.
- *Cheyne-Stokes respiration.* At first, the breathing is slow and shallow; then the respiration becomes faster and deeper until it reaches a kind of peak; then the respiration slows down and becomes shallow again. The breathing may then stop completely for 10 seconds and then begin the pattern again. This type of respiration may be caused by certain cerebral (brain), cardiac (heart), or pulmonary (chest) diseases or conditions. It frequently occurs before death.

$\mathcal{P}$ROCEDURE

Measuring Respirations

1. Assemble your equipment:

Watch with a second hand   Pencil
Pad

2. Wash your hands.

3. Ask visitors to leave the room, if appropriate.

4. Hold the client's wrist just as if you were taking his pulse. This way he will not know you are watching his breathing. Count the client's respirations, without his knowing it, immediately after counting his pulse rate.

5. If the client is a child who has been crying or is restless, wait until he is quiet before counting respirations. If a child is asleep, count his respirations before he wakes up. Always count a child's pulse and respirations before you measure his temperature. (Many children get upset when you measure their temperatures.)

6. One rise and one fall of the client's chest count as one respiration.

7. If you cannot clearly see the chest rise and fall, fold the client's arms across his chest. Then you can feel his breathing as you hold his wrist.

8. Check the position of the second hand on the watch. Count "one" when you see the client's chest rising as he breathes in. The next time his chest rises, count "two." Keep doing this for a full minute. Report the number of respirations you count.

9. You may be permitted to count for 30 seconds. Count the respirations for 30 seconds and then multiply the number you counted by 2. For example, if you count 8 respirations in 30 seconds (a half-minute), then your number for a full minute is 16.

10. If the client's breathing rhythm is irregular, always count for a full minute. Observe the depth of the breathing while counting the respirations.

11. Immediately write down the number you counted.

12. Note whether the respirations were noisy or labored as well as your observations concerning the client during this procedure.

13. Make the client comfortable.

14. Wash your hands.

BLOOD PRESSURE

Blood pressure is the force of the blood pushing against the walls of the arteries. The heart contracts as it pumps the blood into the arteries. When the heart is contracting, the pressure is highest. This pressure is called the systolic pressure. As the heart relaxes between each contraction, the pressure is called the diastolic pressure. When you take a client's blood pressure, you are measuring these two pressures.

When a person's blood pressure is higher than the normal range for his age and condition, it is referred to as high blood pressure or hypertension. When a client's blood pressure is lower than the normal range for his age and condition, it is referred to as low blood pressure or hypotension. One reading of high blood pressure does not mean that a person has hypertension. This diagnosis can be made only by a physician after a complete medical evaluation.

When you take a client's blood pressure, you will be using an instrument called a sphygmomanometer. There are two kinds of sphygmomanometers: mercury and aneroid. However, each is simply called the blood pressure cuff. The four main parts of this instrument are the manometer, valve, cuff, and bulb (Figure 13.12).

Both kinds have an inflatable cloth-covered rubber bag or cuff. The cuff is wrapped around the client's arm. Both kinds also have a rubber bulb for pumping air into the cuff. Regardless of type of equipment, the procedure for measuring blood pressure is the same, except for reading the

MERCURY SPHYGMOMANOMETER

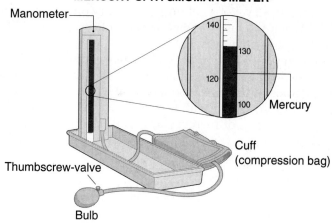

ANEROID SPHYGMOMANOMETER

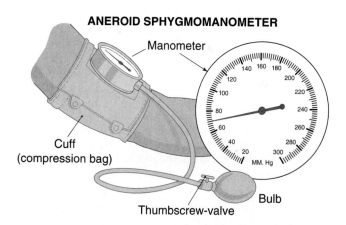

FIGURE 13.12 Sphygmomanometers may look different, but they all measure blood pressure accurately.

measurement. When you use the mercury type, you will be watching the level of a column of mercury on a measuring scale. When you use the dial or aneroid type, you will be watching a pointer on a dial.

When you take a client's blood pressure, you will be doing two things at the same time. You will be listening to the brachial pulse as it sounds in the brachial artery in the client's arm. You will also be watching an indicator (either a column of mercury or a dial) in order to take a reading.

*P*ROCEDURE

Measuring Blood Pressure

This procedure is based on the article "Hypertension—What Can Go Wrong When You Measure Blood Pressure," *American Journal of Nursing* 1980; 8(5): 942–5.

1. Assemble your equipment:
   Sphygmomanometer (blood pressure cuff)
   Stethoscope
   Antiseptic pad to clean earpieces of stethoscope
   Pad
   Pencil
2. Wash your hands.
3. Tell the client that you are going to take his blood pressure.
4. Wipe the earpieces of the stethoscope with the antiseptic pad.
5. Have the client resting quietly. He should be either lying down or sitting in a chair.
6. If you are using the mercury apparatus, the measuring scale should be level with your eyes.

7. The client's arm should be bare up to the shoulder or the client's sleeve should be well above the elbow.

8. The client's arm from the elbow down should be resting fully extended on the bed, the arm of the chair, or your hip, well-supported, with the palm upward.

9. Unroll the cuff and loosen the valve on the bulb. Then squeeze the compression bag to deflate it completely.

10. Wrap the cuff snugly and smoothly around the client's arm above the elbow. But do not wrap it so tightly that the client is uncomfortable from the pressure.

11. Leave the area clear where you will place the bell or diaphragm of the stethoscope.

12. Be sure the manometer is in position so you can read the numbers easily.

13. With your fingertips, find the client's brachial pulse at the inner side of the arm above the elbow. Hold the bell or

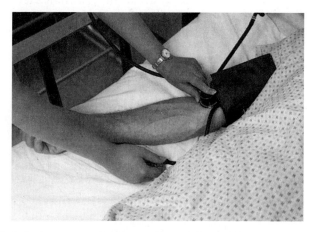

FIGURE 13.13 Part of taking a client's blood pressure is listening to his brachial pulse.

diaphragm there and inflate the cuff until the pulse disappears. Note the reading on the indicator. Quickly deflate the cuff. This is the approximation of the client's systolic reading and is called the palpated systolic pressure (Figure 13.13).

14. Put the earpieces of the stethoscope into your ears and place the bell or diaphragm of the stethoscope on the brachial pulse. Hold it snugly but not too tightly. Do not let the stethoscope touch the blood pressure cuff.

15. Tighten the thumbscrew of the valve to close it. Turn it clockwise. Be careful not to turn it too tightly. If you do, you will have trouble opening it.

16. Hold the stethoscope in place. Inflate the cuff until the dial points to 30 mm above the palpated systolic pressure.

17. Open the valve counterclockwise. This allows the air to escape. Let it out slowly until the sound of the pulse comes back. A few seconds must go by without sounds. If you do hear pulse sounds immediately, you must stop the procedure. Then completely deflate the cuff. Wait a few seconds. Then inflate the cuff to a much higher calibration above 200 mm. Again, loosen the thumbscrew to let the air out. Listen for a repeated pulse sound. At the same time, watch the indicator.

18. Note the calibration that the pointer passes as you hear the first sound. This point indicates the systolic pressure (or the top number).

19. Continue releasing the air from the cuff. When the sounds change to a softer and faster thud or disappear, note the calibration. This is the diastolic pressure (or bottom number).

20. Deflate the cuff completely. Remove it from the client's arm.

21. Record your reading on the client's chart.

22. After using the blood pressure cuff, roll it up over the manometer and replace it in the case.

23. Wipe the earpieces of the stethoscope again with an antiseptic swab. Put the stethoscope back in its proper place.

24. Wash your hands.

25. Record the blood pressure and your observations concerning the client during this procedure.

*P*AIN MANAGEMENT

Every person has the right to be free of pain. That means that we as health professionals have the responsibility to identify, record, and report the presence of pain and take steps to remove the pain. Everyone experiences pain and responds differently to it. It is the result of personal experiences, health status, and cultural norms. Other influencing factors could be age, family dynamics, and time of day.

Acute pain is usually short in duration. It has a beginning and an end. An example is pain after an operation. The pain starts after the surgery and is gone when healing is completed.

Chronic pain is always present. The condition that causes this pain also is usually chronic. An example would be arthritis pain. This pain can be relieved and may even disappear for a time, but will return.

- Plan your care around the administration of the pain medication so that the client will be most comfortable. Discuss this with the client and together you will determine the best schedule for care and medication.

- Observe your client's reaction to the medication. If the reaction is not what is expected, report it to your supervisor immediately!

- If the client is not taking the medication as it has been ordered, report this to your supervisor immediately!

- Observe the family dynamics regarding a person in pain. Discuss them with your supervisor.

Measuring Pain

The reporting of pain is very subjective. A scale has been established which is now used within the health care industry to quantify pain. The scale goes from 1 to 10, with 10 being the worst pain imaginable. (Children use faces instead of numbers.) When asking the client if he is in pain, ask him to rate the pain on this scale. Report that number. Record the time of day and the number. It may also be important to record what the client was doing.

It is also important to note other changes in the client which would indicate the status of his pain:

- Breathing pattern
- Skin: dry, clammy, or sweaty
- Body position
- Facial expression
- Tone of voice

CHAPTER 14

Intake and Output

*F*LUID BALANCE

Water is essential to human life. After oxygen, water is the most important nutrient the body requires. A person can lose half his body protein and almost half his weight and still live, but losing only one-fifth of his body fluid will result in death.

Through eating and drinking, the average healthy adult will take in about 3½ quarts of fluid every 24 hours. This is called fluid intake. The average adult also will eliminate about 3½ quarts of fluid every 24 hours. This is called fluid output. The human body has several ways of keeping the amount of fluid it eliminates balanced with the amount of fluid it takes in. When this balance is disturbed, the body is said to be in a state of fluid imbalance. In some medical conditions, fluid may be held by the body tissues. This causes swelling and is called edema. In other conditions, much fluid can be lost, and this is called dehydration. Fluids can be discharged from the body through:

- The kidneys in the form of urine
- The skin in the form of perspiration
- The lungs during breathing
- The intestinal tract

Many things can affect the fluid balance system, including:

- Medication
- Exercise
- Weather
- Emotional stress
- Nourishment
- General health

The Metric System of Measurement

The term "cc" is an abbreviation for cubic centimeter, a unit of measurement in the metric system (Figure 14.1). In the United States, we normally use one system for measuring liquids (ounces, pints, quarts, and gallons) and a different system for measuring lengths (inches, feet, yards, and miles).

A cubic centimeter can be thought of as a square block with each edge of the block measuring 1 centimeter long. If we filled this block with water, we would have a cubic centimeter (1 cc) of water.

Making an Intake and Output Sheet

The amounts of intake and output (I&O) are written on a special sheet of paper called the intake and output sheet. Some agencies have special forms for this purpose; some do not. The intake and output sheet is divided into two parts, with intake on the left and output on the right (Figure 14.2). After measuring intake and output, record the amount in the proper column. Indicate the time and what was drunk or expelled. The amounts in each column are totaled every 24 hours.

U.S. CUSTOMARY LIQUID MEASURE WITH EQUIVALENT METRIC MEASUREMENTS		
oz	=	ounce
1 cc	=	1 mL
1/4 teaspoon	=	1 cc
1 teaspoon	=	4 cc
30 cc	=	1 oz
60 cc	=	2 oz
90 cc	=	3 oz
120 cc	=	4 oz
150 cc	=	5 oz
180 cc	=	6 oz
210 cc	=	7 oz
240 cc	=	8 oz
270 cc	=	9 oz
300 cc	=	10 oz
500 cc	=	1 pint
1,000 cc	=	1 quart
4,000 cc	=	1 gallon
Abbreviations		
pt	=	pint
qt	=	quart
gal	=	gallon
cc	=	cubic centimeter
mL	=	milliliter

FIGURE 14.1 Liquid measurements must be recorded and reported on the same measurement scale.

A 24-hour intake record is started with the first fluids the client drinks in the morning. The first urinary output of the morning, however, is considered to be a part of the previous day's I&O because the fluid that formed the urine was consumed within the previous 24 hours. Therefore, the first urine recorded on the output sheet will actually be the second urination of the day.

Client name _____ Date _____						
INTAKE			OUTPUT		
Time		Amt.	Time		Amt.
Total			Total		

FIGURE 14.2 Intake and output sheet.

A family member must be taught to keep the record when you are not in the home. It is most important that all people who write on the sheet use the same procedure; otherwise, the total will not be accurate.

*F*LUID INTAKE

Most of the fluids in the body are taken in when a person drinks liquids. A client's intake includes all liquids.

A container or measuring cup is used to measure intake and output. It is marked or calibrated with a row of short lines and numbers. You can use a regular measuring cup. Another calibrated container may be a baby bottle. Be sure that you use one container to measure intake and a different one for output.

In order to record accurately the exact amounts of fluids taken by the client, you will have to measure the amount of liquid contained in each serving container, bowl, glass, and cup that the client uses. It is helpful to make a list of how much each one contains.

*P*ROCEDURE

Measuring the Capacity of Serving Containers

1. Assemble your equipment:

   Complete set of dishes, bowls,   Pen
      cups, and glasses used by the client   Paper
   Measuring cup   Water

2. Fill the first container with water.

3. Pour this water into the measuring cup.

4. Look at the level of the water and determine the amount in cc (cubic centimeters).

5. Write this information on the paper.

6. Repeat these steps for each dish, glass, bowl, or cup used by the client.

Measuring Fluid Intake

Tell the client that his intake is being measured. Encourage him to help you as much as he can by asking him to keep track of how much liquid he drinks. Record the fluid intake as soon as the client has consumed the fluids.

When measuring fluid intake, note the difference between the amount the client drinks and the amount he leaves in the serving container.

PROCEDURE

Determining the Amounts Consumed

1. Assemble your equipment:
   Measuring cup   Paper
   Pen   Leftover liquids in serving containers
2. Pour the leftover liquid into the measuring cup.
3. Look at the level and determine the amount in cc.
4. From your list, determine the amount in the full serving container.
5. Subtract the leftover amount from the full container amount. This figure is the amount the client actually drank.

6. Immediately report this amount on the intake side of the intake and output sheet.

*F*LUID OUTPUT

Measuring Fluid Output

Fluid output is the sum total of liquids that come out of the body. Most fluid is discharged from the body as urine. Output also includes emesis (vomitus), drainage from a wound, loss of blood, and excessive perspiration.

Tell the client his output is being measured and ask him to cooperate. All clients who are measuring their output must urinate in a bedpan, urinal, or container. Ask the client not to place toilet paper in this container. Provide a plastic bag for this purpose. Then dispose of the tissue into the toilet. If at all possible, ask your client not to move his bowels while urinating.

It is important to notice all qualities about the urine when you measure it, and report any changes immediately. Some medications can change the color of urine. Some foods can change the odor of urine.

Qualities of urine that should be noted include:

- Color
- With particles or clear
- Odor
- Amount

PROCEDURE

Measuring Urinary Output

1. Assemble your equipment:
   Bedpan and cover or urinal   Measuring container
   or container for urine   Pad
   Disposable gloves   Pencil

2. Wash your hands and put on gloves.

3. Pour the urine from the bedpan or urinal into the measuring container.

4. Place the container on a flat surface for accuracy in measurement.

5. At eye level, carefully look at the container to see the number reached by the level of urine. Remember it.

6. Rinse and return the measuring container to its proper place. (Pour the urine and the rinse water into the toilet.)

7. Rinse and return the urinal or bedpan to its proper place. (Pour the rinse water into the toilet.)

8. Remove gloves and dispose of them. Wash your hands.

9. Record the amount of urine in cc and the character of the urine on the output side of the I&O sheet.

Measuring Output from an Indwelling Catheter

Sometimes, a client has a catheter (tube) inserted into his urinary bladder by the doctor or nurse. This catheter drains all the client's urine into a plastic urine container, which hangs below the level of the urinary bladder (Figures 14.3 and 14.4). You will empty this container, measure the urine

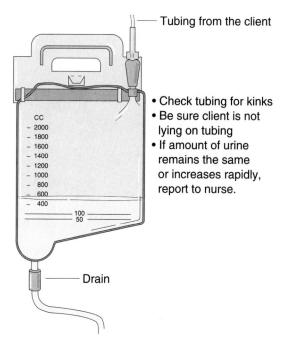

Tubing from the client

- Check tubing for kinks
- Be sure client is not lying on tubing
- If amount of urine remains the same or increases rapidly, report to nurse.

CC
- 2000
- 1800
- 1600
- 1400
- 1200
- 1000
- 800
- 600
- 400

100
50

Drain

FIGURE 14.3 A plastic urine collection container should be hung on the bed frame below the level of the bladder.

for amount, and record the amount. This will always be done whenever it is full and always before the end of your working shift. The measurement is not taken from the soft, expandable, plastic urine container. A hard plastic container is always used because it is more accurate.

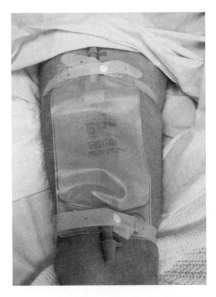

FIGURE 14.4 Leg drainage bag for ambulatory patient.

Procedure

Emptying a Urinary Collection Bag From an Indwelling Catheter

1. Assemble your equipment:
   Measuring container   Pad
   Paper towels   Pencil
2. Wash your hands.
3. Protect the floor with paper towels.
4. Open the drain at the bottom of the plastic urine container and let the urine run into the measuring cup. Then close the

drain. Be sure the urine does not touch the floor. Be sure the tubing from the catheter bag does not touch the floor.

5. Place the measuring container on a flat surface for accuracy in measurement.

6. At eye level, carefully look at the container to see the level of urine. Remember it.

7. Rinse the measuring container and put it in its proper place. (Pour the urine and rinse water into the toilet.)

8. Wash your hands.

9. Record the time, amount in cc, and anything unusual concerning the urine on the output side of the I&O sheet.

Fluid Output from the Incontinent Client

If the client is incontinent (cannot control bowels and/or urine), record this on the output side of the I&O sheet each time the bed is wet. Even though the urine cannot be measured, it will be obvious that the client's kidneys are functioning.

Measuring Fluids Other than Urine

Vomitus and diarrhea are also measured according to the procedure for measuring urinary output. Be sure to indicate on the I&O sheet what fluid you are recording.

If a client bleeds a great deal, has wound discharge, or perspires heavily, indicate this on the I&O sheet. Be sure to indicate:

- What was wet
- How wet (damp, dripping, etc.)
- The size of the area that was wet
- The time this occurred

BALANCING FLUID INTAKE

Clients who need to have more fluids added to their normal intake are told to force fluids. Fluids should never be forced or restricted without discussing this with your supervisor first. FF is the abbreviation for force fluids. A client who is to force fluids often needs encouragement to drink. Be sure you know how much fluid the client is to have within a 24-hour period.

- Show enthusiasm and be cheerful
- Provide different kinds of liquids that the client prefers, as permitted
- Offer liquids without being asked
- Offer hot and cold drinks
- Offer liquids in divided amounts (for example, 800 cc every 8 hours means the client ought to drink 100 cc per hour)

Record the amount taken in by the client in cc and on the intake side of the I&O. Report to your supervisor if the client is unable to drink the amount required.

Some clients must restrict their fluid intake. This means that fluids are to be limited to a certain amount.

- Record the amount of intake on the intake side of the I&O sheet.
- Frequent oral hygiene is often necessary.
- If the restriction is severe, the client may be permitted to suck on ice chips or candy. Check with your supervisor before you start any of these practices.

Straining Urine

Collect the urine in the same manner as if you were to measure it. Be sure the client knows he is to save all his urine and has a container available. The toilet tissue should not be dropped into the container with the urine but disposed of in a plastic bag. The client should not move his bowels at the same time or the specimen is useless.

Procedure

Straining Urine

1. Assemble your equipment.
    Disposable paper strainers or gauze
      that fits into the container
    Specimen container with label
    Urine specimen
    Disposable gloves
2. Wash your hands.
3. Put on gloves.
4. Pour the urine through the strainer into a calibrated container (Figure 14.5).
5. Put the strainer with any particles into the specimen container. Do not remove any particles.
6. Record the amount of urine measured, if appropriate. Record the date and time of the collection.
7. Discard the urine by pouring into a toilet.
8. Clean the containers.

FIGURE 14.5 Straining urine.

9. Put the specimen in the appropriate place until it can be sent/taken to the laboratory.
10. Remove gloves and wash hands.

CHAPTER 15

Specimen Collection

SPECIMEN COLLECTION

One of the body's normal functions is to regularly get rid of waste products. When these products are tested in the laboratory, changes in bodily function can be detected. Specimens are samples of bodily waste products that are collected and sent to the laboratory for examination.

Obtaining a Specimen

Some clients are embarrassed by the procedures involved in obtaining some types of specimens. Your client will be calm and cooperative if you show understanding and assist him when necessary. If your client understands the procedure, he should obtain the specimen himself.

Human waste material has many names. Street language uses one set of terms. Many cultures use other sets of terms. Many people do not know the correct English words for human waste material. It is usually a good idea to try to use the words that the client and his family use (this is especially true of children). If these words are offensive to you, discuss this situation with your supervisor.

Need for Accuracy

Be sure you follow all the "rights" listed here:

- The right client: from whom the specimen is to be collected.
- The right specimen: as ordered by the doctor, free of other matter. Urine must be free of blood and feces.
- The right time: when the specimen should be collected.
- The right amount: amount needed for the laboratory to test.
- The right container: the cup that is correct for each specimen.
- The right label: filled out properly and neatly.
- The right method: procedure by which you collect the specimen.
- The right asepsis: washing your hands before and after collecting the specimen. Use disposable gloves.
- The right attitude: how you approach and speak to the client.
- The right storage: store the specimen correctly before it is sent to the laboratory.

Asepsis in Specimen Collection

Asepsis means "free of disease-causing organisms." It is very important to use good medical aseptic technique to prevent contamination. Wash your hands carefully before and after collecting each specimen. Handwashing before you collect the specimen prevents contamination of the specimen by anything that may be on your hands. Handwashing after you collect the specimen prevents microorganisms from the specimen from remaining on your hands.

URINE COLLECTION

Routine Urine Specimen

This is a single sample of urine taken from the client as he voids in the usual way. No special precautions are taken. At times, you will be told to take a specimen of the first urine of the day, but if you are not given time instructions, this specimen may be taken when convenient.

PROCEDURE

Collecting a Routine Urine Specimen

1. Assemble your equipment:

   Bedpan or urinal
   Disposable gloves
   Measuring container for
        measuring output
   Urine specimen container
        and lid

   Paper or plastic bag
        for toilet tissue
   Label
   Wet washcloth
   Towel

2. Prepare the label. Write clearly the client's name and address, the date, and the time. Also write what type of specimen this is—Routine Urine.

3. Wash your hands and put on gloves.

4. Ask visitors to leave the room, if appropriate.

5. Tell the client a urine specimen is needed. Explain the procedure to him. If he is able to collect the specimen himself, he should do so.

6. If the client is able, he can urinate directly into the container. If he is not, ask the client to urinate into the bedpan or urinal. Remind the client not to put toilet tissue into the bedpan but to dispose of it in a paper bag or a plastic bag. You will discard the tissue in the toilet. Remove gloves and wash hands.

7. Offer the client a washcloth and towel to wash his hands.

8. Make the client comfortable.

9. Put on gloves and take the bedpan or urinal into the bathroom.

10. If the client is on I&O, pour the urine into a clean measuring container and record the amount of urine on the I&O sheet.

11. Pour the urine into the specimen container. Fill it three-fourths full.

12. Put the lid on the container. Wipe off the outside of the container. Secure the label to the container.

13. Pour the urine remaining in the bedpan, urinal, or measuring container into the toilet.

14. Clean and rinse the bedpan, urinal, or measuring container. Put it in its proper place.

15. Remove gloves and wash your hands.

16. Make a notation on the client's chart that you collected the specimen, the time, and anything you observed about the client during this procedure.

17. Store the specimen in the correct place before it is taken to the laboratory.

Collecting a Urine Specimen from a Client with a Foley Catheter

A urine specimen from a client with a Foley catheter in place takes time to collect. Be sure the client has had some fluid to drink before you attempt this. Tell the client what you will be doing, because he will be unable to see the procedure or take an active part in it. Label the specimen and include that the specimen was obtained from a catheter.

*P*ROCEDURE

Obtaining a Urine Specimen from a Client With a Foley Catheter

1. Assemble your equipment:
   Specimen container and lid
   Measuring container
   Label
   Disposable gloves

   Padding to protect the bed
   Protective cap for drainage
   tubing or sterile gauze
   pads
2. Prepare the label. Write clearly the client's name and address, the date, and the time. Write what type of specimen it is and how it was obtained.
3. Wash hands.
4. Explain the procedure to the client.
5. Put on gloves.
6. Clamp indwelling urinary catheter below the port by folding plastic tubing in half and applying a metal/plastic clamp.
7. Wait no more than 15 minutes for a small amount of urine to collect in the tubing above the port.

8. Insert a sterile syringe gently into the port (after swabbing with alcohol) taking care not to poke the needle through the tubing.

9. Withdraw approximately 10 cc of urine.

10. Insert the urine into a sterile specimen cup. Take care not to touch the rim or inside cover of the cap (this prevents contamination of the specimen).

11. Unclamp the tubing and straighten it out. Be sure that the urine is now flowing freely.

12. Apply the correct lab label to the specimen cup and bag according to policy.

13. Report the results of the procedure to your supervisor.

14. Remove gloves and wash your hands.

15. Make a notation on the client's chart that you collected the specimen, the time, and anything observed about the client during this procedure.

16. Store the specimen in the correct place before it is taken to the laboratory.

Midstream Clean-Catch Urine Specimen

A special method is used to collect a client's urine when the specimen must be totally free from contamination. This special type of specimen is called a midstream clean-catch urine specimen. Clean-catch refers to the fact that the urine is not contaminated by anything outside the client's body. The procedure requires careful washing of the genital area. Midstream means catching the urine specimen between the time the client begins to void and time he stops.

PROCEDURE

Collecting a Midstream Clean-Catch Urine Specimen

1. Assemble your equipment:

   Clean-catch kit or sterilized jar
   Sterile cleansing solution
   Sterile gauze
   Disposable gloves
   Waste bag

   Bedpan or urinal, if the
      client is unable to
      go to the bathroom
   Wet washcloth
   Towel

2. Prepare the label if it is outside the kit. If not, wait until the end of the procedure. Write clearly the client's name and address, the date, and the time. Write what type of specimen it is and how it was obtained.

3. Wash your hands.

4. Ask visitors to leave the room, if appropriate. You may want to explain this procedure to a family member.

5. Tell the client you need a midstream clean-catch urine specimen.

6. Explain the procedure. If the client is able, he may collect the specimen himself.

7. If the client is not able to collect the specimen, assist him with the procedure.

8. Open the disposable kit.

9. Put on the gloves. Remove the towelettes and the urine specimen container. Do not put your hand inside the container or lid.

10. For female clients:
    a. Separate the folds of the labia and wipe with one towelette from the front to the back along one labia. Throw away the towelette. The labia must be separated during cleansing and collection of the specimen.

    b. Wipe the opposite labia with the second towelette. Throw it away.

    c. Wipe down the middle using the third towelette. Throw it away.

11. For male clients:

    a. If the male is not circumcised, pull the foreskin of the penis back before cleansing the penis. Hold it back during urination.

    b. Use a circular motion to clean the head of the penis. Use all three towelettes. Throw each one away after you use it.

12. Ask the client to start urinating into the bedpan or the toilet. Then ask him to stop. Place the sterile urine container under the stream of urine and ask the client to start urinating again. Fill the container one-half to three-fourths full. The remaining urine may be discarded.

13. If the client is on I&O, all the urine must first be voided into a sterile measuring container and measured, then put into the sterile specimen container provided. Be sure to note on the I&O sheet the amount of urine that was sent as a specimen.

14. Cover the urine container with the proper lid. Be sure not to touch the inside of the lid or the container. Wipe off the outside of the container.

15. Take off your gloves.

16. Wash your hands.

17. Make the client comfortable. Offer the client a wet washcloth and towel to wash his hands.

18. Clean all the equipment and replace it.

19. Wash your hands.

20. Make a notation on the client's chart that you collected the specimen, the time, and anything observed about the client during this procedure.

21. Store the specimen in the correct place before it is taken to the laboratory.

24-hour Urine Specimen

A 24-hour urine specimen is a collection of all urine voided by a client over a 24-hour period. All the urine is collected for 24 hours, usually from 7 A.M. on the first day to 7 A.M. the following day.

When you are to obtain a 24-hour urine specimen, it is necessary to ask the client to void and discard this voided urine at 7 A.M. This is done because this urine has been in the bladder for an unknown length of time. The test should begin with the bladder empty. For the next 24 hours, save all the urine voided by the client. On the following day at 7 A.M., ask the client to void and add this specimen to the previous collection. This way, the doctor can be sure that all of the urine for the test came into the urinary bladder during the 24 hours of the test period.

It is very important that the client and his family understand the importance of collecting all the urine voided within the 24 hours. If one urine specimen is accidentally thrown away, the test is not accurate and will have to be repeated.

Some specimens must be kept on ice and others not. Ask!

*P*ROCEDURE

Collecting a 24-Hour Urine Specimen

1. Assemble your equipment:

   Large container, usually a 1-gallon bottle (the laboratory usually supplies this)
   Bedpan or urinal
   Disposable gloves

   Measuring container used for measuring output if the client is on I&O
   Label for the container
   Wet washcloth

| Funnel, if the neck of the bottle is small | Towel |

2. Fill out the label. Clearly write the client's name and address, the date, and the time the collection started.

3. Wash your hands and put on gloves.

4. Ask visitors to leave the room, if appropriate.

5. Tell the client that a 24-hour specimen is needed. Explain the procedure to him and his family. Discuss the placement and care of the gallon container of urine.

6. You may be instructed to refrigerate the urine. If so, one way is to keep it in a bucket of ice. This ice will have to be changed as it melts. It may, of course, be kept in the refrigerator if that is acceptable to the client and his family.

7. During the collection of the specimen, ask the client to use the bedpan or urinal each time he voids. Remind him not to throw toilet tissue into the bedpan or urinal and to try to urinate without moving his bowels at the same time. Provide a waste bag for the toilet tissue and then discard the tissue promptly in the toilet.

8. If the client is on I&O, measure all urine each time the client urinates and write it on the I&O sheet.

9. When the collection starts, have the client urinate. Throw away this first urine. This is to be sure that the bladder is completely empty as the collection starts. If this urine is discarded at 7 A.M., then the collection will continue until 7 A.M. the following morning.

10. For the next 24 hours, save all the client's urine. At the end of the collection, write the time the collection stopped on the label. Store the bottle in the proper place until it is sent to the laboratory.

11. Offer the client a washcloth and towel to wash his hands each time he voids.

12. Be sure to clean all equipment after each urination. Note in your charting that the collection was done and your observations about the client during this procedure.

Collecting a Urine Specimen from an Infant

The procedure may appear to be uncomfortable to the child, but it does not hurt him. Reassure the child's parent or guardian that you are not hurting the child and that the information the doctor will have after the laboratory examination of the urine will help in the child's care.

P R O C E D U R E

Collecting a Urine Specimen From an Infant

1. Assemble your equipment:
   Urine specimen bottle   Plastic disposable infant
       or container   urine collector
   Gloves

2. Prepare a label. Write the client's name and address, the date, and the type of specimen. Fill in the time when the actual specimen is obtained.

3. Wash your hands.

4. Ask visitors to leave, except the parent or guardian of the child.

5. Explain to the child and his parent that you want to collect a urine specimen. A child who is not yet toilet-trained can understand language and is more likely to cooperate if he knows what is expected of him. Use language the child understands and is familiar with.

6. Put on gloves and take off the child's diaper.

7. Clean the genital area. Be sure it is dry or the collector bag will not stick.

8. Remove the outside piece that surrounds the opening of the plastic urine collector. Be sure the skin is not folded under the sticky part as you apply it. Place the opening of the bag around the male penis or the female meatus (Figure 15.1).

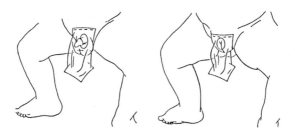

FIGURE 15.1 Collecting an infant's urine specimen.

Do not cover the rectum. The specimen is useless if it is contaminated with fecal matter.

9. Put the child's diaper on as usual.

10. Check every half-hour to see if the infant has voided. You cannot feel the diaper. You must look inside the diaper.

11. When the infant has voided, remove the urine collector gently. Do not spill the urine. Pour the urine into a specimen container.

12. Wash off any excess sticky material on the genitals. Make the baby comfortable.

13. Remove gloves and wash your hands.

14. Make a notation on the client's chart that you collected the specimen, the time, and anything you observed about the client during the procedure.

15. Store the specimen in the correct place before it is taken to the laboratory.

STOOL SPECIMEN

The solid waste from a person's body has many names—"stools," "feces," "fecal matter," "excreta," "excrement," "B.M.," and "bowel movement." The doctor sometimes requires a sample of the client's feces to assist in diagnosing the client's illness or in monitoring the client's progress. A sample of feces is a stool specimen. There are certain tests that must be performed only on a warm stool. You will be told whether the specimen is to be warm or cold.

PROCEDURE

Collecting a Stool Specimen

1. Assemble your equipment:

Bedpan	Plastic bag for warm
Stool container	specimen, if used by your
Disposable gloves	agency
Label	Washcloth
Wooden tongue depressor	Towel

2. Fill in the label with the client's name and address, the date, and the type of specimen. Fill in the time when the actual specimen is obtained.

3. Wash your hands and put on gloves.

4. Ask visitors to leave the room, if appropriate.

5. Tell the client that a stool specimen is needed. Explain that he is to call you whenever he can move his bowels.

6. Have the client move his bowels in the bedpan. If the client is unable to use the bedpan, place several layers of toilet tissue in the bottom of the toilet and have the client move his bowels on the paper (Figure 15.2). This way you will be able to take a specimen easily.

7. Ask the client not to urinate into the bedpan and not to put toilet tissue into the bedpan. Provide him with a plastic or paper bag to dispose of the tissue temporarily. Then discard the tissue in the toilet.

8. After the client has had a bowel movement, take the bedpan into the bathroom.

9. Remove gloves and wash your hands.

10. Offer the client a washcloth and towel for his hands.

11. Make the client comfortable.

FIGURE 15.2

12. Put on gloves. Using the wooden tongue depressor, take 1 to 2 tablespoons of stool from the bedpan and place it into the stool specimen container (Figure 15.3).

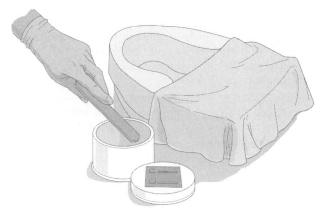

FIGURE 15.3

13. Cover the container. Do not touch the inside of the container or the top of it.

14. Wrap the depressor in a piece of toilet tissue and discard it into a plastic or paper bag.

15. Empty the remaining feces into the toilet.

16. Clean the bedpan and return it to its proper place.

17. Remove gloves and wash your hands.

18. Make a notation on the client's chart that you collected the specimen, the time, and anything you observed about the client during this procedure.

19. Store the specimen in the correct place before it is taken to the laboratory.

SPUTUM COLLECTION

Sputum is a substance collected from a client's lungs. It contains saliva, mucous, and sometimes blood or pus. It is usually clear in color but can be gray, yellow, green, or red. The best time to collect a sputum specimen is in the morning, right after the client awakens.

PROCEDURE

Collecting a Sputum Specimen

1. Assemble your equipment:
   Sputum container with lid   Disposable gloves
   Tissues

2. Label the container with the client's name and address, the date, and the type of specimen. Fill in the time when the actual specimen is obtained.

3. Wash your hands and put on gloves.

4. Ask visitors to leave the room, if appropriate.

5. Tell the client a sputum specimen is needed.

6. If the client has eaten recently, have him rinse out his mouth. If he wants oral hygiene at this time, help him as necessary.

7. Give him the sputum container. Ask him to take three consecutive deep breaths. On the third breath, ask him to exhale deeply and cough. He should be able to bring up sputum from within the lungs. Explain to him that saliva is not adequate for this test.

8. Have the client spit the sputum directly into the specimen container.

9. Cover the container immediately. Be careful not to touch the inside of either the container or the cover.

10. Offer the client oral hygiene.

11. Make the client comfortable.

12. Remove gloves and wash your hands.

13. Make a notation on the client's chart that you collected the specimen, the time, and anything you observed about the client during this procedure.

14. Store the specimen in the correct place before it is taken to the laboratory.

CHAPTER 16

Special Procedures

ASSISTING WITH MEDICATIONS

Medication is prescribed by a physician, dispensed by a pharmacist, and administered or given without client assistance by a nurse or physician. These professionals are licensed by the state to perform their duties. These duties are very specific. Failure to stay within the state guidelines can result in a legal action resulting in a fine, the revoking of a license to practice the profession, and possibly jail. In addition, these people are paid for their services. As a homemaker/home health aide, you are not licensed to administer medication, nor are you paid to do so. You are, however, expected to assist your clients as they take their own medication. When you administer medication to a client, you take all responsibility that goes along with giving medication. When you assist a client, he shares the responsibility. If you ever have a question about a situation with your client, ask your supervisor.

Prescription drugs are prescribed by a physician and cannot be bought without a prescription. Over-the-counter drugs can be bought without a prescription. You will not administer either type of drug and will assist the client only with those drugs about which you have been instructed specifically.

*Y*OUR ROLE AS A HOMEMAKER/ HOME HEALTH AIDE

As a homemaker/home health aide, you probably will spend more time with the client than any other member of the health care team. During this time, you often will be assigned to assist the client with his medication. To do this correctly, you will have to have certain information. Without this information, an accident could happen. Accidents involving medication are very serious because they can cause the client pain, delay his recovery, and sometimes even cause death.

To perform your duties well, you must know the Five Rights of Medication (Figure 16.1). You should also know the side effects of the medication, how to store the medication, and how it reacts with food. If you observe any side effects after your client has taken the medication, report them immediately to your supervisor. Some of the most common side effects are shown in Figure 16.2. However,

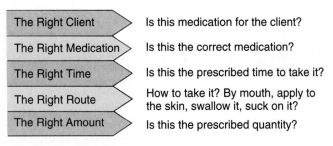

The Right Client   Is this medication for the client?

The Right Medication   Is this the correct medication?

The Right Time   Is this the prescribed time to take it?

The Right Route   How to take it? By mouth, apply to the skin, swallow it, suck on it?

The Right Amount   Is this the prescribed quantity?

FIGURE 16.1 The Five Rights of Medication must be observed every time a client takes medication.

any change in behavior associated with the taking of medication should be noted:

- If your client is not taking the medication exactly as it has been prescribed

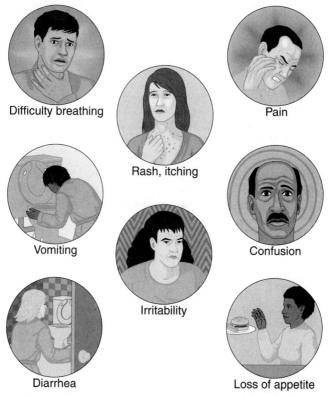

Difficulty breathing

Rash, itching

Pain

Vomiting

Irritability

Confusion

Diarrhea

Loss of appetite

FIGURE 16.2 Changes in usual patterns of behavior may indicate a medication reaction. Report any change you note or are told about immediately to your supervisor.

- If your client is taking medication (prescription or over-the-counter) of which your supervisor is not aware
- If your client does not know why he is taking his medication
- If the client's orientation, concentration, memory, or mood changes soon after he takes his medication
- If your client is confusing his medications

PROCEDURE

Assisting a Client with Medication

1. Assemble your equipment:

Medication	Dressings, if medication is applied to
Spoon	the skin
Water or juice	Tissues or cotton balls

2. Wash your hands.
3. Ask visitors to leave the room, if appropriate.
4. Remind the client it is time for his medication.
5. Check the Five Rights of Medication.
6. Place the medication within reach of the client. Loosen the tops of bottles or tubes.
7. Assist the client as necessary:

   a. *Oral medication.* Hold client's hand, assist him with liquid.

   b. *Ointments and creams.* Assist him as needed with medication and dressing.

   c. *Eye medication.* Guide his hand and wipe excess liquid or ointment from under eye working from nose to outer area.

8. Make the client comfortable.

9. Put the medication in its proper place. Dispose of the used equipment.

10. Wash your hands.

11. Make a notation on the client's chart that he took his medication, the time, and how he took it. Also note your observations of the client during this procedure.

MEDICATION STORAGE

- Some clients save medication, but some of it changes its chemical makeup as it ages. Old medication should be disposed of with the client's permission.

- Many medications have similar names and look alike. Store these separately.

- Do not assist a client in taking a medication from an unlabeled container.

- Do not change the place your client stores his medication without his permission.

- Keep medication out of reach of children and confused, forgetful clients.

- Keep medication away from extreme heat, cold, or light.

- Dispose of medication by flushing it down a toilet or pouring it down a drain. Dispose of old medication so that no one else can make use of it or eat it by mistake.

OXYGEN THERAPY

Oxygen is considered a medication. All the rules and responsibilities that apply to you while you are assisting a client with medication also apply while you are assisting a client with oxygen. Oxygen is prescribed by a physician. The tank may look like a vacuum cleaner canister or a piece of furniture. It may also look like the tanks in the hospital.

The three main kinds of oxygen storage are:

- *Portable liquid unit*. This small unit is intended to be used for short periods of time, usually outside of the house. It is filled from a stationary unit in the house (Figure 16.3a).

- *Stationary unit*. There are several different types of cylinders. They are all designed to remain stationary, however, and will deliver oxygen over a period of several days. The tubing connected from a green cylinder to the client can be adjusted in length to increase client mobility (Figure 16.3b).

- *Oxygen concentrator*. This device removes the oxygen from the air and delivers it, through tubing, to the client. The tubing length can be adjusted (Figure 16.3c).

The company delivering the oxygen is responsible for refilling the tank, servicing the equipment, and teaching the client and his family how to use the equipment. The company should provide a telephone number to call in case of an emergency. If this is not the case, report it to your supervisor.

All oxygen is dispensed from a tank to the client through a rubber tube connected to a nasal cannula or

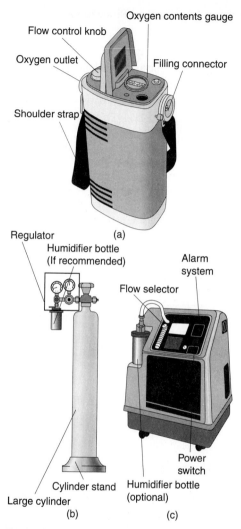

FIGURE 16.3 (a) Portable oxygen unit used to increase client mobility for short periods of time; (b) stationary cylinder is most commonly used for clients confined to their home; (c) oxygen concentrator may be prescribed for prolonged use of oxygen therapy.

catheter. Oxygen is very drying, so a nebulizer filled with water or medication usually is attached to the tank. The oxygen passes through the water and takes on moisture before it goes to the client (Figure 16.4).

- *Nasal cannula.* Nasal cannula tubes are inserted into the client's nostrils. The plastic cannula is a half-circle length of tubing with two openings in the center. It fits about 1/2 inch into the client's nostrils. Nasal cannulae are held in place by an elastic band around the client's head and are connected to the source of oxygen by a length of plastic tubing (Figure 16.5).

- *Nasal catheter.* This catheter is a piece of tubing that is longer than a cannula. It is inserted through the client's nostril into the back of his mouth. The nasal catheter is fastened to the client's forehead or cheek with a piece of tape that holds it steady.

- *Face mask.* This is a piece of plastic shaped like a cup which covers the client's nose and mouth. It has holes

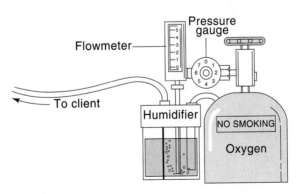

FIGURE 16.4 Although some oxygen delivery systems look different, they all have the same parts and function.

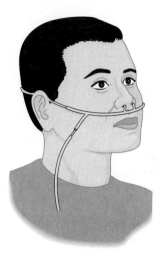

FIGURE 16.5 Nasal cannulae move easily, so check their placement frequently.

in it. A tube connects the mask to the oxygen tank, and a piece of elastic holds the mask securely to the client's face. This mask is used when the client requires more oxygen than can be given by cannula or catheter. This mask must be removed for the client to eat. A client can say a few words with the mask in place, but usually removes it to speak (Figure 16.6).

Safety

- Put up a "No Smoking" sign in the room where the client uses the oxygen. Enforce this rule without any exceptions!

- Report to your supervisor if the client does not use the oxygen as it was prescribed.

- Use cotton bed clothes to decrease static electricity.

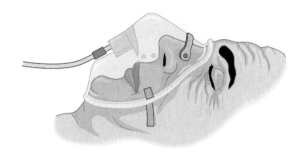

FIGURE 16.6 A client cannot say much with a face mask in place. Be sure the client can signal for assistance.

- Do not use electric shavers or hair dryers while the oxygen is running. Keep the electric plugs out of the walls while the oxygen is running. If an electric plug is pulled from the outlet while the oxygen is running, a spark could cause an explosion.
- Do not use candles or open flames in the room.
- Avoid combing a client's hair while he is receiving oxygen. A spark of electricity from his hair could set off an explosion.
- Ask for careful instructions as to which valve turns the oxygen on and off.
- The setting has been chosen by the physician. Too much or too little oxygen can cause the client to change his breathing pattern, his heart rate, and his speech pattern. Call your supervisor immediately if you notice any of these signs. Do not change the oxygen setting.

Indications of too much oxygen are:

- Sleepiness or difficulty waking up
- Headache

- Difficulty speaking
- Slow, shallow breathing

Indications of too little oxygen are:

- Tiredness
- Blue fingernails and/or lips
- Anxiety, restlessness
- Irritability
- Confusion

Nonsterile Dressings

Dressings that do not require you to use sterile technique or to apply medication to the wound will often be assigned to your care. These are called nonsterile. Keep in mind:

- the protection of the wound
- the protection of the surrounding tissue

Sometimes, a dressing will be secured with tape; sometimes, additional bandage material will be wrapped around the area; and sometimes, an occlusive dressing will be used (Figure 16.7). Do not change the type of dressing being used unless you have discussed it with your supervisor.

When you change a dressing, always note the color, odor, amount, and consistency of the drainage (discharge) on the old dressing. Also, note how big the wound is and the condition of the skin surrounding the wound. Note any change in the wound since you last saw it. If the nurse is scheduled to visit, save the old dressing for her to see.

FIGURE 16.7 A dressing that encloses the wound to keep air away from it is called an occlusive dressing.

Example of Charting

7/3/00—Dressing changed on Mrs. C's right thigh at 10 A.M. Old dressing has light red drainage, 25-cent size, no odor. Wound 5-cent size. Surrounding skin had several small red raised areas. Clean dressing applied. Tape not applied to red areas. Called supervisor to report this. Mary Jones H/HHA.

PROCEDURE

Changing a Nonsterile Dressing

1. Assemble your equipment:

Clean dressing	Paper bag or plastic bag for old
Tape	dressings
Cleansing solution	Medication the client will apply
Disposable gloves	

2. Wash your hands and put on gloves.

3. Ask visitors to leave the room, if appropriate.

4. Tell the client you are going to change his dressing.

5. Open the paper bag.

6. Open the clean dressings without touching the center of them. Prepare the tape in a convenient place.

7. Position the client so that the wound is exposed.

8. Remove the old dressing. Note the drainage for amount, color, odor, and consistency. Note the size of the wound and the condition of the surrounding skin.

9. Cleanse the wound and the skin as you have been instructed. Use circular motions and clean from the clean areas to the dirty areas. The wound is considered clean and the skin dirty.

10. Allow the client to assist you as much as possible.

11. If a medication is to be applied to the wound, assist the client with the application as needed.

12. Apply clean dressings. Hold all dressings by the corners as you apply them. Do not contaminate the center of the bandages. Tape the dressing in place, leaving the edges free. Do not put tape completely around the edges of the bandage (Figure 16.8).

13. Make the client comfortable.

14. Discard the dressing in a covered container. Clean the equipment.

15. Remove gloves and wash your hands.

16. Make a notation on the client's chart that you changed his dressing. Also note your observations of the client during this procedure.

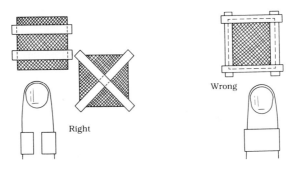

Right

Wrong

FIGURE 16.8

/NDWELLING URINARY CATHETER

The urinary catheter is the most common kind of catheter used for taking fluids out of the body. This catheter is made of plastic or rubber and is inserted by a nurse or physician through the client's urethra into his bladder. A catheter may be used when a client is unable to urinate naturally, or it may be used to measure the amount of urine left in the bladder after a client has urinated naturally. It may also be used to help keep an incontinent client dry. An incontinent client is one who cannot control his urine or feces.

Sometimes, a urinary catheter is used for only one withdrawal of urine. Sometimes, it is kept in place in the bladder for a number of days or even weeks. This type of catheter is called an indwelling catheter or Foley catheter (Figure 16.9). This catheter is specially made so that it will stay in the bladder. It has two tubes, one inside the other. The outside tube is connected at one end to a balloon. After the catheter has been inserted, the balloon is filled with water or air so the catheter will not pass out through the urethra. Urine drains out of the

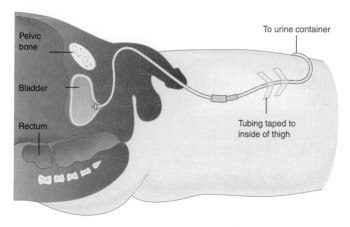

Pelvic bone

To urine container

Bladder

Rectum

Tubing taped to inside of thigh

FIGURE 16.9 A catheter is a possible source of irritation and infection. Tend it carefully and according to the plan of care.

bladder through the outer tube and collects in a container. The container is attached to a point located lower than the client's urinary bladder. An indwelling catheter is always a closed system, which means it is never opened except when the urine collecting bag is emptied.

Sometimes, in male clients, the catheter is secured to the abdomen rather than the thigh. This reduces the pressure on the catheter and provides the straightest route for the urine drain.

Urinary indwelling catheters drain by straight drainage from the client into a bag. This type of drainage gets its name from the fact that the tubing from the bed to the bag must be kept straight and all other tubing must be kept above this. When the tubing is in its proper position, the urine will drain freely into the bag. If the tubing is not in the proper position, the urine could back up into the bladder or the kidneys (Figure 16.10).

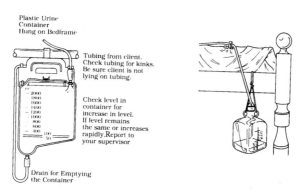

Plastic Urine
Container
Hung on Bedframe

Tubing from client.
Check tubing for kinks.
Be sure client is not
lying on tubing.

Check level in
container for
increase in level.
If level remains
the same or increases
rapidly. Report to
your supervisor

Drain for Emptying
the Container

FIGURE 16.10 Check the tubing from the client to the drainage bag frequently to be sure it is free of kinks.

It is normal for urine to change from light yellow to dark yellow, depending on the concentration and the amount of fluid the client has consumed.

- Check from time to time to make sure the level of urine has increased. If the level stays the same, report this to your supervisor immediately.

- If the client says he feels that his bladder is full, or that he needs to urinate, report this to your supervisor immediately.

- If the client is allowed to get out of bed for short periods, the bag must always be held lower than the client's urinary bladder to prevent the urine in the tubing and bag from draining back into the urinary bladder.

- Check to make sure there are no kinks in the catheter and tubing.

- Be sure the client is not lying on the catheter or the tubing. This would stop the flow of urine.

- Be sure the tubing from the bed to the bag is always kept straight.

- The catheter should be secured at all times to the client's inner thigh or, in the case of some male clients, the abdomen. This keeps it from being pulled on or being pulled out of the bladder. Tape or special straps made for this purpose can be used.

- Most clients with urinary drainage through a catheter are on intake and output (I&O) measurement.

- If urine leaks around a catheter, report this to your supervisor.

- A male client may have an erection while the catheter is in place. Assure him there is nothing the matter with him, and maintain a concerned attitude.

- Empty the collection bag frequently from the correct port. Protect the floor from spillage. There are many types of collection bags. If you find one that is new to you, ask your supervisor for assistance.

- Clean the collection tubing and the bag as instructed by your agency. Some agencies discard collection equipment after a specified amount of time. Some agencies use a cleansing procedure.

- Keep the client's urinary opening clean. Even though he is not urinating, mucous and perspiration collect in the area.

- Be sure the tubing is free of fecal matter and mucous.

- Cover the exposed ends of tubing only with sterile covers.

- Notify your supervisor immediately if you see sediment or blood in the tubing or collection bag.

PROCEDURE

Catheter Care

Note: This procedure may be incorporated into the morning bath routine. Be sure you use clean water for this procedure.

1. Assemble your equipment:

   Basin of water and mild   Paper or plastic bag for waste
   soap or cleaning solution   Disposable gloves
   Washcloth or gauze pads

2. Wash your hands.
3. Ask visitors to leave the room, if appropriate.
4. Tell the client you are going to give him catheter care.
5. Position the client on his back so the catheter and urinary meatus are exposed. Put on your gloves.
6. Wash the area gently. Do not pull on the catheter, but hold it with one hand while wiping it with the other.
7. Observe the meatus for redness, swelling, or discharge.
8. Wipe away from the meatus when caring for a female client. Wipe from the meatus to the anus (Figure 16.11).
9. Wipe one way and not back and forth.
10. Remove your gloves.
11. Dry the area.
12. Apply lotion, cornstarch, or powder in small quantities to the thighs. Ask your supervisor if this area should be kept dry or moist.
13. Make the client comfortable.
14. Dispose of the dirty water into the toilet. Clean your equipment, and put it in its proper place.
15. Wash your hands.
16. Make a notation on the client's chart that you have completed this procedure. Also make a note of your observations of the client during this procedure.

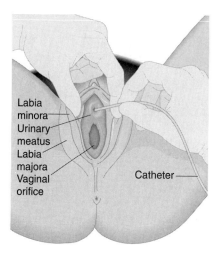

Labia minora
Urinary meatus
Labia majora
Vaginal orifice
Catheter

FIGURE 16.11 Be sure to keep the entire perineum clean in female clients to prevent irritation and possible infection.

*L*EG BAG

A leg bag is a small plastic bag worn on the client's leg. This apparatus allows the client to be more active than when using the traditional straight drainage. It cannot be used when the client is lying down because the drainage is improper in that position (Figure 16.12). The same rules of asepsis that apply to changing a straight drainage bag apply to putting on a leg bag. Be sure to put the top of the bag at the top and the bottom at the bottom. Empty the bag immediately after it is removed or when it gets full. If the client is on I&O, record the amount of urine collected. Clean the bag as you have been taught.

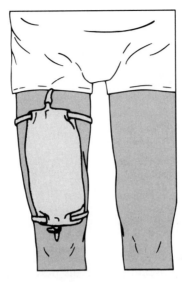

FIGURE 16.12 The use of a leg bag increases the client's mobility but must be emptied frequently.

PROCEDURE

Changing a Catheter From a Straight Drainage Bag to a Leg Bag

1. Assemble your equipment:

   Leg bag with straps
   Disposable gloves
   Alcohol wipes or antiseptic solution

   Sterile cover for straight drainage tubing
   Sterile 4 × 4 bed protector

2. Wash your hands and put on gloves.

3. Ask visitors to leave the room, if appropriate.

4. Tell the client you are going to put on his leg bag.

5. Expose the end of the catheter and the drainage tubing. Put the bed protector under this area.

6. Disconnect the drainage tubing from the catheter and allow it to drain. Put a sterile cover on the end of the tubing, and place it out of the way but not on the floor. Do not put the catheter on the bed.

7. Wipe the attachment tube of the leg bag with an alcohol swab, and insert the tube into the catheter.

8. Secure the leg bag to the client's thigh.

9. Make the client comfortable.

10. Empty the drainage bag. Measure the urine, and note it on the chart.

11. Remove gloves and wash your hands.

12. Make a notation on the client's chart that you have completed this procedure. Also make a note of your observations of the client during this procedure.

USES OF EXTERNAL URINARY DRAINAGE SYSTEMS

When a male client is incontinent of urine, the nurse may suggest the use of an external drainage system that will collect the urine and keep the client dry. One end of the catheter is kept in place at the end of the penis and one end is connected to straight drainage (Figure 16.13).

This device should not be left on for more than 24 hours at a time and must be removed at least that often so that the penis may be washed and inspected. If there is any change in the skin and/or the client complains of pain or

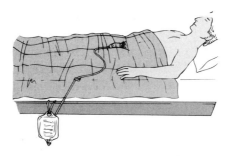

FIGURE 16.13 Check the placement of external drainage frequently and change it at least every 24 hours.

discomfort, or the catheter does not drain, remove the entire device, discard it, and call your supervisor. Observe the client shortly after you put on the catheter and then frequently when you are with him. The cleaning of the bag and the catheter should be discussed with your supervisor.

PROCEDURE

External Urinary Drainage

1. Assemble your equipment:
   External urinary system, consisting of a condom, a catheter, and a straight drainage system
   Material to secure condom to penis (tape, strap, or adhesive foam)
   Soap
   Water
   Towel
   Disposable gloves

2. Wash your hands.

3. Ask visitors to leave the room, if appropriate.

4. Tell the client you are going to put on an external urinary collection device. Put on gloves.

5. Position the client on his back so that the penis is exposed. Cover the client so he is not exposed.

6. Wash the entire penis and dry thoroughly. Observe the penis for any discharge or redness.

7. Roll the condom onto the entire length of the penis.

8. Secure the condom. Be sure the strap is tight enough to hold the condom in place but not so tight as to hurt the client.

9. Attach the catheter to the condom and to the straight drainage. Secure the collection bag on a bed or chair.

10. Make the client comfortable.

11. Dispose of the dirty water into the toilet. Clean your equipment and put it in its proper place.

12. Remove gloves and wash your hands.

13. Make a notation on the client's chart that you have completed this procedure. Also make note of your observations of the client during this procedure.

UNDERSTANDING INTRAVENOUS (IV) THERAPY

Intravenous (IV) therapy is prescribed by a physician and administered by a registered nurse. During this procedure, the nurse inserts a needle into the client's veins to provide a way to give fluids or medication. The medication or fluids are either given by single injection, continuous drip slowly from a bottle or bag, or by a pump which regulates the flow of the medication or nourishment through a tube secured to the needle (Figure 16.14).

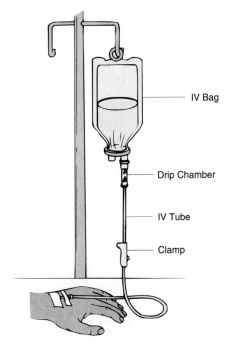

IV Bag

Drip Chamber

IV Tube

Clamp

FIGURE 16.14 Clients with IVs do not have to be in bed, but they must be in a relaxed environment.

- *Continuous infusion*. Fluid and/or medication is always running; prescribed for a client who has a family member or friend who is able to assume responsibility for the insertion site and care of the bottles or bags.
- *Intermittent infusion*. Small amounts of fluid or medication are given over short periods of time; each time a dose is needed, the IV must be started again.

There are three types of IV therapy:

- *Peripheral lines*. Veins, usually of the upper extremities, are used.
- *Central venous lines*. A catheter that has been surgically implanted into one of the large veins. The placement of this type of catheter is made when the medication is very irritating to the blood vessels or must be given frequently or when large amounts of medication must be given. The end of the catheter used for medication administration is visible on the chest area. The care of the catheter will be carefully discussed with you and the family. Do not touch the catheter until you have received the instructions (Figure 16.15).

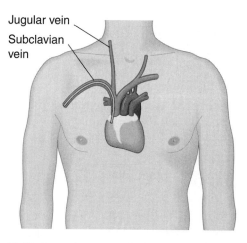

Jugular vein
Subclavian vein

FIGURE 16.15 Central venous lines should be cared for as prescribed by the physician. Be sure to report any discomfort that the client describes to your supervisor immediately.

▪ *Peripherally inserted central venous catheter (PICC).* The catheter is inserted at the bedside by a specially trained nurse or physician. The care of this catheter and the dressing will be discussed with you and the family. Do not remove the dressing unless you have been instructed to do so.

If the client has a continuous infusion, he may walk around as long as the bottle of fluid is above the insertion site and does not pull on the tubing. Remind the client not to sit or lean on the tubing.

You will not be responsible for the care or dressing changes of the IV site. Central venous lines will be covered by a dressing when they are not in use. Sometimes, a peripheral line will have a cap on it when it is not in use. This cap is usually covered by a dressing. Do not disturb either type of dressing. You will be asked to keep the dressing dry and clean. Check the dressing at least every 8 hours to be sure it is secure. You should also be alert to changes in the site and report them immediately. Report to your supervisor if:

▪ The client complains of pain in the area.
▪ The area is red, hot, and/or swollen.
▪ You notice blood or any drainage from the area.
▪ The client removes the needle or tubing, or if either one falls out.
▪ The tubing has blood in it.
▪ The level of fluid in the bag or bottle does not decrease.
▪ The bag or bottle breaks.

Be sure to document when you check the dressing. Write down that you checked the area and the condition of the dressing and the skin.

Example: April 11, 2000 2:00 P.M. IV site on left arm checked. Client did not complain of discomfort. Skin intact. No drainage noted on dressing, which was secure and dry. Mary Cummings, H/HHA

*C*AST CARE

A client who has broken a bone or sprained or strained a muscle may have a cast or splint placed on the body part to immobilize it. The procedure provides support to the injured part and prevents deformity by keeping it in the correct body alignment. Splints and casts are temporary. Permanent support to the bones in the form of pins, plates, and replacement of joints also may be necessary (Figures 16.16).

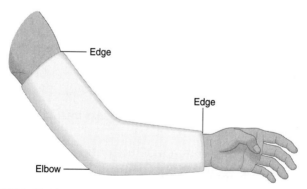

Edge

Edge

Elbow

FIGURE 16.16 Report immediately any changes in the casted limb or the cast that you notice or the client reports.

Casts are wet when applied, then allowed to dry. Once they are hardened, the casts should not be allowed to get wet. Do not wash them. Plastic or fiberglass casts perform the same task but are lighter, cleaner, and easier to use and remove. Check the cast edges several times a day. Report any sharp edges immediately to your supervisor.

While a plaster cast is drying, the client's position must be maintained and the cast left uncovered. It is normal for the cast to feel hot to the touch and to the client as it is drying. Pillows can be placed to support the cast so it will not move while it is still soft.

- A cast should not restrict circulation to the part.
- A cast should not cause pain. The pain should be only from the healing bone or muscle.
- The skin under a cast frequently itches. Do not put anything into the cast. This might cause a scratch and lead to a skin infection.
- Protect a cast while a client is using the bedpan or toilet.
- There are casts that can be wet and allowed to air dry. Check with the client and your supervisor as to how to care for each cast.

Call your supervisor immediately if:

- The client complains of numbness or tingling of toes or fingers.
- There is discoloration of toes or fingers.
- There is swelling of the limb at the edge of the cast.
- There are unusual odors coming from the cast.

- The cast is loosely fitting
- You notice discolorations on the cast

*T*HE OSTOMY

The creation of an ostomy is a surgical procedure. An ostomy is a new opening in the abdomen for the release of wastes from the body. The opening is called a stoma. This operation is necessary when the colon or urinary system is diseased or injured. Ostomies are created for many reasons—not only because a client has cancer. Sometimes, the surgery is done to permit the colon to heal following an injury. Some ostomies are temporary and others are permanent. The word ostomy means "opening into." A colostomy is an opening into the colon. An ileostomy is an opening into the ileum. A ureterostomy is an opening into the ureter. The opening is from the abdominal wall to the affected organ. The part you see, the stoma, will look like a pink rosebud (Figure 16.17).

A person with an ostomy must wear an appliance to collect the matter released through the stoma (Figure 16.18). This collecting bag is held over the stoma by special paste, adhesive, and/or a belt. Some ostomy appliances are permanent. This means that they are reused after they are cleaned and dried. Some bags are disposable and used only once (Figure 16.19).

Having an ostomy is usually a traumatic occurrence. It requires changes in the daily routine of the client and often of family members. The client's body image changes. Having an ostomy is a life-altering experience.

Everyone reacts differently to this experience. Some people learn the new routines and return to their previous

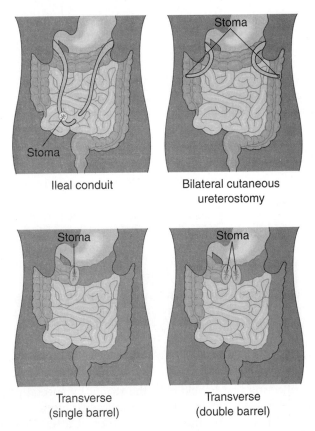

FIGURE 16.17 The placement and type of ostomy is decided by the physician before surgery.

lifestyle. Some people do not. Be alert to the coping mechanisms of your client and his family. Support them as they learn how to care for the ostomy and become familiar with the appliances.

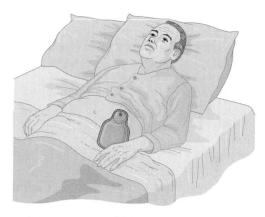

FIGURE 16.18 The choice of a collection device is a personal one.

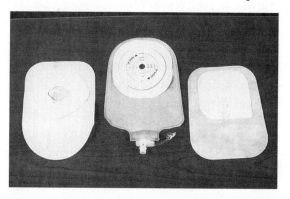

FIGURE 16.19 There are various types of ostomy appliances.

PROCEDURE

Assisting With an Ostomy

Note: Each client has his own routine for caring for his ostomy. This procedure is a general guide.

1. Assemble your equipment:

   Bedpan

   Disposable bed protector

   Bath blanket

   Clean ostomy belt, adjustable

   Ostomy appliance

   Toilet tissue material to secure
   the ostomy appliances

   Basin of water

   Soap or cleanser

   Washcloth

   Disposable gloves

   Towels

   Lubricant or skin cream,
   as ordered

   Plastic waste bag

2. Wash your hands.

3. Ask visitors to leave the room, if appropriate.

4. Tell the client that you are going to assist him with changing his ostomy appliance.

5. Cover the client with the bath blanket. Ask the client to hold the top edge of the blanket. Without exposing him, fanfold the top sheet and bedspread to the foot of the bed under the blanket.

6. Place the disposable bed protector under the client's hips. This is to keep the bed from getting wet or dirty.

7. Place the bedpan within easy reach.

8. Put the wash basin, soap, washcloth, and bath towels near the bed. Put on gloves.

9. Open the belt. Protect it if it is clean and can be used again. If the belt is dirty, remove it. It must be replaced with a clean one.

10. Remove the soiled plastic stoma bag from the belt carefully.

11. Put the soiled plastic bag into the bedpan. Wipe the area around the ostomy with toilet tissue. This is to remove any loose feces. Place the dirty tissue in the plastic bag. Flush the tissues down the toilet later.

12. Wet and soap the washcloth. Wash the entire ostomy area with a gentle circular motion.

13. Dry the area gently with a bath towel.

14. Apply a small amount of lubricant or protective cream (if ordered) around the area of the ostomy. The lubricant is to prevent irritation to the skin around the ostomy. Wipe off all excess lubricant so that the ostomy device will adhere to the skin.

15. If using a wafer, secure it around the stoma. Be sure the size is correct (Figure 16.20).

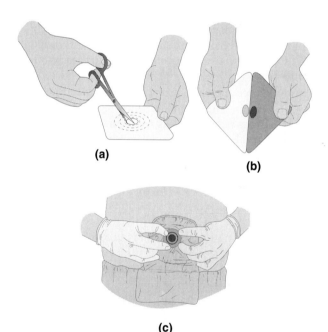

(a)

(b)

(c)

FIGURE 16.20 (a) Cut the hole in the center of the wafer ⅛-inch larger than the stoma. (b) Peel the backing from the wafer. (c) Place the wafer around the stoma and attach a clean bag.

16. Put a clean adjustable belt, if the client wears one, on the client. Place a clean stoma bag in place through the loop.

17. Remove the disposable bed protector. Change any damp linen.

18. Replace the top sheet and bedspread, and remove the bath blanket.

19. Make the client comfortable.

20. Remove all used equipment. Dispose of waste material into the toilet. Do not throw the plastic collection bag down the toilet but into the plastic liner in the wastebasket.

21. Clean the bedpan, and put it in its proper place.

22. Empty the wash basin into the toilet. Wash it thoroughly with soap and water. Rinse and dry it, and return it to its proper place.

23. Remove gloves and wash your hands.

24. Make a notation on the client's chart that you have completed this procedure. Also make a note of your observations about the client during this procedure.

A client and his family may want to discuss this operation with you. They will ask you questions. Do not lie to them. Frequently, a client or family member will ask you the same question many times. This is a way of confirming that the first answer you gave was the real one. Report this to your supervisor. Your supervisor can then help you plan your care to meet this client's needs.

All ostomy care is based on several considerations. They are:

- Aseptic technique (rules of cleanliness)
- Client and family reaction to the procedure
- Client prognosis
- Frequent changing of the collection bag

A collection bag must be changed when it is full or when the adhering seal is broken. Some clients will be well enough to sit the toilet in the bathroom to do this procedure. Also, many clients will be learning to do this procedure independently, in which case you will assist them less and less.

Some clients will have to irrigate their colostomy. Irrigating a colostomy is like giving an enema into the ostomy. You may, after you have been instructed, assist the client as he carries out this procedure.

Gastrostomy, duodenostomy, and jejunostomy are surgical openings made directly into various parts of the upper gastrointestinal tract. These incisions are kept open by the presence of a tube or a screw cap. The client will receive part or all of his nourishment through this opening. Sometimes a pump will be used to give the feeding. He may also take his medication through this opening (Figure 16.21).

Cleanliness is an important part of the care. Be sure that the client's or family member's hands are clean before he cares for the site and before he starts the feeding.

Assist the client in making the feeding or in preparing commercially prepared feeding. Label the container with important information such as date and time of mixing and initial use. It is wise to discard any feeding that is more than 24 hours old. Warm the solution to room temperature. Observe the client as to how he tolerates the feeding. Report your observations to your supervisor.

Note the time of the feeding, how long it lasts, and how the client tolerates it. Also note if he complains of any nausea, vomiting, diarrhea, cramps, or sweating after the feeding.

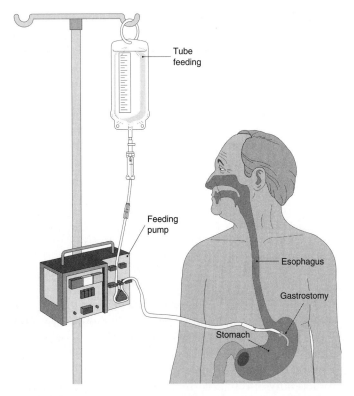

FIGURE 16.21 A pump keeps the tube feeding drain at a predetermined rate.

Creating a Safe Environment for a Client Having a Seizure

A seizure is caused by an abnormality within the central nervous system and is thought to be an electrical problem in the nerve cells. Seizures can occur from the time of birth or may be the result of a head injury or disease. Often, the cause of seizures is unknown. Seizures are often controlled by medication. A client who has been diagnosed as having epilepsy or who has seizures due to another disease often leads a normally productive life. Other people's ignorance about seizures is his biggest enemy.

A client may know when he is going to have a seizure. He experiences what is called an aura. An aura may be a smell or sensation that always occurs before the client has a seizure. There are two types of seizures:

- A person having a *grand mal seizure* may demonstrate stiffness of the total body followed by a jerking action of the muscles. Usually, the client becomes unconscious. Sometimes, the client bites his tongue. Sometimes, he becomes incontinent. These seizures can last for several minutes.

- In the *petit mal seizure*, the client may appear to be daydreaming. His eyes may roll back and there may be some quivering of the body muscles. The petit mal seizure usually lasts less than 30 seconds. The client usually has no memory of the seizure.

Safety During a Seizure

If you are present at the beginning of a seizure, you may place a padded tongue depressor, padded tongue blade, or a belt in the client's mouth, depending on the policy of your health care agency. Some health care agencies prefer that you simply turn the client's head to the side. If the client's jaw is already tight or he has his teeth clenched, do not try to pry his teeth apart to insert a tongue depressor. Help the client to lie down on the floor. Loosen his clothing and move any furniture that he might hit as he moves. Place a pillow or something soft under his head. Turn his head to the side to promote drainage of saliva or vomitus. Never try to move or restrain the client. Protect the client from people who may stare at him. Protect him from embarrassment.

Comfort the client after the seizure. Clean him of any saliva, urine, or fecal matter. Assist him with mouth care and care of his body after the seizure. After the client is comfortable and safe, chart the client's actions and your actions during this occurrence. Notify your supervisor of the entire incident.

*T*ESTING FOR BLOOD GLUCOSE

The amount of glucose in the blood indicates the amount of medication and food the diabetic person must have. Diabetic clients are taught how to monitor their blood glucose levels by using one of several testing devices. They are also instructed how to record their findings and how to adjust their medication. The device and the timing of the tests are prescribed by the physician and may be different for each client.

*P*ROCEDURE

Testing Blood Glucose Level

1. Assemble your equipment:
   Blood glucose meter, such as
     a One-Touch Profile meter
   Test strips
   Penlet and lancet

   Disposable pipet
   Disposable gloves
   Adhesive bandage like a
     Band-Aid®

2. Wash your hands.

3. Explain to the client that you are going to test his blood glucose.

4. Make the client comfortable and wash his hands with soap and water.

5. Put on disposable gloves.

6. Match the code on the test strips to the number on the meter. Check the expiration date on the test strips. Discard them if they have expired. The code number may have to be reset. Follow the manufacturer's instructions.

7. Remove the test strip from container. Close the container. Do not touch the white area of the strip.

8. Press "Power" and insert the strip into the meter (Figure 16.22).

9. Insert the lancet into the Penlet according to the manufacturer's directions.

10. Place the end of the lancet firmly against the side of the client's fingertip.

11. Press the button on top of the Penlet.

12. Squeeze the finger gently to obtain a large drop of blood.

FIGURE 16.22 (Photo courtesy of Johnson & Johnson.)

13. Using a disposable pipet, slowly draw up the drop of blood and apply the sample to the test strip. This method prevents contamination of the client and is preferred in a hospital or nursing home setting where several patients or residents use the same blood glucose meter. An alternative method for individual use (at home, for example) is to apply the blood sample directly to the strip (Figure 16.23).

14. Wait a short time for the results to appear on the blood glucose meter (Figure 16.24).

15. Apply the bandage to the client's finger.

FIGURE 16.23 (Photo courtesy of Johnson & Johnson.)

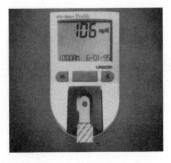

FIGURE 16.24 (Photo courtesy of Johnson & Johnson.)

16. Remove disposable gloves and wash your hands.
17. Record the results. Notify the supervisor if the results are above or below normal.

DEEP-BREATHING EXERCISES

Shallow breathing takes place in the upper lobes of the lungs, which are surrounded by bony areas on all sides. The lungs cannot expand very much in the bony enclosure, so they cannot take in much oxygen or exhale much carbon dioxide. People who have had lung disease for a long time have "barrel chests." The chest cavity has taken on this shape in an attempt to have the lungs inhale more oxygen.

Deep breathing helps people inhale more air with less effort than their usual type of breathing. When people breathe deeply, the lower lobes of the lungs push the soft tissue of the abdomen out of the way and expand to take in more air.

Continue to reinforce the reasons why deep breathing is important.

- When the client takes a deep breath, his shoulders and chest should not move. His abdomen should expand. When he exhales his abdomen should get flat. If the client is confused about how to do this, tell him to cough. The squeezing of the abdominal area will make him aware of where the muscular activity should take place.

- Coughing is forced expiration. Deep breathing sometimes produces a coughing response. This is true especially if the lungs are congested. Keep a basin, tissue, or specimen container (if ordered) near the client. Collect any mucous he may bring up. Encourage him to spit it out. Note the color, amount, and odor.

■ Protect the client from visitors and friends when he is coughing. Deep breathing is frequently unpleasant, although it is very important. Because it also makes some people cough and bring up mucous, plan to carry out this exercise between mealtimes. By doing this, it will not cause vomiting or loss of appetite.

■ Sometimes the client will use a machine to help him do this exercise. Be sure you understand how to assist the client as he uses it.

Procedure

Helping a Client With Deep-Breathing Exercises

1. Assemble your equipment:
   Equipment for mouth care   Plastic bag for waste
      following this procedure
   Tissues and basin or
      specimen container
2. Wash your hands.
3. Ask visitors to leave the room, if appropriate.
4. Tell the client you are going to help him with deep-breathing exercises.
5. Direct the client to breathe in deeply through his nose.
6. Direct the client to blow out through his mouth with his lips "pursed," as though he were blowing out a match (Figure 16.25).

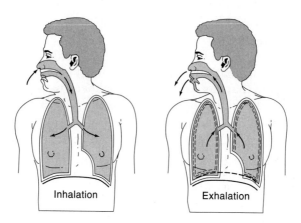

Inhalation   Exhalation

FIGURE 16.25

7. The steps should be repeated 10 times.
8. Offer the client mouth care. Wear gloves if offering mouth care.
9. Dispose of the tissues into a plastic bag.
10. Make the client comfortable.
11. Make a notation on the chart that you have completed this procedure. Also note anything you observed about the client while doing this procedure.

*T*HE SITZ BATH

The term sitz bath means "seat bath" or a bath that is taken while seated. The area that is bathed is the perineal area. Such a procedure may be ordered to promote healing of the area, to decrease pain following surgery or a procedure, and to increase relaxation of the muscles in the perineal area.

A sitz bath can be taken by the client either in a specially designed bath that fits into the toilet or commode or in a bathtub that has had a covered rubber ring placed in it so that the perineal area is suspended off the tub floor (Figure 16.26).

- Be sure the water is the correct temperature. It should be comfortable to the touch and measure between 95° and 110°F or between 35° and 43°C.

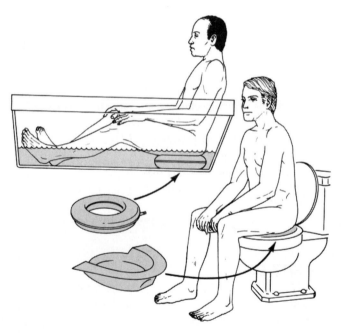

FIGURE 16.26 Provide a safe and private place for the client during a sitz bath. Be sure he can signal for assistance.

Water that is too hot will burn the client, and water that is too cold will cause the muscles to tighten up rather than relax. Maintain the water temperature by adding warm water when necessary.

- Help the client start and finish the procedure. Safely getting on and off the commode, or in and out of the tub, should be done slowly and at the client's speed. Protect the client from slipping and falling on towels, clothes, or dressings.

- The usual length of time for a sitz bath is between 10 and 15 minutes. You will be told how long and how often your client should have a sitz bath. Check on your client frequently and tell him how long he has yet to go. Ask your client how he feels, and observe him, too.

Chart your activities.

- The length of time the client remained in the bath
- The client's reaction to the bath
- A description of any drainage from the wounds
- How the client finished the procedure—new dressing, returned to bed, and so on

*W*ORKING WITH HYPERALIMENTATION

Clients who are severely malnourished and who are unable to eat often receive their nutritional requirements by means of hyperalimentation. For long-term administration, a catheter is surgically placed in a large vein and the nutrition is administered directly into the blood stream. A physician orders the exact dose of the supplement, which must be mixed by a pharmacy. A pharmacy or company specializing in this service has the responsibility for delivering the correct feeding to the client every 24 hours. The catheter that is used for the feeding is not used for any other purpose. Some bottles or bags must be kept refrigerated. Some must be at room temperature. If the delivery does not arrive on time or you notice that the feedings are not stored properly, call your supervisor. Do not discard any unused feedings. Return them to the pharmacy.

Clients may receive this treatment for a short amount of time or for several years. Some clients receive their feedings in the evening and work during the day. Others receive feedings over a 24-hour period. Clients who receive this treatment must be able to assume the responsibility for the feedings or have responsible family members who can do it. Teaching of this procedure usually takes place in the hospital and will be reinforced in the home by the company that brings the feedings. Be sure you and the client have the emergency telephone numbers that can be called with questions. The professionals from the supply company will take responsibility for checking the pump and the catheter insertion site. You will not be asked to administer the feedings or change the dressings on the catheter, but you will be responsible for assisting with preparation of the bottles.

If you are to keep a record of I&O, vital signs, and weights, do so accurately.

- Report any shortness of breath, tingling in arms or feet, weakness, or temperature change.
- Report any irritation or drainage near the catheter site.
- Report any change in the client.
- Help the client maintain a comfortable position during the feeding. The tubes should be straight and not under the client.

CHAPTER 17

Common Diseases

*H*YPERTENSION

Hypertension, or high blood pressure, is a treatable chronic disease. Hypertension contributes to death from heart disease and kidney disease. Treatment for hypertension is available, but must be continued for the client's lifetime. The fact that a client's blood pressure has been brought to an acceptable level does not mean the disease has gone away; it only means that the disease has been brought under control, and this control must be continued.

Hypertension has been called "the silent killer" because it gives no warning. In the early stages of this disease, there often are no symptoms. As the disease develops, people may complain of headaches, vision changes, or problems with their urinary output. If they would consult a physician at this point in their disease, permanent damage to a vital organ could be avoided.

Risk factors for hypertension include:

- A family history of hypertension, heart disease, or kidney disease
- Cigarette smoking
- Obesity (overweight)
- A lot of salt in the diet

413

- African American heritage
- A large amount of saturated fats in the diet

Many conditions seem to cause hypertension, and some of the causes are still unknown. Research scientists are investigating diet, heredity, birth control pills, kidney infections, and chemicals as possible causes of this chronic disease. Treatment may consist of a combination of diet, medication, and exercise.

- Support your client in complying with his medication plan, diet, and exercise. Because he will always be on some treatment for this disease, it is important that the treatment become a regular part of his day. Report to your supervisor any deviation from the care plan.

- Listen to your client. If he has questions about hypertension and/or his treatment, answer him honestly. If you do not know the answer, call your supervisor and be sure that the client gets answers to his questions.

- Be observant for possible side effects from the medication. Depending on the drug and the client, side effects range from a stuffy nose to muscle cramps, weakness, nightmares, and impotence.

*M*YOCARDIAL INFARCTION (MI) OR HEART ATTACK

Myocardial infarction (MI), or heart attack, is a general term that describes sudden damage to the heart. There are many medical reasons people have heart attacks, but they all have the same results—a decrease in the blood supply to the heart, which eventually leads to heart muscle damage and possiblypermanent tissue death.

The word infarct means "the death of tissue due to lack of blood." The word myocardial refers to heart muscle. So a myocardial infarction, or MI, is really the death of part of the heart due to a blockage in a blood vessel. If the blood vessel involved is a small one and only a small amount of heart muscle is affected, this may be called a minor or small heart attack. If the blood vessel involved is a large one and a large portion of the heart is damaged, it is often called a massive heart attack. The ultimate recovery of the injured heart depends on the location of the MI within the heart; presence of atherosclerosis; and the age, sex, and the health history of the individual.

Arteriosclerosis and Atherosclerosis

Arteriosclerosis is hardening of arteries and leads to a decrease in the blood supply to body tissue due to a thickening of vessel walls (Figure 17.1). Atherosclerosis is a form of arteriosclerosis that takes place in several steps:

- A fatty streak develops in the vessel.
- A fibrous plaque develops on top of the fatty streak. Depending on the size of this plaque, the vessel remains open or becomes completely obstructed.
- Sometimes, a clot develops in the same spot as the fibrous plaque.

If atherosclerosis is discovered and treated after the first stage, the condition is reversible. However, once a vessel is completely blocked by plaque, it usually remains that way.

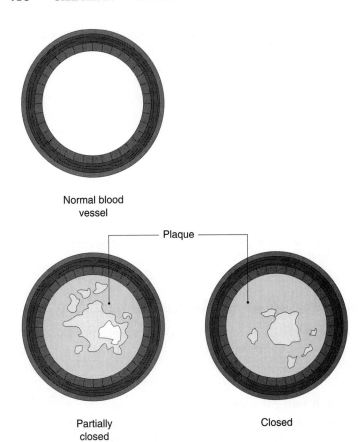

Normal blood
vessel

Plaque

Partially
closed

Closed

FIGURE 17.1 The elimination of plaque-forming foods from the diet should begin in early childhood.

Signs and Symptoms of MI

The following signs and symptoms may appear in your client or in a member of the family. Call for emergency help immediately and keep the client quiet and warm until help arrives.

- Chest pain that may or may not radiate to the arm or jaw
- Wet, clammy skin
- Weak and/or rapid pulse rate
- Pale color
- Low blood pressure
- Shortness of breath
- Nausea

The single best way to prevent or minimize permanent damage to the heart is to get help at a hospital as soon as possible. Every minute is important!

After hospitalization, your client will return with an individualized plan of care based on:

- The type of heart attack he had
- His recovery up to that point
- His home situation
- His prognosis

The plan of care will include instructions about:

- Activity restrictions
- Diet restrictions
- Medications
- Emotional support

Every caregiver balances the desire to allow the client to be a self-sufficient person and the need to restrict his activity level.

A client usually is given an exercise regimen. If your client is unable to progress with the exercise or tries to advance too quickly, report this to your supervisor.

After a heart attack, a person may become a "cardiac cripple." He is so afraid of having another heart attack that he does not exert himself at all or take any part in his care. He even removes himself from family relationships. The opposite of this is a total disregard for one's condition. The client denies any disability. He does not follow any suggestions from his physician, take his medication, or adhere to his diet.

A client often is concerned about how his heart attack will affect his sexual activities. A client usually will return to a full sexual life. Do not give the client any opinions or folktales, but rather say, "I know you are concerned about this, and I will tell the nurse. She will get you the information you want."

A family member may need help in dealing with the stress of lifestyle changes and fear caused by cardiac disease. Suggest that any family member who needs help or expresses these fears seek the assistance of a support group or his or her own physician.

PACEMAKERS

A pacemaker is an electrical device placed either in the left or right upper chest under the skin. The job of this device is to regulate the heart rhythm. A pacemaker can be temporary or permanent. There are three types of pacemakers:

1. *Fixed-rate*. Stimulation rate is fixed usually between 60 and 70 beats per minute. This is only used if the heart is totally dependent on electrical stimulation and is used only temporarily. It is rarely seen in the home.

2. *Synchronous.* Stimulation occurs after a predetermined lack of the heart's own activity. This type is not seen often in the home.

3. *Demand.* When the heartbeat falls below a predetermined rate, the pacemaker takes over. This is the most common type of pacemaker seen in the home.

Care of a Pacemaker

It is helpful to know what type of pacemaker your client has. It is also important to know the rate at which it is set.

- Electrical appliances may be used around pacemakers.

- Microwave ovens should not be used around pacemakers. Some clients have difficulties being around lawn mowers and cellular telephones.

- If your client has hiccoughs, report this immediately. This could be an indication that the electrical wires are out of place.

- If your client's pulse is below the preset level of the pacemaker, report it immediately.

- Report pain or discoloration near the pacemaker.

- Detecting devices in airports should be avoided.

- Report any complaints of dizziness, edema (swelling), shortness of breath, or irregular heart beat.

- Batteries have to be replaced from time to time. The physician decides when this is to be done.

- Assist your client with his telephone monitoring procedure.

ANGINA

Angina is a brief, temporary pain or heaviness in the chest that results from lack of oxygen to the heart. Usually after resting and medication, the client no longer experiences discomfort. An episode may be brought on by stress or physical activity. Angina differs from person to person.

Causes of Angina

Angina is due to the narrowing of the coronary arteries that bring oxygen to the heart. As these vessels narrow, the amount of oxygen decreases, causing pain and discomfort. This is not a heart attack or myocardial infarction because it is a temporary condition. However, if angina is allowed to continue without treatment, the sufferer could have a heart attack, and sustain permanent damage to the heart.

Risk factors for angina include:

- High blood pressure
- High blood cholesterol
- Cigarette smoking
- Obesity (overweight)
- High stress levels

Treatment

There is no sure cure for angina. However, most people with the disease learn to live productive and meaningful lives. The aim of all treatment is to increase the flow of blood and oxygen to the heart through:

- *Medication*. The physician will prescribe a regimen of medication that will help the client and decrease his pain.

- *Control of risk factors*. The client may be put on a weight-reducing diet, told to decrease his use of cigarettes, and advised to decrease his stress level.

- *Surgery*. This treatment will be discussed with the client by his physician.

DIABETES MELLITUS

When the body cannot change carbohydrates (sugars and starches) into energy because of an imbalance of insulin, the result is the chronic disease known as diabetes mellitus. The pancreas usually produces insulin on a feedback mechanism. When the body needs insulin following a meal or when extra energy is needed, the pancreas is alerted and it pumps extra insulin into the bloodstream. If, however, the body needs insulin and none is produced, starches and sugars cannot be converted into energy and absorbed by the cells. Glucose (sugar) remains in the bloodstream and is eventually excreted in the urine as waste.

Signs and Symptoms of Diabetes

- Fatigue, tiredness
- Loss of weight
- Sores heal poorly and slowly

- High blood glucose levels
- Glucose in the urine
- Frequent and large amounts of urine
- Excessive thirst
- Poor vision
- Inflammation of the vagina

There are two types of diabetes. Type 1 results in the person having to take insulin. In Type 2 diabetes, the pancreas produces some insulin, but not enough for normal body function. In this type of diabetes, the person may take oral medications or just regulate his diet. Because a diabetic has a regulated amount of insulin in his body, his food intake also must be regulated. If the amount of food is greater than the amount of insulin available, there will be too much unmetabolized glucose left in the blood. If the amount of insulin is greater than the amount of food available, there will not be any carbohydrates for the insulin to metabolize, and this will cause other problems.

Diabetes can be controlled, but never cured. A diabetic must maintain a special diet and must sometimes take medication by mouth or insulin by injection for the rest of his life. A person with diabetes can live a full and productive life if he follows his prescribed diet and medication schedule. Diagnosis of this disease can be made only by a physician following laboratory tests.

Diabetic Coma and Insulin Shock

Be alert for signs and symptoms of diabetic coma and insulin shock or insulin reaction, and follow the emergency procedure for your client.

Signs and Symptoms of Diabetic Coma (Hyperglycemia/High-Glucose Diabetic Ketoacidosis)

Diabetic coma (ketoacidosis) occurs when the blood has too many carbohydrates and not enough insulin to metabolize them. The symptoms include:

- Air hunger; heavy, labored breathing; increased respiration
- Loss of appetite
- Dulled senses
- Nausea and/or vomiting
- Weakness
- Abdominal pains or discomfort
- Generalized aches
- Increased thirst and parched tongue
- Sweet or fruity odor of the breath
- Flushed, dry skin
- Increased urination
- Soft eyeballs
- Upon examination: large amounts of glucose and ketones in the urine and high blood glucose levels

Signs and Symptoms of Insulin Shock (Hypoglycemia/Low-Blood Glucose Insulin Reaction)

Insulin shock, or insulin reaction, occurs when a person's blood has more insulin than the amount of carbohydrates available for metabolism. The symptoms include:

- Excessive sweating, perspiration
- Faintness, dizziness, weakness

- Hunger
- Irritability, personality change, nervousness
- Numbness of tongue and lips
- Inability to awaken, coma, unconsciousness, stupor
- Headache
- Tremors, trembling
- Blurred or impaired vision
- Upon examination: low blood glucose level and no glucose in the urine

Helping a Client Live With Diabetes

- Help the client and his family learn to live with this disease and the routine of medication and diet. Point out the positive aspects of the client's situation. Help the family adapt the prescribed diet to its lifestyle. If this diet seems to be difficult to follow, report to your supervisor.
- Assist your client with his medication, but never give him an injection or oral medication. Insulin is always taken by injection, not by mouth. Insulin should be kept in a cool place, away from heat and strong light. Notify your supervisor if the client does not keep to his medication schedule or has any reaction to his medication.
- A diabetic may have difficulty with his feet. Observe nails and toes for infection or pressure areas. Report these immediately. Do not cut toenails or fingernails. This is a procedure that should be done by a podiatrist or a family member who has been specially trained.
- Notice the condition of the client's skin. Is it dry, is it flaky, are there bruises, and are any bruises

healing? Because a diabetic has a harder time healing than a nondiabetic, it is important to prevent bruises and pressure areas. If the skin is dry, lubricate it. Dry skin often itches, and a client who scratches himself could injure the skin, causing bruises or infection.

CEREBROVASCULAR ACCIDENT

The term cerebrovascular accident (CVA) has three important parts:

1. **Cerebro:** having to do with the brain
2. **Vascular:** having to do with the blood vessels
3. **Accident:** something unpredictable and unexpected

A CVA (stroke or "brain attack"), the third leading cause of death in the United States, occurs when the blood supply to a part of the brain is stopped due to a blocked blood vessel. When blood flow is stopped, the tissue dies. Because each part of the brain controls a different function, the result of a CVA depends on which blood vessel is blocked and which brain center is destroyed (Figure 17.2).

It is important to remember that the results of the CVA may be paralysis, loss of speech, or loss of vision, but that the cause of the problem is disruption of nerve impulse transmission due to brain tissue damage.

In some brains, when a blood vessel is blocked, the surrounding blood vessels take over to supply the injured part of the brain. This is called collateral circulation. In this case, the damage may not be as great as when there is no collateral circulation.

The speech center of the brain is on the left side, so if the CVA occurs on that side, speech may be affected. If the

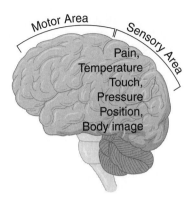

FIGURE 17.2 Each part of the brain governs a specific function.

CVA occurs on the right side, varying degrees of muscle weakness may be the result.

Causes of a CVA

There are four main causes of a CVA:

1. A blood clot can form elsewhere in the body, travel to the brain, and lodge in a small vessel. This is called an embolus (Figure 17.3a).
2. A blood clot can form in the brain itself and remain there. This is called a thrombus.
3. Plaque can accumulate in the blood vessels and eventually close them.
4. A blood vessel can burst, causing a hemorrhage. This is most common in people who have hypertension (Figure 17.3b).

It is impossible to predict when and if the function of a body part will return following a CVA. Do not promise!

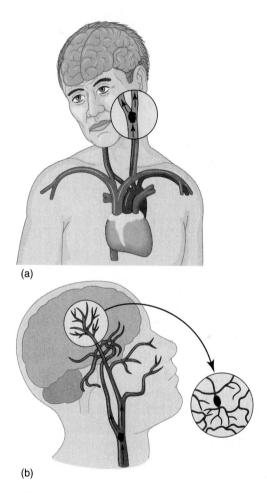

(a)

(b)

FIGURE 17.3 (a) An embolus can form anywhere and travel to the brain. (b) A hemorrhage can take place in any part of the brain.

People who have suffered a CVA resulting in severe speech and/or motor loss have been known to live 30 or 40 years with tender care from their family.

Follow the principles of good personal care and the instructions of the physical, occupational, and speech therapists. The care will be planned with the following in mind:

■ Prevention of complications due to decreased mobility

■ The need for proper nutrition

■ Safety

■ Emotional aspects of the chronic condition for both the client and his family

As you care for your client remember:

■ Always encourage the client. Point out the positive aspects of his progress.

■ Use simple instructions in words that are familiar to the client and his family. Speak slowly and clearly while looking at the client. Do not use baby talk.

■ Always show patience and understanding.

■ Do only the exercises you have been told to do. If you have a question, call the appropriate therapist.

■ Assist the client with his medication.

■ If visitors tire your client, tactfully suggest that they leave so that your client can rest.

Arthritis

Arthritis means inflammation and destruction of joints. At times, there may be other symptoms. The shoulders, ankles, elbows, wrists, fingers, and toes are the most common joints affected by this disease. Arthritis or inflammation can be due to an allergy, an injury, or an infection. The cause of some arthritis cannot be determined—it just appears.

The four most common types of arthritis are:

- *Osteoarthritis*. This is the most common type. The joints and their linings just wear out and become very thin (Figure 17.4). The bony surfaces become thick and develop little spurs that cause pain and inflammation every time the joint moves. Then the bones rub against each other, causing pain and inflammation. This type of arthritis is most common among the elderly.

- *Rheumatoid arthritis*. This is a crippling, chronic disease. All connective tissue may be affected (Figure 17.5). If the disease starts in the joints, connective tissue in other organs eventually may be affected. This type of arthritis usually starts in young adulthood or childhood. Women are three times more likely than men have this type of arthritis.

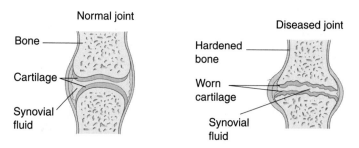

FIGURE 17.4 Osteoarthritis causes a deterioration in the joints.

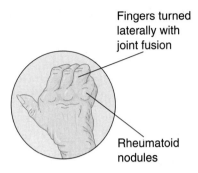

Fingers turned laterally with joint fusion

Rheumatoid nodules

FIGURE 17.5 Rheumatoid arthritis causes joints to become deformed.

- *Gout.* This disease is most common among men. Uric acid crystals build up in the blood and lodge in the joints, causing inflammation and pain. Onset can be sudden and very painful. Any joint can be affected.
- *Ankylosing spondylitis.* This disease, more common in men than in women, may start in childhood and almost always before the age of 35. It attacks only the spine and/or the shoulders and hips. Following treatment, persons with the disease usually remain stiff but are able to function and lead normal lives.

Arthritis is a chronic disease, which means the client will have it forever. Help him to establish a routine for daily care that is safe and efficient and that decreases muscle stress and fatigue.

Exercise and rest are important parts of the client's plan of care. Follow the exercise routine. Do not change it unless you have discussed the change with your supervisor. If you notice that your client's response to the exercises has changed, report it.

A client may try unconventional methods of treating his arthritis. Do not assist in these treatments, and make your supervisor aware of them.

Listen to the client. He may have many feelings about this disease, and he may require emotional counseling from a mental health clinician or psychiatric nurse.

*C*ANCER

Cancer, or a malignancy, is a tumor made up of cells that have changed from normal ones to abnormal ones. This change can happen in any organ, at any time, and at any age. As the abnormal cells reproduce and multiply, they destroy the normal tissue and usually form a tumor. The course of the disease depends on many factors:

- Location of the tumor
- Type of tumor
- When the cancer was discovered
- Type of treatment available
- General health of the client

Causes and Symptoms of Cancer

There is no known cause of cancer, but many possible causes are being investigated. Although a change in the way your body functions may mean many things (not necessarily cancer), there are eight changes, usually called early warning signs of cancer, that should be reported to a doctor immediately.

The spread of cancer cells from one area to another is called metastasis. This does not always occur when there is cancer in the body, but it may. The first site of the cancer is called the primary site, and the place it metastasizes to is called the secondary site.

The only way a tumor is known to be malignant (cancerous) or benign (not malignant) is by taking a small piece of it and examining it under a microscope. This is called a biopsy. It is usually done in the operating room in the hospital.

Treatment

The client may undergo surgery, radiation therapy, chemotherapy, or a combination of these. The choice of treatment is usually made by the doctor after discussion with the client and his family. Sometimes, a family will choose not to tell the client he has cancer. You must go along with it. Discuss this situation with your supervisor so that you will know what to tell the client if he asks you. Do not lie to the client and tell him he will get better unless this is what the family and doctor have decided to tell him.

If the client is terminally ill, you and your supervisor will make a plan of care to meet his specific needs. A person is usually said to be terminally ill when there is little or no hope for recovering from the disease.

Cancer is not contagious. Encourage the family members to visit the client and be supportive. Follow the principles of good personal care.

If the client wishes to talk, let him. If he does not seem to be able to talk to you, ask him if you can call the nurse or someone else.

Many people live for several years with cancer. Help family members deal with this diagnosis by letting them take part in the client's care if they wish. Encourage them to talk to someone who can help them accept this diagnosis.

ALZHEIMER'S DISEASE

Alzheimer's disease is the major cause of mental deterioration in people. This disease is chronic, progressive, and ultimately renders the client totally dependent on others. There is no known cure.

Behavior of Clients With Alzheimer's Disease

You may see a client in any one of three stages of this disease. If you care for a client for a long time, you will see him progress from one stage to the next.

Stage I

At this beginning stage, a person may be able to cover up his memory loss; decreased speech; and even his emotional agitation, depression, or apathy. A person may sense that something is changing and, rather than be embarrassed, simply withdraw from his familiar activities. Family members may not recognize the pattern of this deterioration, may not admit to it, or may feel that all older people are forgetful and withdrawn. Family members may label the client careless or disinterested.

Stage II

During this period, extending over many years, the client's memory progressively worsens. He may stop speaking, may wander, and may repeat movements in a meaningless way. The client becomes less involved in his care and less a contributing member of the family. He may put all types of things in his mouth. His appetite may increase, and his activity may be in the form of continual pacing in small areas. The client starts to need 24-hour supervision.

Stage III

This is the terminal stage. It is a time when families must give continual supervision to the client. His appetite may decrease, and he must be coaxed to eat and drink. The client may become unresponsive.

The maintenance of a routine is one way to ease the care of the client. If you feel the need to change the plan of care, be sure to discuss it with the family and your supervisor.

- Be alert for the safety of the client. Remember, he is unable to remember your instructions so you must be aware of his activities and movements.
- Provide a quiet, unstressed environment.
- Maintain the personal hygiene of the client.
- Maintain a toileting routine. If the client is incontinent and can no longer participate in his personal hygiene, discuss with your supervisor the use of various appliances.
- Small nutritious meals should be offered. Frequent sips of water will decrease the chance for dehydration.
- Monitor the client's sleep habits and report if they are markedly disturbed or they change.
- Be supportive of the family who cares for the client. Encourage them to leave the house when you are there.

- Be alert to family tension. Report this to your supervisor, who will discuss with the family the appropriate counseling or support groups.
- Do not be judgmental.
- Be alert to your feelings.

CHRONIC OBSTRUCTIVE PULMONARY DISEASE

Chronic obstructive pulmonary disease (COPD) refers to all diseases that cause irreversible damage to the lungs over a period of time. People with a diagnosis of severe asthma or emphysema are often said to have COPD. This means that their lungs are not able to expand; remove oxygen from the air that is breathed in; or expel the waste products, such as carbon dioxide. These clients also find it difficult to perform activities that require exertion of any kind. Eating and speaking can be difficult, and exercise is often impossible.

Most of these clients are susceptible to infection due to the pooling of pulmonary secretions in their lungs. When the levels of carbon dioxide and other gases in the blood are not correct, these clients exhibit unusual behavior and are unable to make decisions or be left alone. When the blood gases are corrected, this behavior disappears.

Clients with COPD also suffer from a change in body image. They must learn to live with machines as constant companions because they depend on oxygen equipment and suction equipment to help them breathe. Some clients may have tracheostomy tubes, IVs, or even feeding tubes.

Effects of COPD on the Family

As the client demands more and more care, the family function changes. The primary caregiver becomes isolated from friends because the care of the client takes up so much time. Family members become socially isolated and depressed and often suffer from sensory deprivation. Relationships with friends change.

You will assist the primary caregiver so that there is a break in his or her routine.

- Encourage the caregiver to go out and tend to personal needs while you are in the house.

- Assure both client and family that you will adhere to the routine they have established and will not make changes without discussing them with your supervisor and the client.

- Encourage the client to adhere to his medication schedule. Report any change in behavior. No change is too small.

- Try to interest the client in eating nutritious, small meals. Because eating is a chore for this client and his taste buds are often not as sensitive as yours, every bit of food should be nutritious and tasty. Fluids may or may not be restricted. Prepare foods the client likes. This is not the time to introduce new foods.

- Expose the client to some activities to occupy his time. If the client does not have any hobbies, discuss with him and his family what type of activities he might enjoy. If the client liked to play sports but is no longer able to participate in games, be sure to have him listen to the radio when ball games are on or make him comfortable so he can look at TV. Plan your schedule around these important times in his day.

- Many of the clients you care for will be using oxygen therapy in some form. Remind the client and the family that oxygen and smoking is a dangerous combination and that you will have to report this situation.

Common Neurological Diseases

Three neurologic diseases you will see in the home setting are Parkinson's disease, multiple sclerosis (MS), and amyotrophic lateral sclerosis (ALS) also known as Lou Gehrig's disease. Clients who have these diseases usually remain in the home setting, using adaptive aids. Some remain at home until they die. Although the diseases are different, there are many similarities in the care of these clients. All three diseases result in the need for assistance with care, attention to safety, and support for clients and their families.

Causes of Neurological Disease

Parkinson's disease is a progressive disease that affects the part of the brain controlling movement and balance. The first signs are usually tremors of the hands or legs, difficulty walking, and slowness of movement. Other symptoms may be changes in vision, drooling, difficulty swallowing, and inability to control bowel and bladder function. The cause of the disease is unknown, but most clients respond to drug therapy that replaces certain chemicals they seem to be lacking. People with this disease often work for many years after the diagnosis. Drugs must be carefully and continuously regulated. Side effects from the drugs often occur many years after the therapy has started. Sometimes, clients may appear to be getting better and conclude that they no longer need the medication or may change their routines. This is a great mistake and should be reported to their physician immediately.

MS is a progressive disease that affects the transmission of impulses through the central nervous system. The first signs are usually fatigue, emotional changes, and difficulty with speech. This disease affects young adults who often have young families. People with MS are often able to work for many years if they are protected from infection and have a safe environment. There are medications that help some people, but no one medication has been found to be useful for all clients. The cause is unknown, and the course of the disease varies.

ALS is a progressive disease resulting in the degeneration of the neurons. The cause is unknown, and most clients die within 3 years of diagnosis. Many of these clients choose to stay at home.

Treatment of neurologic diseases is prescribed by a physician. Most clients find that it is important to follow the same routine every day. Assist them as they incorporate the regimens into their daily lives. If you have suggestions for change, discuss them with the clients and their families. Do not change the routine without first telling everyone involved. Areas of concern are:

- *Medication*. It must be taken as prescribed and should not be stopped unless the client's physicians are notified. Report clients' reactions to medication. Be sure to report the slightest changes because they may indicate that dosage changes are necessary.

- *Regular exercise*. This can take the form of active or passive exercise. It could be walking, swimming, or riding a bike. Exercises should be supervised and done regularly. Report fatigue or pain. Be alert to safety needs during exercise. Clients who tire easily should have several short exercise periods rather than one long one. Do not alter the exercise routines without discussing the changes with your supervisor.

- *Nutritional intake.* Small meals high in nutrients and fiber are important. Swallowing of liquids may be difficult, so monitor fluid intake. Safety is important. Be sure the foods are at an acceptable temperature and not too hot. Pieces of food should be small enough to chew easily. Report bowel and bladder changes.

- *Support.* Encourage the clients to be as independent as possible. Encourage the family members to pursue their own interests. There are many local support groups for clients and families. Allow all family members time to express their feelings. Do not be judgmental. Be alert to changes in roles. Listen attentively.

TUBERCULOSIS (TB)

Tuberculosis (TB) is a disease caused by a bacteria. It is spread by people when they laugh, cough, sneeze, or speak to one another. Coughing or sneezing into a tissue or a handkerchief is one way to decrease the spread of the disease. The other way is to wash hands frequently and not touch the hands to the eyes, nose, or mouth.

Today, the disease is seen in all countries and in people in all living conditions. People are at higher risk, however, when living in crowded, poorly ventilated conditions; when malnourished; and when in poor health.

Some people have TB infection. This mean the bacteria is in their body, but it is inactive and cannot be spread or cause harm. Medication is often prescribed for these people to prevent the germs from becoming active.

Signs and Symptoms of TB

There are many signs and symptoms of TB:

- Weight loss, loss of appetite
- Feeling sick, weak, or tired
- Fever
- Sweating, especially during the night
- Chest pain
- Coughing
- Coughing up blood
- Unexplained pain in any body part

Postponing medical help may result in the person getting worse and spreading the disease to people with whom he comes in contact.

How is TB Diagnosed?

The diagnosis of TB, whether active or inactive, can be made only by a physician after a skin test, an x-ray, and/or a sputum sample is taken. Any hospital, clinic, or health department can assist with finding a place to have these tests done quickly and inexpensively.

Usually, once the diagnosis of tuberculosis is made, close contacts of the infected person are also tested. It is important that all contacts be tested, including those who are family members, live in the same house, or are close by.

Treatment for Tuberculosis

Medication is always prescribed and is taken for a long time. It is important that the medication be taken exactly as it is prescribed. If not, the disease may not be cured and may return. Often, more than one medication is given. Other activities, such as physical exercise, diet, and breathing exercises, may also be part of the regime.

When the medication is first started, the client is usually hospitalized and isolated to decrease contact with others. As soon as the disease is under control, the client can go home and be around others without fear of infecting them.

ACQUIRED IMMUNODEFICIENCY SYNDROME (AIDS)

Acquired immunodeficiency syndrome (AIDS) is one type of disease caused by the human immunodeficiency virus (HIV). This viral cause of all related HIV infections, often referred to as AIDS, is spread through contact of blood and body fluids. It cannot be transmitted by holding hands, by giving blood, or by being near someone who has the disease. There is no evidence that AIDS can be spread from sharing the same equipment or bathroom. You will not get sick if you sit next to someone who has any form of AIDS. The virus is not spread by food or sharing a kitchen. It is only transmitted by contact with blood, seminal fluid, or vaginal fluid in the mouth, rectum, vagina, penis, or open wound on the body.

Often, a person has a form of this disease and does not know it. Therefore, it is always important to practice Standard Precautions with all clients. There are several forms of this infection. Only a physician can diagnose the disease. Anyone who thinks he has been exposed to AIDS should go to a physician, a hospital, or health department immediately. Although a person may not appear to have the disease, if he is infected in any form, he can transmit it to another person.

Risk Factors of AIDS

You are at risk of giving, getting, or having AIDS if:

- You are an IV drug user who shares needles.
- You received blood or blood products before 1978.
- You have several sexual partners and do not use condoms.
- You do not know your sexual partners well.
- Any of your sexual partners have had "unprotected" sex since 1978.

Forms of Aids

There are three forms of AIDS:

1. *AIDS carrier*. The only sign of the disease in these people may be a positive blood test. Some carriers never show active signs of the disease. Some carriers remain healthy for many years and then gradually show signs and symptoms. There is no way to predict which course the disease will take. The carriers can, however, transmit the disease.

2. *AIDS-related conditions*. Some people may be healthy for years after the first positive blood test and then show related symptoms. Whether they have mild or severe symptoms, they can transmit the disease.

3. *AIDS*. The disease may appear years after the first positive blood test and years after AIDS-related conditions have appeared and been treated. When this happens, the immune system is compromised and the body is no longer able to protect itself against infection. Death occurs.

You will be asked to demonstrate standard precautions while caring for AIDS clients just as you would when caring for other clients. Use these precautions only when necessary so that neither the clients nor their families feel you are afraid of catching the disease. AIDS clients are often very lonely. Family and friends often do not want to spend time with them, touch them, or hold their hands. Your demonstration that this activity is without danger will help decrease needless fears and dispel myths.

AIDS clients often take medication and have set routines to conserve strength and maintain their muscle tone. If family members are unavailable to assist the clients when you are not there, discuss with your supervisor the availability of support groups or community volunteers.

Report all changes in behavior, pain tolerance, activity tolerance, and skin integrity. Often, AIDS clients have difficulty breathing, so be alert to possible changes in their ability to breathe or speak. Protect the clients from friends and neighbors who may have slight colds or infections. If you feel that any visitor is not 100-percent healthy, suggest he return at another time or speak to a client on the telephone.

Should you have any questions about the disease or the safest way to care for the clients, discuss these openly with your supervisor to increase your knowledge and decrease your fears.

Index